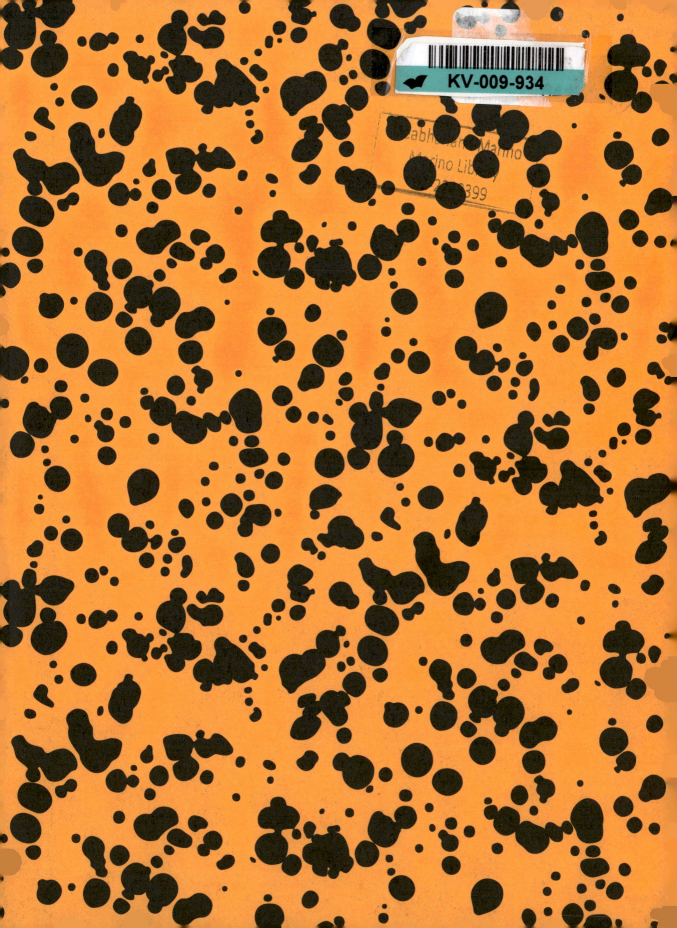

ANNA JONES Easy Wins

Also by Anna Jones:

A Modern Way to Eat
A Modern Way to Cook
The Modern Cook's Year
One: Pot, Pan, Planet

ANNA JONES
Easy Wins

12 flavour hits, 125 delicious recipes,
365 days of good eating

Photography by Matt Russell

4th Estate · *London*

Anna Jones is a cook, writer, the voice of modern vegetarian cooking and the author of the bestselling *One: Pot, Pan, Planet*, *A Modern Way to Eat*, *A Modern Way to Cook* and *The Modern Cook's Year*.

Her books are sold in ten countries and have been translated into five languages. *One: Pot, Pan, Planet* was a Sunday Times bestseller and *The Modern Cook's Year* won the coveted Observer Food Monthly Best New Cookbook Award and The Guild of Food Writers Cookery Book Award. Her previous books have been nominated for the James Beard, Fortnum & Mason and Andre Simon awards.

Anna believes that vegetables should be put at the centre of every table, and is led by the joy of food and its ability to affect change in our daily lives. She lives in Hackney, East London, with her husband and two children.

For Esca. You bring the sun out

Introduction

Standing at my kitchen counter, chopping some vegetables, throwing them into a pan and then ending up with a meal that tastes incredible will forever amaze me. Simple ingredients shown a little love and attention come together to make more than the sum of their parts. This to me is an Easy Win. A little moment of kitchen alchemy that reassures me. Recipes that are reliable sources of joy in a world that is ever-changing.

Unbelievably, I've been cooking as my job for twenty years, and in that time I've seen the way we cook and eat at home change almost completely. The time we spend in the kitchen is less, but we expect much more flavour from our food. A recipe must be fast but clear, easy but layered with taste. We are all on a quest for flavour, especially in vegetable-led cooking. There has been nothing short of a revolution when it comes to putting plants at the centre of our plates. We are all eating more vegetables, and that thrills me. Now I want to help you find a new roster of classic, repeatable recipes that become favourites – to help you make the most of every meal you cook.

That's where the twelve ingredients in this book come in. I also think of them as Easy Wins, ingredients that exceed expectations. They sit quietly in your cupboard or fridge, asking nothing, staying fresh for weeks or months, but when called on add a serious hit of flavour for very little effort.

Lemons, olive oil, vinegar, mustard, tinned tomatoes, capers, chilli and harissa, tahini, garlic, onions, miso and peanut butter. These are the twelve ingredients I use most often in my kitchen to make food taste great, and I know they will be the favourite ingredients in your kitchen too. They seem to be favourites for almost everyone I talk to – loved ingredients that are already in our kitchens. I landed on these twelve after months of observing, note-taking and asking friends about the things that help them cook the best food. They are all ingredients that last a long time, are relatively affordable and easily available. All of them add an element of flavour that I love and crave.

I have chosen only twelve ingredients, so there is a full chapter on each ingredient and a generous number of recipes for you to

Easy Wins

delve into. If you buy an ingredient mentioned in this book, there will be many ways to use it. There is nothing more annoying than a recipe book that asks you to buy sumac or yuzu, for instance, to only use it once.

It's important to mention that some of the ingredients I have chosen come from cultures that are not my own and that I use with respect and reverence, honouring the traditions they come from, the artisans who make them and the memories and meaning they hold for the people to whom they belong. Dotted through the book are recipes from some friends and favourite cooks whose knowledge and knowing of these ingredients is far greater than mine.

My hope with this book is that you cook a few, or maybe even all, of the recipes from a chapter, and in doing so get to know each ingredient, its nuances and its multifaceted flavour. In the tahini chapter, you might learn how bitterness can be a good thing and how it can counter sweetness. In the miso chapter, you will build umami in different ways when you mix it with cheese in a rarebit or with mustard to roast beetroots. It's only by actually cooking that we create the balance of flavour and texture that tastes good to us, and then we learn and adapt how we cook to suit our own palates.

When I had my son Dylan, I had post-natal depression and felt wholly unlike myself. For those months I felt mostly panicked about cooking, not knowing what to choose and not being able to find the time to shop for that night's dinner. It shifted how I think about cooking; it was something that had always come quite easily to me, but for a time it was a stress, another thing on my very full plate that I grew to begin to resent having to do. Luckily those days passed, and my love of cooking returned, but it shifted my perspective permanently to make my recipes as easy as they could be, from the shopping to the table.

This book was written during a summer heatwave, very pregnant with my son Esca and in the months when he was a baby. In those days before and after, my focus was sharply pulled, using the time I had in the most efficient way. Often, I was not sure when my next window to write or cook might be. The recipes in this book are a reflection of that time and of my life.

Recipes with an outrageous amount of flavour for the work it takes to put them together, leaning on ingredients that add an immediate and upfront hit of flavour. All the recipes are, as usual, choreographed and carefully thought out so that they take the least time possible. Each window of time where something might be boiling or roasting is used to do another small task, such as making a topping or cooking something to serve it with, so your cooking window is compact but calm, clear and ordered, wasting no time.

A lot of the work of cooking happens before and after you put a pan on the heat. That is often not the hard part. The deciding, shopping, unpacking, the washing-up. It's often not a lack of skill or desire that stops us from cooking but a lack of other things – from the headspace to plan and shop, to budget or accessibility. I can't make your life less busy, but I have tried to stick to a palate of ingredients that are easily available and for the most part affordable, and to write recipes that are pared back and don't ask you to use every pan or dish in the house.

I have tweaked how I write my recipes in this book to make shopping and cooking as easy as possible. This book lists the amount of each ingredient needed not just in the ingredients list but also in the method at the point at which you use it, so you don't need to cast your eye back over to the ingredients list. It may seem like a small thing, but I've found it much easier to cook from recipes this way. I hope you do too.

And lastly but perhaps most importantly, there is a guide to the ways in which we can shop, cook and eat in a way that treads more lightly on the planet. From how we can reduce waste to the ways in which we can use less energy when we cook. Things we might know and need a reminder of, and hopefully some new tricks too. Saving food, time, energy and money.

I want this book to become full of recipes that are reliable friends and that bring a smile to your face. Dinners that come together so quickly and easily that you no longer need to look at the book. Meals that are so delicious you end the day on a high, patting yourself on the back, because you made something so good. Daily moments of triumph. Easy Wins.

Golden rules for easy wins

'Taste at every stage of the recipe, then taste again.'

1. Think sustainably

It has never been more important to consider the sustainability of how we eat, cook and store our food. If you are reading this book, you have already made a great start by eating more vegetables and cooking from scratch. When planning meals, make sure you use up food you already have – do a quick fridge and cupboard check before you shop. When shopping, opt for food less travelled – local and seasonal. If food is from further afield, choose long shelf-life food that is less likely to be flown in. Think of the energy you are using when you cook. Do not waste.

2. Shop well

The food you make is only as good as your ingredients. Buy the best you can within your means. Eating in-season fruit and veg will taste better and be lighter on the planet. For so many of us, budget is a huge consideration, so simpler recipes with fewer ingredients are your friends.

3. Cooking with a recipe

Read the recipe first. I am guilty of charging into a recipe without looking ahead, but reading over the recipe before you start is key: you might think you know what's coming, but often there will be key things ahead which will be useful to know at the start. Reading the recipe will let you see the big picture and what you are aiming for.

4. Cooking without a recipe

Think about balancing flavour. Read over the chart on pages 230–231, which will help you ask some useful questions about the decisions you will make as you cook. You want to balance flavour and texture, while also having some contrast in flavours and textures, and also think about when to season and when to add acidity before you start cooking.

5. Be flexible

A recipe or a dish is a framework, and if you don't have every ingredient or every piece of equipment you can usually improvise. I am not saying you can replace the hero ingredient, but you could swap capers for olives or parsley for basil. You could use a hand-held blender instead of a food processor. Swap like for like, spice for spice, herb for herb, dairy for dairy, keeping things roughly the same consistency if possible.

6. Season

Season well, season evenly and layer; think of the salty ingredients that will be part of your dish and balance those with the salt you add. See pages 10–15 for more on salt and seasoning.

7. Work methodically

I am not by nature a neat cook, but one thing I learnt as a chef was the benefit of working cleanly. Getting your ingredients and equipment out first, using a mixing bowl to gather waste, and cleaning as you go will make you a better cook and your cooking more successful.

8. Control your heat

Remember, you are in control of the cooking process and your hob or oven. You can always take the pan off the heat or the tray out of the oven if things are cooking too quickly. Don't feel like once you start cooking a recipe you have to keep pace. I have added notes on all the cooking times in the recipes, which encourage you to use visual markers like browning and softness as well as timings.

9. Taste, taste, taste

Tasting and adjusting is the one thing that chefs do that home cooks tend to miss. Taste as you go. Taste at every stage of the recipe, then taste again. Tasting and adjusting the seasoning and balance of acidity, sweetness and umami will make your food as delicious as it can be.

10. Make it your own

This is your dinner. Make it taste good to you. Your taste buds are unique, so this food should reflect that – that could mean more dill, more capers, less lemon, more crispy breadcrumbs. It should be a plate of food you are proud of and want to eat. Recipes are a guide; you are cooking for yourself and the people around your table.

11. The final layer

Making your food sing. Often what sets great food apart is a finishing touch. Crispy sage in brown butter spooned over pasta or fried eggs. A coriander and green chilli chutney on top of a dal. A salsa verde next to some roasted veg. It's this final element, a last topping that takes the flavour and texture to the next level. Often, a flavour-boosting finish is something that can be made in the time the 'main' element is cooking. It could be as simple as chopping some herbs or nuts to top a bowl of soup. This is the extra bit that makes food great.

12. Eat with your eyes

We eat with our eyes. I know that when I make a bit of extra effort to make my food look good, it makes me value what I am eating more and makes me feel sated in a different way, whether that's putting the food on a plate you love, scattering over some herbs or just taking care of how you put each spoonful on the plate.

13. Fill your plate with plants

We all know that eating plants is good for us and the planet. If you have this book in your hands, I'll take that as a given. Eating a wide variety of plants is important. According to Tim Spector, aiming for thirty plants a week, including nuts, seeds, pulses, whole grains, fruit and vegetables, will help us have a healthy gut microbiome, which is key to overall health. We counted up our weekly plant tally, and we all got to thirty much more easily than I expected. And Dylan found it a fun challenge. Bonus points for fermented foods.

Planet-friendly cooking

Sustainability can be a complicated topic. Let's start with some good news. The fact that you are reading this book means you are already off to a good start – eating lots of plants and cooking from scratch.

Here are some simple, positive changes we can make every day in our kitchens. Some of these might feel obvious, but we all need a reminder now and then. You might already be doing a lot of this; if so, could you encourage someone else to make these changes? We need an army of people making small, repeatable everyday changes.

Eat mostly plants

If we want to help slow, and begin to reverse, climate change, it is widely agreed that the most powerful thing we can do is eat fewer animals and more plants. That might mean one meal a day without meat (though I would encourage much more if you can); for others it might mean fine-tuning your vegan diet. Try to make sure that as many of the food decisions you make as possible line up with how you want the world to look.

Waste less

After putting vegetables at the centre of your diet, reducing your waste is the next most impactful thing you can do. It's an easy win; it costs nothing. Think about how you shop so as not to overbuy food. Store it carefully and do a quick, regular mental inventory of what needs to be used before shopping. Use best-before dates only as a guide – your instinct will tell you if it is good to eat. Be flexible – don't be afraid to swap and change recipes to use up what you have.

Eat a diverse plate

The world's capacity to produce food is being undermined by our failure to protect plant and animal life – biodiversity. You can help by varying what you eat, the fruit, the veg, the pulses, the grains and dried goods. If we eat a wide range of different foods, not only is it more nutritious, we also support farmers in growing lots of different crops and encouraging biodiversity. We currently rely on a handful of crops, many of which are being drastically over-farmed and are decimating the soil

Support sustainable farming and eat as much variety as you can fit into your diet. Additionally, this can help with supporting your gut microbiome – it's suggested 30 plants a week is a good aim to keep your gut healthy.

Eat locally and seasonally

Ensure your diet is as seasonal and local as possible within your means. Eat fruit and vegetables that are in season and are grown as close to you as your circumstances and budget allow. Trying to buy UK-grown dry goods is also a great idea: there are great pulses, grains, honey, oils and vinegar produced in the UK.

Consider air miles

Food miles are a huge part of the discussion around sustainability. But it's often hard to know exactly which foods are high on the food miles scale and what impact that has on their carbon footprint. I generally check labels and try to buy fresh foods as locally as possible and only buy dry goods from further afield that are likely to have been shipped not flown. Foodmiles.com is a good resource.

Protect soil

Soil is essential, home to 98% of life on Earth, and we need it to sustain all life. But our soils are degrading at an alarming rate, and soil is being lost 40 times faster than it is being made. We have taken soil for granted and now one-third of the world's arable soils are degraded. The situation is urgent, as it takes a thousand years for one centimetre of topsoil to form. It is generally accepted that if nothing is done, we only have 60 harvests left. If we do not radically change how we grow and produce food now, our children will not be able to feed themselves.

You can help by switching your shopping habits. If you have the means and access, choose to buy produce from growers practising conservation or regenerative farming. If that is a bridge too far,

consider buying organic – your money will be supporting farmers and farming methods that put soil health at the core of their business. It is my sincere hope that these farming practices will become more widespread in the coming years and more accessible and affordable to all.

Choose fairtrade

While I base my shop around local and seasonal food as much as I can, we live in a world with a global food system. Buying foods from communities on the other side of the planet can help support and regenerate local economies, good farming practices and hence the environment. By buying fairtrade, you are guaranteeing fair prices and investing in local communities. Buying fairtrade means you are sending a clear message to the food system that you care about the people who grew or made your food. Fairtrade also requires farmers to adhere to sustainability targets.

Consider energy

Consider the energy you use when you cook. It's not something which is often part of the sustainability conversation. A third of the energy we use at home is used in the kitchen, so try to cook things in one pan or tray, and only turn on one heat source (either the hob or the oven, not both) to reduce the energy use in your kitchen. If you turn the oven on, don't preheat it for more than five minutes, and try to cook a couple of things at once. If you are cooking in a pan, put a lid on it. Make sure your fridge is not overfilled, but your freezer is more efficient if it is full.

Do what you can

Make the changes that you can within your lifestyle, time and budget. Don't look back or feel guilty, look forward, with every day an opportunity for positive change.

'We need an army of people making small, repeatable everyday changes.'

Salt and seasoning

If you want good-tasting food, after buying quality ingredients the next most important thing you can do in your kitchen is season your food well. It's said that salt makes food taste more like itself. All you need to season your food well is salt and your taste buds. It's a part of cooking everyone can get excited about, no matter your skill or means.

Salt is a mineral. It's one of a few key nutrients we need to stay alive, to maintain our body's balance, so we need to eat it daily. We are wired to crave the salt that keeps our bodies working, so to us salt makes everything taste better.

Salt amplifies flavour but can alter texture and enhance or mellow other flavours. There is a skill to adding salt, or seasoning. Adding good salt at the right time in cooking will give you well-seasoned food. If you season well while cooking, you won't need to add salt to your food on the table. Home-cooked food as a rule will almost always be lower in salt than processed food.

Salt doesn't just enhance flavour, it reduces our perception of bitterness, enhances sweetness and reduces our perception of acidity in food. Salt should taste clean and flavourless, like the taste on your lips after a dip in the sea. For us to taste salt, it must be dissolved in water, either the water we cook with or our saliva when we eat it.

Types of salt
Salt of the earth

- Table salt
  Likely sourced from an underground salt mine (though all salt originally comes from the sea). Dense and very salty, it is purified to remove other minerals and usually has added iodine. I don't use this salt unless I am in a pinch.

- Coarse or rock salt
  Like table salt but with bigger crystals.

Sea salt
The salt left behind when seawater evaporates; the processes used to extract the salt yield different types of salt:

- Fine sea salt
  I use fine sea salt for seasoning water for pasta and veg and for anything where I need to measure it in tea-spoons, like breadmaking or baking.

- Flaky sea salt
  This is my most-used salt for seasoning almost everything, from veg before roasting to finishing salads. It forms miraculous pyramids. I always use Halen Môn sea salt.

- Sel de gris and fleur de sel
  A special, originally French, type of sea salt, sel de gris is coarser and fleur de sel has a flower-like grain. These can be used instead of flaky sea salt; sel de gris will sometimes need grinding first.

- Kosher salt
  Popular in America, this is salt with no additives which is finer than flaky salt and good for cooking with. Different brands have different grain sizes, so they are not interchangeable.

How to season

A pinch of salt
I keep my salt in a shallow, wide bowl on the kitchen surface next to the hob. It's important to be able to get all five fingers into the bowl; small bowls and salt pigs do not allow for that.

The four-finger pinch
When recipes say a pinch of salt, most of the time they don't literally mean a two-finger pinch. Every chef I have worked with uses a more solid pinch, using three or four fingers to scoop up a good pinch of salt. I use four fingers, leaving out my little finger but using my other three fingers and my thumb to form a little platform for a good amount of salt to sit on. You can use this pinch for when you are seasoning a small area or when the salt will dissolve (like a dressing).

The upturned sprinkle
One way chefs ensure an even distribution of salt is to take a generous pinch, turn their hand around so the pinched fingers are facing upwards, then, with the fingers still facing up, wriggle the hand back and forth to scatter the salt evenly. The upturned sprinkle is for when you have a large surface to season evenly – like a tray of veg for roasting or the top of a focaccia. There is a useful video on what is called the 'wrist wag' salting technique if you need to see it.

The palm pinch
For things that need a generous seasoning – think water for blanching veg or pasta water – I use a palm pinch. I gather salt from my bowl with all four fingers and my thumb so I have a decent half-palm pinch of salt. Remember here, a lot of this salt will stay in the water when you boil or blanch, so you are not literally adding this much salt.

Season evenly
It might feel like the annoying behaviour of a TV chef, but seasoning from a height is actually a good thing to do. It means the salt falls evenly over whatever you are trying to season. It goes without saying that this is not needed if the salt is going into a liquid.

'Salt should taste clean and flavourless, like the taste on your lips after a dip in the sea.'

Season often – layering

When you season is as important as how. Good cooks season little and often throughout the cooking process, adding salt at every stage and building saltiness slowly in each part of what's being cooked. Adding it to ingredients throughout the cooking process can actually transform not just how they taste but the molecular structure of the food, for example changing the texture, colour and aroma of the ingredients too.

How to taste

When tasting food, you are not tasting for saltiness but for the food to taste at its peak, for the flavour to be bright, upfront and immediate, not flat. Well-salted food does not taste of salt.

Salting different foods

Vegetables

Vegetables contain pectin, which is the stuff that makes jam set and keeps vegetables crunchy. When we cook, we soften the pectin in fruit or vegetables. This happens through ripening, heat or seasoning with salt. I can't think of a vegetable that doesn't benefit from salt.

· Roasted vegetables
Salt and toss in oil before roasting and then again at the end of cooking.

· Blanched or boiled vegetables
Very generously salt water for blanching; most of the salt will go down the drain. Salting also helps vegetables hold on to more nutrients. I taste this water to check how salty it is. Obviously, it will be hot, so use a spoon and allow it to cool a little before tasting. It should taste decently salty to you. By tasting time and time again, you are developing a sense of the perfect level of salt for you and for the veg you are cooking.

· Pan frying or sautéing vegetables
Add at the beginning of cooking and then again at the end.

Pre-salting

Watery veg (and fruit) benefits from salting before you cook it. This will allow the salt to do its work and season the veg more evenly, and it will draw some of the water out, so be sure to pat veg dry beforehand if you are cooking them. Aubergines are a good example here.

Raw fruit and veg

Salt is hygroscopic (that means it loves water). When it hits the surface of fruit or veg, it draws out the moisture. There is then an imbalance of a salty layer on the outside and less salty cells inside – so the non-salty cells start to move outwards and the effect is the veg sheds its water. This is useful in salting tomatoes, or for any veg you want to be less watery.

Potatoes

They need a good amount of salt. I use about one-third more salt when I'm seasoning potatoes than I do with any other root vegetable. I just think potatoes need more salt.

Tomatoes

Like potatoes, tomatoes absolutely need salt. I always season my tomatoes, if I'm going to eat them raw, with a generous amount of salt and a splash of acid, usually red wine vinegar, and let them sit and absorb the salt and the acid for at least ten minutes.

The exception: mushrooms

I always salt mushrooms after they have cooked or browned, as salting them earlier encourages them to release liquid, which means they take longer to brown and may be tougher when cooked.

Eggs

Eggs absorb salt easily – it helps their proteins come together at a lower temperature, which keeps them tender. I add a pinch to any eggs I am whisking before cooking,

Easy Wins

or I add salt to the water if I am poaching them. Salt does not get through the shell of an egg, so season boiled eggs after cooking, and the same goes for fried.

Pulses and grains

As a young chef, I was taught never to salt my beans while cooking. I can safely say this is nonsense. I have cooked beans both with and without salt to compare, and the salted beans are softer and, it goes without saying, tastier. If you are soaking your beans, season the soaking water; if not, add salt to the beans from the beginning of cooking. As beans are cooked for a long time, more of the salt from the water will have a chance to get into the bean, so you don't need as much salt in the water as if you were boiling veg or pasta.

Pasta

There is an idiom that pasta water should be 'as salty as the sea'. To me, it's an exaggeration, though I have seen pasta cooked in seawater. If you have ever had a full gulp of seawater, you will know it is unbearably salty. Pasta water should be heavily seasoned with salt (remember most of it will go down the plughole when it's drained): I usually add 2 very generous four-finger pinches to a 5-litre pot. You will get to know how much salt to use – how much your pot needs for the amount of people you regularly cook for. As with the water for cooking veg, I taste the water I am going to cook pasta in to check for salt. Be careful to let it cool and then taste and add more if you think it needs it.

Rice

Basmati rice has a delicate fragrance and adding salt can mask this, so, thanks to cook Nik Sharma, if I am cooking plain basmati I will not season it with salt. The delicateness of the basmati comes through, and I make sure the food I am serving with the rice is well seasoned to balance it out.

Bread and baking

There are many theories on when to season your dough, especially if you make sourdough bread. Ideally, you add it after mixing the flour and water and letting that sit to come together first, but if you add it sooner your bread will still work.

Fat

Salt needs water to dissolve, so it won't dissolve in pure fat like olive oil. Most fat has a little water content – butter, yoghurt, salad dressing, etc. It takes salt longer to dissolve in fat or anything with a low water content, so season it as early as possible to allow time to absorb.

Sweet

Salt is just as important when it comes to sweet food. A little salt can amplify the flavour and sweetness in a dessert. Think of salted caramel; a sea salt-topped cookie. Fine salt should be used in batters, pastries and custards, etc., and flaky salt should be used for topping things before baking or finishing.

Other ways to add salt

As well as using actual salt to season when we cook, it's important to take into account that many ingredients we add to our cooking are inherently salty and will add to the overall seasoning of a dish. I like to think about what I am adding to the dish before I start cooking, and adjust the level of salt I add accordingly at each moment when I would season. If I am making a tartare sauce, for instance, using both salty capers and cornichons, I would start by making an unsalted mayonnaise and then add the capers and cornichons, the lemon and parsley, and taste to see if it needed actual salt as well. It may need more capers, more lemon, more herbs, not just more salt. So: taste, think, adjust, taste, think, adjust, adding each thing you think it's missing little by little until it's perfect.

'I can't think of a vegetable that doesn't benefit from salt.'

Salt and seasoning

Two of the twelve ingredients I picked to focus on in this book are 'salty' ingredients. Capers and miso, on page 150 and 284 respectively. Reading and cooking your way through these chapters is a good way of understanding how salty ingredients can be used to create well-seasoned food.

Salty ingredients I use in my kitchen:
· Capers
· Chutney
· Ketchup
· Kimchi
· Mayonnaise
· Miso
· Mustard
· Olives
· Pickles or cornichons
· Preserved lemons
· Salted butter
· Salty cheese
  (Parmesan and pecorino)
· Seaweed
· Soy sauce
· Vegetarian fish sauce

Rescuing oversalted food

We have all overseasoned food; I have many times. Sometimes the level of saltiness can be past repair, but, most of the time, one of the tricks below will bring back a salty pot of food.

Dilute the salt
Add more unsalted ingredients to dilute the level of salt. Starchy things are particularly good here – potatoes, rice, pasta, grains. Add more water if it's a liquid dish.

Add acid
Acid helps neutralise saltiness, so adding lemon, lime or vinegar, or even tinned tomatoes or yoghurt (which are acidic), will help. Start by adding a little on a spoon to see what the acid does, then correct the whole dish.

Add dairy or oat milk
Adding dairy will do two things – it will add some sweetness and acidity, which will both counter the saltiness

and coat your mouth when you eat, creating a kind of barrier for the salt.

Add raw potatoes or dough
A piece of raw potato or dough added to a soup or stew will absorb some of the salt and therefore reduce the saltiness. Take it out before eating, obviously.

Add a little sweetness
Sweetness can help counter saltiness, so a pinch of sugar or a drop of maple syrup or honey could help. Equally, if a salad has been oversalted, try adding something sweet: think slices of peach to a tomato salad or some sliced grapes to a herby green salad.

Halve it
Halve the oversalted dish or sauce, then correct it a half at a time; diluting it can work well here. You can refrigerate or freeze the second half and tackle that another time.

If all else fails, order takeaway
There is always another chance to make dinner, so don't beat yourself up.

What about pepper?

Pepper is a spice and, to me, does not have a place in every dish or on every dinner table. Spicing is flavour but also part of culture and tradition. I use many other spices (cumin, coriander seed, smoked paprika) just as much as I use pepper. See page 338 for more on spices.

Lemons

Lemons the colour of the sun sit heaped in a bowl on my counter. A constant in my cooking, second only to salt. A seasoning. A brightening. Sharp juice squeezed over, food stands to attention with pips left behind in my hand. Zest the skin and a haze of misty oil creeps up to my nose and fills the room with freshness and promise. My cooking is a love letter to lemons. A foil for richness, a lift when something is lacking, sharp against sweet. To me, almost everything benefits from lemon. Sometimes I scratch the skin and sniff and stand at the bowl, not cooking, just smelling, spirits lifted.

On Lemons

Lemons are a third seasoning in my cooking. So often when a dish is lacking something, lemon will complete it. Once I have tasted for salt, my next thought is lemon – juice added at the end of cooking for a lift, or zest for zing. Like salt, adding lemon helps food taste more like itself.

You can harness so many different flavours from a lemon: the sharp, refreshing acidity from juice; the brightening sherbet of fresh zest; the rounded lift of a roasted lemon, with its sharp but caramelised notes. And then there's the preserved lemon, which brings something altogether different to the table, salty, tangy, full.

Sharp, Acid, Sour, Bitter

Types

- Amalfi lemons
  From the Italian coast, these are pitted and knobbly. They taste a bit sweeter than your average variety.

- Meyer lemons
  A cross between lemon and mandarin/pomelo. They are my favourite lemons. You don't see them much in the UK, but I eat more than my fair share when I travel to California.

Goes well with

Almost everything

asparagus	feta
basil	ginger
blueberry	honey
broccoli	mint
caper	olive
chilli	parsley
chocolate	potato
coconut	rosemary
coriander	saffron
courgette	sesame
corn	thyme
cumin	tomato
dill	turmeric

Favourite uses

Juice needs to be added late on in cooking, as the sharpness will be lost if it's heated for too long.

- Grated over feta before baking
- To finish a dal
- Whole slices cut thinly then chopped small in a salad
- Cut into wedges and roasted with potatoes
- Squeezed into a glass of water with maple syrup and a pinch of salt
- Zested over squares of chocolate
- Cooked into a pickle with mustard seed and chilli

Storage and tips

I keep as many as I will use in a week on my counter, with the rest stored in the fridge, replacing the ones in the bowl as they are used.

Lemons past their best can be squeezed and the juice frozen in ice-cube trays.

Half a lemon is almost always enough; the other half will sit for days in your fridge until needed, as will a zested lemon.

Most lemons are unripe. Keep them in your bowl until you can dent them with a finger – they will be juicier. If you don't have time for that, rolling them quite hard under your palm on a surface will help release the juice.

Waxed and unwaxed – most lemons have an edible waxed coating so that they keep for longer. It's waxy and greasy to the touch and turns sticky when wet. Run under hot water, then rub enthusiastically with a tea towel to get some of it off.

Extend the life of a squeezed lemon by putting it halved into your dishwasher for sparkling dishes.

What to buy

Buy unwaxed organic lemons if you can, or, even better, ones with leaves – they are a marker of the lemon's freshness.

Quick preserved lemons

4 large unwaxed lemons, roughly
    chopped into 1cm pieces
2 tablespoons fine sea salt
1 tablespoon golden caster sugar

Preserving lemons in their whole state, adorned with nothing but salt, relies on an essential ingredient many of us are short of: time. By chopping the lemon into smaller pieces, adding a little sugar to balance the immediate acidity of the fruit and accelerating the process with a little heat, you can have a batch of preserved lemon pieces much quicker than whole ones. These are a good thing to make if you don't always keep fresh lemons on hand, or to preserve them when lemons are in season in your part of the world.

MAKES 2 MEDIUM JARS

Prepare your lemons
Halve 4 large unwaxed lemons then chop them into rough 1cm dice, removing seeds and trying to keep as much juice as possible. Add the pieces to a small saucepan as you go.

Bash the lemons
Using the blunt end of a rolling pin, push and pound the lemons lightly in the pan to extract the juice. Add 2 tablespoons fine sea salt and 1 tablespoon golden caster sugar and pound again to mix well.

Cook the lemons
Bring the lemons to a simmer, then turn the heat down to the very lowest setting and cook until the peel just starts to soften, about 4–5 minutes. Set aside to cool completely, then transfer to a large sterilised jar. These lemons will keep very happily in their jar in the fridge for up to a month.

One-pot pasta al limone

400g spaghetti or linguine
2 large unwaxed lemons
1 clove of garlic, peeled and
    bashed but kept whole
100ml olive oil
1 teaspoon flaky sea salt
50g salted butter or vegan butter
40g Parmesan or vegan
    Parmesan-style cheese
    (I use a vegetarian one),
    grated
½ a bunch of basil (15g), leaves
    picked and torn (optional)

Pasta al limone. I can't think of a plate of food that shines a light on lemon flavour in quite the same way. Pasta, lemon and Parmesan come together in alchemy to create something worthy of any table.

I tested out a lot of pasta al limone recipes before I landed here. Some had cream, some had finely chopped lemon but none came close to the creaminess of this one and none was as easy. The one-pan method (where you cook the pasta and sauce in one pan) was made for pasta al limone. The starchy water it creates is exactly what is needed to thicken the lemony sauce and coat the pasta. I like to keep this pretty simple. I have suggested some basil as an option at the end, but these simple lemony noodles are enough on their own and a true pantry pasta. If you like, you could add some greens or even stir through some warmed cannellini beans.

SERVES 4

Fill the pasta pan
Put 400g spaghetti or linguine into a large lidded saucepan. Grate in the zest of 2 large unwaxed lemons and add 1 clove of garlic, peeled and bashed but kept whole, 100ml olive oil and 1 teaspoon flaky sea salt.

Add water and cook
Add 1 litre boiling water, cover with a lid and bring to the boil. As soon as it boils, remove the lid and simmer for 8 minutes, using a pair of tongs to turn the pasta in the thickening pasta water every 30 seconds or so as it cooks.

Add the lemon juice
Once the pasta has had 8 minutes, squeeze in the juice of one of the zested lemons and simmer for a final 2 minutes with the lid off.

Finish the pasta
Once almost all the water has evaporated, take the pan off the heat, stir in 50g salted butter or vegan butter and 20g grated Parmesan or vegan Parmesan-style cheese and leave to sit for a minute or two, so the pasta can absorb most of the remaining water and form a lemony sauce. Taste and add more salt, lemon juice and butter or olive oil as needed. Tangle into 4 bowls and finish with the rest of the Parmesan and ½ a bunch of torn basil leaves, if you like.

Lemon, green chilli and Cheddar tart

1 organic egg, beaten (or oat milk for vegans)
320g ready-rolled all-butter puff pastry (vegan pastry if needed)
1 unwaxed lemon
2 tablespoons extra virgin olive oil
150g good-quality mature Cheddar or vegan Cheddar-style cheese, grated
½ an onion, peeled and very thinly sliced
1 green chilli or jalapeño chilli, finely sliced
½ a bunch of parsley and/or coriander (15g), leaves picked
½ a bunch of mint (15g), leaves picked

The idea for this came from watching pizza man Chris Bianco put loads of thinly sliced lemon on top of his ciabatta. I thought the same thing would work with a tart. This tart is fresh, the richness of the pastry is countered by the zip of lemon, the sweetness of onion and the pep of green chilli and it's rounded out with the bite of the Cheddar. It's also a very friendly recipe that looks like it took a lot longer to make than it did. I've doubled this to feed a crowd.

The pastry has a very quick and fuss-free pre-bake to make sure it's crisp, then it's topped with the Cheddar, onion, lemon and chilli. It's essentially an assembly of a dish. You need to use a cold baking tray at the start so that the pastry holds its nice layers when it gets into the oven.

SERVES 4

Preheat the oven and prepare the pastry base
Preheat the oven to 200°C/180°C fan. Beat 1 organic egg, if using, in a small bowl. Lay out the 320g ready-rolled all-butter or vegan puff pastry on a cold baking tray. Working quickly to keep it cold, score the pastry to form a rim about 1cm around the edge of the rectangle – this will form the edge of the tart once cooked. Prick the middle of the base all over with a fork and lightly brush with the beaten egg or a little oat milk. Bake in the oven for 20–25 minutes until golden.

Slice and dress the lemon
Slice three-quarters of 1 unwaxed lemon, leaving a final quarter for later. I want you to slice it really thinly here, discarding the ends, seeds and any slices that have too much pith as you go. A mandoline can be helpful. Toss the slices in 1 tablespoon extra virgin olive oil and a pinch of sea salt.

Take your pastry out of the oven
As soon as the pastry comes out of the oven, press down on the middle rectangle of the base (which will have puffed up a little), flattening the middle of the pastry ready for the toppings and leaving a nice risen border around the outside. Turn the oven up to 220°C/200°C fan.

Assemble the tart and bake
Scatter 150g grated Cheddar or vegan Cheddar evenly over the baked pastry base, followed by ½ an onion, peeled and very thinly sliced, the dressed lemon and finally 1 finely sliced green chilli. Return to the oven for 15 minutes and bake until the pastry is deep golden and the cheese is bubbling.

Make the herb salad
Put the picked leaves from ½ a bunch of parsley and/or coriander and ½ a bunch of mint into a small bowl with the juice from the remaining quarter of a lemon and 1 tablespoon olive oil. Season with salt and pepper, then toss to dress the leaves.

To serve
Remove the tart from the oven and allow to cool for a few minutes before serving with the dressed herbs.

Double lemon pilaf with buttery almonds

300g basmati rice
75g unsalted butter
100g whole almonds,
    roughly sliced
2 onions or shallots, peeled
    and finely sliced
½ teaspoon ground turmeric
1 tablespoon nigella seeds
3 unwaxed lemons
½ a bunch of coriander (15g),
    leaves picked
½ a bunch of mint (15g), leaves
    picked

This double lemon pilaf uses lemon first in the rice, which mellows a little as it cooks, and then a shock of bright lemon juice to finish. I have kept the recipe simple, but I've suggested a few vegetables that I often add at the end as the seasons change. It's great on its own, though, with some sautéed greens and yoghurt.

SERVES 4

Preheat the oven and prepare the rice
Preheat the oven to 180°C/160°C fan. Wash 300g basmati rice well then soak in cold water for 20 minutes, or as long as you have.

Brown the butter and toast the almonds
Heat a large, ideally heavy-based, lidded, ovenproof sauté pan over a medium heat, then add 75g unsalted butter and 100g roughly sliced whole almonds. Once the butter has started to brown and the almonds look toasty, use a slotted spoon to scoop the nuts out, leaving most of the butter behind.

Cook the onions
Add 2 peeled and finely sliced onions or shallots to the browned butter and cook for 5 minutes, until softened and beginning to brown. Add ½ teaspoon ground turmeric and cook for another minute.

Add the rice and bake
Drain the rice well and add it to the sauté pan. Cook over a medium heat for a couple of minutes, stirring all the time to seal the rice. Add 1 tablespoon nigella seeds, the zest and juice of 2 unwaxed lemons, 750ml boiling water or vegetable stock and a teaspoon of sea salt. Cover the pan and place in the preheated oven for 15–18 minutes, or until the rice is fluffy and all the water has been absorbed.

Finish the pilaf
Top with the buttery almonds, the leaves from ½ a bunch of both coriander and mint, and finish with a squeeze of juice from the final lemon.

Seasonal additions:
Add the vegetables to the sauté pan with the onions and stir through the rice before putting in the oven.

Spring
Podded or frozen peas and asparagus (tips left whole, stems sliced; add for the last 5 minutes of cooking).

Summer
Green or runner beans, topped and tailed, runners sliced, and a handful of cherry tomatoes.

Autumn
Sautéed sliced leeks and shredded sweetheart cabbage or greens (sauté the leeks and cabbage in butter or olive oil first).

Winter
Shredded kale or cavolo nero and very thinly sliced or grated squash.

Lemon traybake with green olives and herbs

2 onions, peeled and cut into
    wedges
5 tablespoons extra virgin
    olive oil
4 long green Turkish peppers,
    halved and deseeded, or
    1 large green pepper, halved
    and quartered
1 unwaxed lemon
2 medium courgettes
150g runner beans or green beans
a bunch of spring onions
100g stone-in green olives
a bunch of mint (30g),
    leaves picked
a bunch of parsley (30g),
    leaves picked
1 clove of garlic, peeled and grated
150g Greek or oat Greek yoghurt

I will eat lemon in any form. I've considered eating the sweet Amalfi ones like an apple. I do understand, though, that some people do not share my overenthusiasm for all forms of lemon – no matter how sharp or bitter. And I appreciate that, for some, adding pieces of whole raw lemon to salads, as I love to do, may be a step too far. This traybake uses chopped whole lemon slices, but they are roasted, which tempers their sharpness and acidity and sweetens them. This is entry-level whole-lemon eating.

This is a late spring to summer combination of vegetables but you could swap out the runner beans for asparagus in spring and for purple sprouting broccoli in winter.

SERVES 4

Roast the longer cooking vegetables
Preheat the oven to 240°C/220°C fan. Put 2 onions, peeled and cut into wedges, in a large shallow baking tray with 3 tablespoons extra virgin olive oil, 4 Turkish peppers, halved and deseeded, and a good pinch of sea salt and freshly ground black pepper. Toss to coat everything, then roast in the oven for 20 minutes.

Prep the rest of the veg
Roughly cut 1 unwaxed lemon into thin slices, then halve each slice. Chop 2 medium courgettes into large 3cm chunks. Cut 150g runner beans in half at an angle or trim 150g green beans, leaving them whole.

Add the rest of the veg
Once the onions and peppers have been roasting for 20 minutes, add the lemon slices, courgettes and beans to the roasting tray. Reserve 2 spring onions for later and add the rest to the tray, keeping them whole. Toss

so everything is coated in oil. Return to the oven for a further 10–15 minutes until everything is tender and roasted.

Make the green olive and herb dressing
Destone 100g green olives and roughly chop them. Roughly chop a bunch of both mint and parsley and finely chop the reserved spring onions. Put everything in a bowl with 2 tablespoons extra virgin olive oil and 1 peeled and grated clove of garlic, season with freshly ground black pepper and mix together. Taste and add some salt or more olive oil as needed.

Put everything together
Spread 150g Greek or oat Greek yoghurt over the bottom of a serving platter, then pile on the lemon-roasted vegetables. Spoon over the olive dressing, finishing with a little more olive oil if needed. Serve with warm flatbreads.

My perfect lemon salad

2 heads of butter lettuce or
    4 Little Gems
2 handfuls of peppery leaves
    (I like rocket or mustard leaf)
2 unwaxed lemons
4 tablespoons extra virgin
    olive oil
1 teaspoon runny honey or
    maple syrup
½ teaspoon Dijon mustard
hard cheese for grating
    (I use a vegetarian pecorino
    or Parmesan), optional

This is my platonic ideal of a salad. Very lemony and very bright. It sits perfectly next to almost anything and cuts through even the richest foods. I have included the washing instructions for the leaves, because it is so important that they are clean and dry for the dressing to cling to them properly.

SERVES 6

Prepare the lettuce
Remove any wilted or bruised leaves from 2 heads of butter lettuce or 4 Little Gems, then trim each head at the root to break the lettuce into individual leaves. Drop them into a sink filled with tepid water. Trim and discard bruised leaves or stalky bits from the peppery leaves and drop the remaining leaves and tender stems into the sink too. Swirl the greens in the water then drain them well. Wash the leaves once more in cold water. Spin dry in a salad spinner.

Chop the lemon
Slice then finely chop 1 unwaxed lemon, removing the seeds as you go. You want both the flesh and the lemon peel here. Be sure to chop both as small as possible. Grate the zest from the other lemon into a jam jar and squeeze in the juice from the second lemon.

Make the dressing
Put 4 tablespoons olive oil into the jam jar with 1 teaspoon runny honey, ½ teaspoon Dijon mustard, a good pinch of sea salt and freshly ground black pepper, and shake to mix. Taste the dressing by dipping a leaf of lettuce into it – the water in the lettuce will mellow the dressing so this is always the best way to taste it.

Finish the salad
Put the leaves into a large mixing bowl with the lemon pieces, add a good pinch of salt and pepper, then a few tablespoons of the dressing. Toss together gently with your hands to coat each leaf. Taste and add more dressing if needed. Pile high on a serving plate and finish with some grated Parmesan or pecorino cheese if you like.

Lemon chickpeas with halloumi and seeded honey

5 tablespoons olive oil
1½ teaspoons nigella seeds
½ teaspoon ground turmeric
1 × 700g jar chickpeas
½ teaspoon coriander seeds
½ teaspoon Turkish chilli flakes
50g runny honey or maple syrup
200g kale, spring greens or
    cavolo nero
1 unwaxed lemon
1 × 200g block of halloumi

This was a quick dinner one night when reserves were low but the need for flavour and texture was high. Jarred chickpeas are a quick dinner staple in our house. Plump, rich and pleasingly salty, they are perfectly seasoned already, so make an almost foolproof base for a meal. I like to hit them up with a good jolt of lemon and here they get frizzled with spices and served with lemony greens and a honeyed halloumi. This is inspired by something I ate at Bubala, a great Middle-Eastern vegetarian restaurant in London. I try to use jarred chickpeas here, as tinned don't work as well. If you are using tinned, add less liquid from the tin.

SERVES 4

Cook the chickpeas
Add a tablespoon of olive oil to a medium saucepan. Add 1 teaspoon nigella seeds and ½ teaspoon ground turmeric and cook on a medium heat until sizzling and fragrant. Standing back a little in case they spatter, add a 700g jar of chickpeas and their liquid to the pan. Cook for 10 minutes, stirring occasionally, until soft and starting to break down a little.

Mix the seeded honey
While the chickpeas are cooking, put the remaining ½ teaspoon of nigella seeds, ½ teaspoon coriander seeds and ½ teaspoon Turkish chilli flakes in a pestle and mortar and bash until fine, then add a good grinding of black pepper. Stir the spices through 50g runny honey or maple syrup and set aside.

Prepare the greens and lemon
Remove the leaves from the stalks of 200g greens. Tear or cut any very large leaves and finely slice the stalks, discarding any super tough bits. Thinly slice half an unwaxed lemon, then chop the slices so you have small lemon pieces. Save the other half of the lemon for later.

Cook the greens
Put a large frying pan over a medium heat. Add 3 tablespoons olive oil and the stalks of the greens and cook for a couple of minutes to soften the stalks. Add the leaves and the lemon pieces, stirring so the lemon and oil coat the greens. Fry for 3–5 minutes until slightly crisp and bright green. Remove the greens from the pan and set aside for a moment.

Cook the halloumi
Cut a 200g block of halloumi into thick slices lengthways. Put the kale pan back on a medium heat and add the halloumi with a tablespoon of oil and cook for a minute or two on each side until golden brown. Put the golden halloumi on a plate and pour over the seeded honey.

To serve
Squeeze the remaining lemon half over the greens and stir to coat. Divide the spiced chickpeas between shallow bowls and top with the honeyed halloumi and a handful of greens.

Emily's lemony celeriac schnitzel

½ a bunch of thyme (10g), leaves
    picked
3 unwaxed lemons
1 large celeriac (800g), peeled and
    sliced into roughly 2cm-thick
    discs
125g panko breadcrumbs
3 cloves of garlic, peeled
70g blanched hazelnuts
3 tablespoons olive oil
250g roasted red peppers from
    a jar, drained
1 tablespoon pomegranate
    molasses
1 teaspoon Turkish chilli flakes
1 teaspoon cumin seeds,
    coarsely ground
1 teaspoon tomato purée
1 preserved lemon, deseeded and
    finely chopped
60g Parmesan or vegan
    Parmesan-style cheese
3 tablespoons plain or spelt flour
2 large organic or free-range eggs
200ml groundnut oil
a handful of coriander leaves,
    parsley and dill to serve
peppery salad leaves, to serve

My great friend Emily loves lemon as much as I do. So much in fact that Dylan calls her Aunty Lemony. Emily has been by my side in the kitchen and as a friend for the last fifteen years and has been a huge part of all of my books and recipes. So it would not have been right to have a lemon chapter without a recipe from Em.

SERVES 4

Preheat the oven and cook the celeriac
Preheat the oven to 180°C/160°C fan. Bring a large half-full pan of salted water to the boil. Add the picked leaves from ¼ a bunch of thyme and the juice and zest of 1 unwaxed lemon. Peel and slice 1 large celeriac into 2cm-thick discs and, once the water is boiling, simmer them for 8 minutes until they are soft when pierced with the tip of a knife but still holding their shape. Remove, drain and set aside.

Toast the breadcrumbs
Meanwhile, put 50g panko bread-crumbs with 3 peeled cloves of garlic and 70g blanched hazelnuts on a large baking tray, drizzle with olive oil and season with salt. Bake for 10 minutes or until golden. Remove from the oven and leave to cool a little. Turn the oven down to 170°C/150°C fan.

Make the muhammara
Put 250g drained roasted red peppers, 1 tablespoon pomegranate molasses, 1 teaspoon Turkish chilli flakes, 1 teaspoon coarsely ground cumin seeds and 1 teaspoon tomato purée into a food processor and pulse until well combined. Add the breadcrumb mixture to the blender with the juice and zest of another unwaxed lemon. Pour in a tablespoon of olive oil and pulse to a textured, dippable

sauce. Stir through 1 finely chopped preserved lemon and season if needed.

Prepare the breadcrumbs
Get out three shallow bowls and put 75g of panko breadcrumbs into one then grate in the zest of the last unwaxed lemon and 60g Parmesan into the bowl. Season with pepper and set aside. Put 3 tablespoons plain or spelt flour into the second bowl with the remaining picked thyme leaves, season and set aside. Crack 2 eggs into the last bowl, give them a good whisk and set aside.

Heat the oil
Pour 200ml groundnut oil into a wide high-sided frying pan and place over a medium heat. While the oil is heating, breadcrumb the celeriac.

Breadcrumb then fry the celeriac
Dip the celeriac in the seasoned flour, dusting off any excess, then into the eggs, followed by the breadcrumbs, making sure each piece is evenly coated. Continue until all the celeriac is coated.

Once the oil is hot enough (about 180°C), add 2 of the celeriac schnitzels to the pan and fry for 2 minutes on each side until golden and perfectly crisp. Carefully remove the schnitzels from the oil, put them on a baking tray and into the oven while you fry the other two.

When all the schnitzels are fried, put a good spoonful of muhammara on a plate, top with the schnitzel and scatter over the herbs dressed in lemon juice, and the peppery salad leaves.

Dylan's lemony ice lollies

Strawberry, apple and lemon
10 strawberries, plus a few
    extra slices
1 red apple, cored and roughly
    chopped
200ml apple juice
juice of 1 unwaxed lemon

Watermelon, pear and lime
1 pear, cored and chopped
juice of 2 unwaxed limes
200ml apple juice
2 large slices watermelon (15g)

Many of the recipes for this book were cooked during a blistering July heatwave in London. There were pies in 40 degrees, which got eaten after the temperatures dropped each evening. But in the daytime all we wanted was cold, refreshing, citrussy things. Dylan was on ice-lolly duty, coming up with his favourite refreshing combinations of fruits. These were the winners: a sherbety strawberry one and lime, pear and watermelon. (I know it's a lemon chapter, but I'm making an exception.) We each ate at least 2 a day.

MAKES 6 MEDIUM-SIZED ICE LOLLIES

Strawberry, apple and lemon
Put 10 strawberries, 1 cored and roughly chopped red apple, 200ml apple juice and the juice of 1 unwaxed lemon into a blender and blend until smooth. Add some extra strawberry slices to each mould then pour the mixture into your lolly moulds and freeze for at least 5 hours.

Watermelon, pear and lime
Put 1 cored and chopped pear, the juice of 2 unwaxed limes and 200ml apple juice into a blender and blend until smooth. Cut 15g watermelon into slices that will fit within your lolly moulds, add to each mould, then pour in the mixture and freeze for at least 5 hours.

Hot lemon and bay pudding

25g unsalted, room temperature
    butter, plus extra for greasing
225g caster sugar
3 large free-range or organic eggs
30g plain flour
zest and juice of 3 unwaxed
    lemons
250ml whole milk
1 fresh bay leaf
icing sugar, to serve

This is one of those magical puddings that is spooned into the dish as one unassuming batter and comes out of the oven transformed into a double-textured pudding: a light lemon sponge top and a rich lemony custard at the bottom. One of the best examples I know of kitchen alchemy and one of the easiest puddings. I add bay here, as I love lemon and bay together. The bay brings some grounding depth to the sherbety hit of lemon. This pudding is inspired by one made by JR Ryall of Ballymaloe. You can skip the bay if you like things more classic, though. I've not found a good way to make this without eggs, so there are no vegan switches here.

SERVES 4

Cream the butter and sugar
You will need approximately a 1.2-litre pie dish, lightly greased with softened butter. Preheat the oven to 180°C/160°C fan. Put 25g of butter into a mixing bowl or the bowl of a stand mixer and turn the mixer on low. Gradually add 225g caster sugar. As there is not much butter it won't go creamy and fluffy but will remain sandy.

Separate the eggs
Carefully separate 3 large free-range or organic eggs and put the yolks into one bowl and the egg whites into another very clean bowl (a spotless bowl will help to get the best lift out of your egg whites when you whip them).

Add the yolks to the batter
Add the egg yolks to the sugar mixture, then mix in 30g plain flour. Then add the zest and juice of 3 unwaxed lemons followed by 250ml milk.

Whisk the egg whites
Using a hand-held electric whisk or the whisk attachment of your stand mixer, whisk the egg whites until they form stiff peaks (when the bowl is held upside-down the whites should stay put in the bowl).

Fold in the whites
Use a metal spoon or spatula to carefully fold the egg whites into the batter. Be gentle to keep as much lightness from the egg whites as possible. Trust the process here; it will seem too liquidy and split but it will come together in the oven.

Bake
Put 1 fresh bay leaf into the bottom of the dish, then pour in the batter and bake for 40 minutes until the top is golden and set. Dust with icing sugar and serve immediately. It's also good cold from the fridge the next day.

Citrus and maple sherbet

4 big unwaxed lemons, 8 if you
want to serve in lemons
(the Amalfi ones are best
if you can get them)
1kg ripe cantaloupe melon
8 clementines, peeled, deseeded
and roughly chopped
150ml maple syrup, plus more
if needed

This sorbet is bright, pink and refreshing. I grew up eating lemon sorbet in hollowed-out lemons in restaurants on holiday. To a seven-year-old me there was nothing more delicious, chic or fun than dessert in a lemon, and I still stand by that at forty-four. Please know, though, that there is absolutely no need to hollow out a lemon to serve this in. I often make it as a quick dessert in little glasses.

I love making ice cream and sorbet. I have an ice-cream machine, but I rarely get it out. It's heavy and feels like a faff, so I only use it on special occasions (see the chocolate caper ice cream on page 170). Here I ask you to freeze the fruit first, then use a food processor to blitz to an instant sorbet with some maple syrup. It feels like magic. I make this for me and my kids a lot in the summer, scooped into cones, which feels almost as fun as a lemon.

MAKES A BIG TUB OF SORBET, ENOUGH
TO FILL LOTS OF LEMONS

Prepare the lemons

If you don't want to go all in on the kitsch filled lemons, you can cut the top and bottom off 4 lemons, then place on a chopping board and use a knife to cut away the zest and white pith from 4 lemons. Cut the flesh in half and pick out any seeds, then roughly chop the flesh into 2–3cm pieces. The zest from the outside can be kept for making tea or cooking.

If you want to serve the sorbet in lemons, cut the bottom off 8 big unwaxed lemons at the stalk end so they sit flat, then cut the top third off each lemon (keeping these tops). Use a spoon to scoop out the flesh from all 8 lemons. You will be using the flesh from 4 lemons in this recipe (see above), so for these pick out

any seeds and chop the flesh into 2–3cm pieces. The rest can be kept for something else. If using them to serve in, you want to keep the lemons whole so you can fill them later and keep the lemon flesh for the sorbet. Put your 8 hollowed-out lemons and tops into the freezer.

Prepare and freeze the melon and citrus

Cut 1kg ripe cantaloupe melon in half and spoon out the seeds. You will need about 500g of the flesh. Roughly chop the flesh into 2–3cm pieces and put it into a container with 8 peeled, deseeded and roughly chopped clementines (you should end up with about 600–700g of peeled clementines) and the roughly chopped flesh of the 4 lemons. Freeze the fruit for 8 hours, or ideally overnight. It can be kept frozen for up to a month, until needed.

Make the sorbet

Remove the frozen fruit from the freezer and put in a high-powered food processor, along with 150ml maple syrup. Blend for 3–4 minutes, until smooth. You might need to stop a few times and use a spatula to scrape down the sides to make sure the food-processor is catching everything. Taste and add more maple syrup if needed; how much you need will depend on the sweetness of your fruit.

Scoop straight into bowls or the hollowed-out lemons and eat immediately, or put into a tub to keep in the freezer. You can keep any leftovers in the freezer, and leave it out for 5 minutes before scooping – if it becomes icy you can blend again before serving.

Double lemon cake with streusel topping

250g plain flour, plus 80g for the streusel topping
20g porridge oats
250g plus 2 tablespoons golden caster sugar
zest of 4 unwaxed lemons
200g unsalted butter at room temperature, plus 70g cold unsalted butter and a little extra for the tin
80g ground almonds
1½ teaspoons baking powder
1 teaspoon bicarbonate of soda
½ teaspoon sea salt
3 large organic or free-range eggs
1 teaspoon pure vanilla extract
250g natural yoghurt or oat yoghurt
100g good-quality lemon curd, plus extra to serve
crème fraîche, to serve

This is my ideal cake. Lemony, soft-crumbed and streusel-topped. The idea for this recipe comes from baker Thalia Ho, who has a cake in her book *Wild Sweetness* that ripples lemon curd through it. This cake is loaded with three types of lemon: lemon zest studded through the cake batter, the curd on top and a hit in the streusel topping.

MAKES A 23CM CAKE, SERVES 12

Make the streusel topping
Put 80g plain flour, 20g porridge oats, 2 tablespoons caster sugar and a pinch of sea salt into a bowl and mix well. Add the zest of 1 unwaxed lemon, then add 70g of cold unsalted butter. Use your fingers to rub the butter into the flour like a crumble mixture until large sticky clumps have formed. This is your streusel.

Preheat the oven and line your tin
Preheat the oven to 180°C/160°C fan. Grease a 23cm cake tin with butter, then line with baking paper.

Mix the dry ingredients
Put 250g plain flour, 80g ground almonds, 1½ teaspoons baking powder and 1 teaspoon bicarbonate of soda into a mixing bowl with ½ teaspoon sea salt and mix with a whisk until there are no lumps.

Cream the butter and sugar
In a stand mixer with the paddle attachment, or in another mixing bowl with an electric hand whisk or wooden spoon, cream 200g unsalted butter and 250g golden caster sugar until pale and fluffy. This will take about 3–4 minutes in a stand mixer and longer by hand.

Add the eggs
Scrape down the bowl and add 3 large organic or free-range eggs one at a time, mixing on a low speed until each one is incorporated, then mix in 1 teaspoon pure vanilla extract, the zest of another unwaxed lemon, and 250g natural yoghurt or oat yoghurt.

Add the dry ingredients
Add the dry ingredients to the batter in the mixing bowl and mix until just combined. This is a very forgiving cake, but minimal mixing will make it as light as possible.

Put the batter into the cake tin and add the lemon curd
Scrape the batter into the prepared tin and level it gently with a spatula, then spoon over 100g good-quality lemon curd in little patches and use your spoon to swirl it in a little. Scatter the streusel topping evenly to the very edges of the cake; don't pile it into the middle or it will sink.

Bake the cake
Bake for 1 hour, or until a skewer inserted into the middle of the cake comes out clean. Cover the top of the cake with foil if it looks like it's browning too fast. Allow to cool for 15 minutes in the tin, then remove from the tin and leave to cool completely on a wire rack. Serve with some crème fraîche rippled with a little lemon curd.

Lemon soda bread

400ml whole milk or oat
milk, plus a little extra for
brushing
3 unwaxed lemons
350g plain or plain spelt flour,
plus extra for dusting
350g wholemeal flour
2 teaspoons bicarbonate of soda
2 teaspoons flaky sea salt
150g unsalted butter or vegan
block, at room temperature
2 teaspoons good-quality runny
honey or maple syrup

This is one of the most moreish things
I have made in a while. This recipe is
a lesson in how lemon can lift even
something hearty like soda bread.
Lemon is used in lots of ways here: the
juice turns milk into buttermilk; the
zest lifts the flavour of the bread and
is also added to a honey and lemon
butter to spread on the just-out-of-
the-oven slices. Soda bread is a great
entry-level bread to make if breadmaking or sourdough scares you. It's
so easy and needs no kneading, rising
or shaping. This is best served fresh
on the day it is made. After that it
needs toasting. Once cooled, you can
slice and freeze it, then toast the slices
from frozen as needed.

MAKES ONE GOOD-SIZED LOAF

Preheat the oven and prepare the tray
Preheat the oven to 180°C/160°C fan
and line a shallow baking tray with
baking paper and a dusting of flour.

Make the buttermilk
In a jug, measure out 400ml whole
milk or oat milk, then add the zest
and juice of 2 unwaxed lemons. Give
it a good stir and set aside for 15
minutes to thicken up and curdle.
Oat milk won't thicken or curdle but
the recipe will still work perfectly.

Make the dough
In a large mixing bowl, mix together
350g plain flour, 350g wholemeal flour,
2 teaspoons bicarbonate of soda and
1 teaspoon of flaky sea salt. Make
a well in the middle of the flour
and pour in the thickened, lemony
buttermilk mixture, stirring until
there are no dry floury patches, then
use your hands to bring it together
to a rough dough. Don't over-mix
here. The less you mix it, the lighter
the bread will be; this is not like a
normal yeasted bread dough.

Shape and bake the loaf
Tip the dough out on to a well-
floured surface, use your hands to
bring it together into a rough ball,
then scoop it on to the lined and
floured tray. Use a knife or dough
scraper to make a large, deep cross
on the top of the bread, brush with
a little extra milk, then bake in the
oven for 40 minutes until golden
brown all over.

Make the lemon honey butter
In a small bowl, mix and mash 150g
unsalted butter or vegan block, at
room temperature, with the zest of
1 lemon and 2 teaspoons good-quality
honey or maple syrup. Taste and add
as much of the second teaspoon of
sea salt as needed; this will depend
on the saltiness of your butter.

Take your loaf out
Remove the bread from the oven and
tap the bottom of the loaf. If you get
a hollow sound, it's perfect, so pop it
on a wire rack to cool. Leave to cool
for about 30 minutes to an hour. Slice
and serve warm with a thick spread
of the lemon honey butter and/or
jam. Keep any leftover bread well
wrapped and eat within 2 days, or
slice and freeze in a freezer bag.

Olive Oil

The first pressing of olives, oil pouring in a thin, steady stream from a spout, green as grass and shimmering. Sipped from a spoon – buttery, peppery, like a freshly mown lawn. Like nothing I have tasted before or since. The oil on my counter is not green but golden; a bottle lasts barely a week for all its uses. A thick layer in a pan for sizzling. A plentiful pour over pasta, to season, coat and add richness. Beaten into cake batter. A deep layer to slow cook in, the vegetables taking on its blonde butteriness. Drizzled onto yoghurt with honey. To top vanilla ice cream. Glugged onto focaccia. Drinkable.

On Olive Oil

I couldn't cook without olive oil. A good olive oil improves almost anything – it's one of my most-loved and most-used ingredients. Your food will taste good if you start with a good oil. It can feel hard to know which oil to use. There are so many, and they vary hugely in taste, quality and cost. And the expensive ones are not necessarily the best.

Oils will range from peppery to buttery, and while it may seem silly to taste your oil like you might a wine, it's not. Finding an oil you like the taste of in your price range will make all your cooking better. To me, the most important factor in olive oil is freshness. So when you buy oil, use it quickly and don't keep it for ages in your cupboard.

It's often said that olive oil should not be heated high for fear of its compounds breaking down and becoming unhealthy for us. Actually, the smoke point of extra virgin olive oil is quite high – 190°C or above – and most cooking in a home kitchen will be done far below this, so I use it for almost all my cooking.

In my kitchen, I have three olive oils. I use a decent but affordable extra virgin olive oil for almost all frying and cooking. A favourite more expensive olive oil is used for best – it's for finishing food that's already cooked, from soups to salads. Lastly, there is a light olive oil I use occasionally for making mayonnaise and for frying when I don't want an olive flavour.

I am generous with olive oil when I am cooking, and some of the amounts in these recipes might be more than you are used to adding. I use olive oil for the texture and mouth-feel it gives, as well as its flavour, and for that you need more than a thin drizzle. Many of the recipes in this chapter rely on a brave use of olive oil. Olive oil is a fat our body likes and needs, and I am sure these home-cooked dishes will still have far less fat than processed food.

Peppery, Buttery, Rich, Spicy

Types

- First pressing
  The bright green, grassy oil from the first pressing of the olives. Worth seeking out.

- Extra virgin
  Other than grinding and pressing, no other chemicals or processes are used in its production. Good extra virgin will often taste peppery, grassy, fruity or spicy.

- Virgin
  One down in quality (and price) from extra virgin, it has minimal flaws.

- Light
  This refers to a lighter colour rather than a lower fat content. A refined oil with fewer nutrients and less flavour – produced using heat after the first pressing of the olives.

Goes well with

almond	ice cream
caper	lemon
chilli	pulses
chocolate	rosemary
cucumber	soft herbs
garlic	tomato
greens	yoghurt

Favourite uses

- For drizzling over almost anything
- For drizzling over focaccia, pasta, salads, scrambled eggs
- For finishing chocolate desserts
- For olive oil-roasted tomatoes
- To confit garlic
- Instead of butter in cakes
- To braise runner beans
- In a thick layer on top of a ribollita

Storage

Store somewhere cool and dark with a consistent temperature: temperature fluctuations from a fridge, stove or oven are not good for your oil. It's best stored in dark bottles out of the sun in a cool place.

What to buy

- Spanish
  Belazu and Brindisa both import really good oil from Spain and are widely available. I use these oils a lot.

- Palestinian
  Zaytoun is a warm, peppery and affordable Palestinian oil I buy often.

- Greek
  Two Fields and Citizens of Soil offer a subscription of beautifully golden oil delivered straight to your kitchen.

- Italian
  Saint Rosalia is a verdant oil in excellent packaging. Selvapiana and Fontodi are oils I have been cooking with for years.

Easy Wins

Jalapeño and coriander oil

1 large bunch of soft herbs
    (I used coriander)
2–4 chillies, depending on heat
    (I used 3 jalapeños)
500ml extra virgin olive oil

Most of the time I use olive oil as it is, unadorned. A good olive oil needs nothing added to it. But I do know a lot of people who buy chilli oil, so this recipe encourages you to make it, not buy it. Most chilli oil in the shops uses rubbish oil and focus on chilli heat. I make this when I have lingering herbs or chilli to use up, and I often have both. I used coriander and jalapeños here, but any chilli and soft herb would work well. The oil keeps for ages, and I use it to top tacos, beans, soups and dips. Use a decent extra virgin but not the very best olive oil here. You want the oil to be mellow and buttery; the most important thing is to make sure it's fresh. I encourage you to use limp bunches of herbs, as it won't matter if they have started to droop, and the same goes for the chillies.

MAKES ABOUT 500ML OF OIL

Blanch and ice the herbs
Put a pan of water on to boil and get a large bowl of iced water ready next to your sink. Once boiling, blanch the herbs in the water for 20 seconds, then drain and immediately dunk under the iced water. Drain and pat dry on a tea towel.

Blitz the oil
De-stem the chillies and put the chillies, seeds and all, into a blender with the blanched herbs and pour in the oil. Blitz on high for a minute or so until you have a smooth, very green oil.

Set up the sieve/muslin for draining
Put a piece of muslin or a thin, clean tea towel over a sieve and set that over a mixing bowl or wide-mouthed jug. It's best to do this in or near the sink.

Sieve your oil
Carefully pour the oil into the centre of the muslin, allowing as much to drip through on its own as possible. Once the dripping has stopped, gather the corners of the muslin to create a little bag with the green herby oil in the middle. Use your hands to squeeze the top of the bag, pushing as much of the green oil through as possible. This might take a few attempts. You only want the herby paste left in the muslin. You can use the paste in the base of a curry or freeze it.

Store the oil
Pour the oil into a jug or bottle, where it will keep at room temperature for a couple of weeks, or in the fridge, where it will keep for a couple of months. If you keep it in the fridge, the oil will solidify. Just bring it to room temperature before you use it, or spoon it straight from the jar on to something hot, and it will turn back to oil immediately.

Ways to use the oil:

- To top tacos
- To spoon over pasta
- On a tomato salad
- To make a dressing
- Mixed with chopped fresh herbs for a quick topping

Frizzled spring onion and olive oil dip

1 bunch of spring onions,
    trimmed
150ml extra virgin olive oil
1 teaspoon Turkish chilli flakes
    or ½ teaspoon chilli flakes
1 teaspoon caster sugar
½ teaspoon ground turmeric
150g thick strained Greek
    yoghurt
zest and juice of 2 unwaxed
    limes

John is obsessed with dips. He will dip almost anything, especially pizza crusts. I can't quite get into the pizza crusts into sour cream and chive dip he loves, but I do love a dip. This one is a take on the traditionally Chinese spring onion oil, but with a hit of chilli and turmeric, and sits on top of a thick lime yoghurt.

You can buy really good thick Greek yoghurt from the supermarket or your local shop. If your yoghurt is not thick (and by that I mean spoonable, almost the consistency of clotted cream), then you can strain the yoghurt yourself. Hang it in a piece of muslin or a clean thin tea towel over a mixing bowl overnight or for as long as you have to thicken it. It's fine out of the fridge overnight.

SERVES 4

Prep and frizzle the spring onions
Trim then thinly slice both the white and green parts of 1 bunch of spring onions, then put them into a small pan with 100ml olive oil and 1 teaspoon Turkish chilli flakes and cook over a low–medium heat until you can hear everything begin to sizzle. Cook until the edges of the spring onions are beginning to brown and crisp. Add 1 teaspoon sugar and ½ teaspoon ground turmeric and cook for another minute.

Cool and season
Take the pan off the heat and allow the oil to cool in the pan. Once cool, season with salt and pepper.

Season the yoghurt and serve
Mix 150g thick strained Greek yoghurt with the juice and zest of 2 limes, season well with sea salt, then put into a shallow bowl or on a plate. Swirl in the oil and serve with warm bread or raw veg for dipping.

Olive Oil

Spiced aubergines with cucumber salsa

150ml extra virgin oil, plus
    2 tablespoons
3 medium aubergines (about
    750g), trimmed and sliced
    lengthways into wedges
1 teaspoon cumin seeds
1 teaspoon coriander seeds
1 teaspoon ground turmeric
2 cloves of garlic, peeled and
    very thinly sliced
a small thumb-sized piece of
    ginger (15g), peeled and sliced
    into thin matchsticks
1 cucumber, peeled and roughly
    diced
zest and juice of 1 unwaxed
    lemon
a small bunch of mint, leaves
    picked
pinch of Turkish chilli flakes,
    plus extra for sprinkling
200g Greek yoghurt or oat
    Greek yoghurt
a drizzle of pomegranate
    molasses or runny honey,
    to serve
4 warm flatbreads, to serve

Aubergines love olive oil like no other vegetable. They literally lap up the oil, and the flavour. Thanks to the oil, these aubergines should be so soft and buttery that you can cut through them with a spoon. This way of cooking the aubergines in a good amount of decent olive oil and a little water is an easy route to the best aubergines I've ever tasted. It's all done in a tray, layering the flavours as you cook; the olive oil brings a warm golden richness to the aubergine.

SERVES 4

Preheat the oven and the tin
Preheat the oven to 180°C/160°C fan. Pour 150ml extra virgin olive oil into a large, deep roasting tin and put it in the oven to heat up.

Prep the aubergines
Salt 3 aubergines, sliced lengthways into wedges, generously. Carefully remove the hot oil from the oven, add 1 teaspoon cumin seeds, 1 teaspoon coriander seeds and 1 teaspoon ground turmeric, then lay the aubergine wedges in a single layer on top so they sizzle a little. Carefully add 150ml cold water (the oil will spit, so be careful) and roast in the oven for 15 minutes.

Turn the aubergines and add the garlic and ginger
Take the tray out of the oven, turn the aubergines so they cook evenly, then scatter 2 cloves of garlic, peeled and very thinly sliced, and 15g ginger, peeled and sliced into thin matchsticks, into the tray around the aubergine. Return to the oven for a further 15 minutes until the ginger and garlic are lightly golden and cooked.

Make the cucumber salsa
Put 1 peeled and roughly diced cucumber into a bowl with the zest and juice of 1 unwaxed lemon and 2 tablespoons extra virgin olive oil. Roughly chop a small bunch of mint leaves and stir into the cucumber with a pinch of Turkish chilli flakes. Season with a pinch of sea salt and a few grinds of freshly ground black pepper.

Finish the aubergines
Put 200g Greek yoghurt or oat Greek yoghurt on a platter or a few plates, then top with the aubergines, a spoonful of cucumber salsa, extra Turkish chilli flakes and a drizzle of pomegranate molasses or honey. Serve with 4 warm flatbreads.

Pappa pomodoro

400g ripe cherry tomatoes
150ml good-quality extra virgin
    olive oil, plus extra for frying
    and drizzling
2 cloves of garlic, peeled and
    finely sliced
a bunch of basil (30g), leaves
    picked and stalks finely
    chopped
800g fresh tomatoes, roughly
    chopped, or 2 × 400g tins
    good-quality plum tomatoes
200g stale good-quality bread,
    like sourdough (2 slices) or
    ciabatta

I cooked this a lot as a young chef, both in the restaurants I worked in during stints cooking in Mallorca and Tuscany and at home, when tomatoes were cheap and plentiful.

This soup is a lesson in how olive oil can lift something from simple to incredible. Here it adds some buttery olive flavour but also when it hits the tomato it makes this soup creamy and many times more satisfying than it would be without it.

SERVES 4

Char the cherry tomatoes
Heat a large pan big enough to cook your soup in. Add 400g ripe cherry tomatoes and cook on a high heat until softened and charred at the edges. Add 100ml water to the pan to pull all the tomato flavours up off the bottom of the pan. Keep the heat on high to reduce the liquid by three-quarters.

Fry the garlic
When the tomato juices have all but cooked away, add a glug of oil to the pan and turn the heat down to medium. Add 2 cloves of peeled and finely sliced garlic and the chopped stalks from a 30g bunch of basil and simmer for a couple of minutes with the tomatoes, or until softened but not browning.

Add the tomatoes
Tip in 800g chopped fresh or tinned tomatoes. If you are using tinned, break them up with the back of a spoon, then add 600ml or 1½ tinfuls of cold water. Bring to the boil, then reduce to a simmer and cook for 15 minutes, stirring every now and then.

Add the bread
Tear 200g stale good-quality bread into the tomatoes in smallish pieces. I keep the crust on here, but if you prefer take yours off. Stir in the bread and add a good pinch of sea salt and ground black pepper. Tear in almost all the basil leaves and let the soup sit on a low heat for 10 minutes.

Finish the soup
Pour over 150ml good-quality extra virgin olive oil, stirring it in. The soup should be a thick, almost porridge-like consistency. If you need to, add a few splashes of hot water to loosen it. Taste and check the seasoning, adding more salt and pepper if needed. Serve with the remaining basil torn over the top.

Buttery green veg and herb braise

2 bulbs of fennel, trimmed and
    sliced into 6–8 wedges
650g medium waxy potatoes,
    peeled and halved if small, or
    cut into 3cm chunks if bigger
1 medium courgette, cut into
    irregular 3cm pieces
150ml extra virgin olive oil,
    plus 3 tablespoons
3 cloves of garlic, peeled and
    finely sliced
1 heaped teaspoon coriander
    seeds, crushed
a few sprigs of oregano or
    thyme (10g), leaves picked
1 unwaxed lemon, ½ thinly
    sliced, the remaining half
    to serve
150g green vegetables (e.g. green
    beans, podded broad beans
    or peas, asparagus or runner
    beans), cut into bite-sized
    pieces
200g thick natural yoghurt
a small handful of parsley leaves
    (15g), roughly chopped
a small handful of fresh dill (10g),
    and/or chives, finely chopped

Cooking vegetables in olive oil and water in this way brings out a buttery sweetness and allows the richness of the oil to lap around them as they cook. The result is beautifully cooked vegetables with a rich olive oil broth. I often make this as it is, but if you want a more filling meal then adding some cooked giant couscous or a tin of white beans for the last few minutes of cooking is a great idea.

SERVES 4

Prepare the vegetables
Trim 2 bulbs of fennel, then slice into 6–8 wedges, depending on the size of your bulbs. Peel and roughly chop 650g waxy potatoes into halves or 3cm chunks if they are bigger. Then roughly chop 1 medium courgette into irregular 3cm pieces.

Heat the oil and cook the fennel
In a large, wide, lidded heavy-based pan, heat 3 tablespoons extra virgin olive oil over a medium-high heat. Add the fennel and cook for 5 minutes, turning over occasionally until lightly golden on both sides.

Add the garlic, herbs and oil
Stir in 3 peeled and finely sliced cloves of garlic, 1 heaped teaspoon coriander seeds, crushed, and fry for a further minute, then add the potatoes, the leaves from a few sprigs of oregano or thyme, ½ an unwaxed lemon, cut into thin slices, and 150ml extra virgin olive oil along with 250ml cold water (or enough to cover the vegetables) and a big pinch of flaky sea salt.

Cover and cook
Cover, bring to a boil, turn down to a low simmer and cook for 15 minutes. After 15 minutes, stir in the courgette pieces and plenty of freshly ground black pepper along with 150g green

vegetables cut into bite-sized pieces and cook for a further 10–15 minutes until everything is soft. You may need to add the longer-cooking green veg with the courgettes first, and any quicker-cooking veg like peas only for the last 5 minutes.

To serve
Spoon the veg and some of the broth into bowls and top with a big spoonful of thick natural yoghurt and an extra squeeze of lemon, some chopped parsley and dill and a little more flaky sea salt and freshly ground black pepper.

Stanley Tucci's spaghetti alla Nerano

about 200ml of olive oil
8–10 small courgettes, sliced
  into thin rounds
a large bunch of basil (75g),
  leaves picked
extra virgin olive oil, for
  drizzling
500g spaghetti
100–200g grated Parmesan
  cheese

This recipe comes with the kind permission of Stanley Tucci. It's the pasta I dream about most. After watching Stanley and Felicity (my friend and agent) eat it on his TV show, I made it every week over the summer. This plate of pasta is a lesson in the beauty of a few ingredients, cooked simply and with care, which Italians in my opinion do best. And also a lesson in how olive oil is the maker of greatness in a dish.

It takes a while to fry all the courgettes but the sweetness it brings out will pay you back. Try to use little sweet courgettes for this; the big ones can be more bitter which you don't want here.

SERVES 4

Cook the courgettes
Put about 200ml olive oil in a large pot and bring to a low boil over a medium-high heat. Slice 8–10 small courgettes into thin rounds and fry in batches in the oil until they are golden brown. Remove and set aside on paper towels. Sprinkle them with sea salt and scatter over 75g basil leaves. Transfer to a bowl and drizzle liberally with extra virgin olive oil.

Cook the pasta
Cook 500g spaghetti in plenty of salted boiling water until al dente and strain, reserving about 2 cupfuls (500ml) of the pasta water.

Finish the spaghetti alla Nerano
Place the cooked pasta back into the pan over a low heat with the courgette mixture and stir together gently. Add the pasta water, a little at a time, to create a creamy texture. You may not use all of the pasta water. Now gradually add 100–200g grated Parmesan to the mixture and continue to combine by stirring

gently and tossing. When the mixture has a slight creaminess, remove from the stove and serve immediately.

Note: The fried courgettes can be refrigerated for about 5 days for use at a later date. Best to bring them to room temperature before using.

Butter beans with green olives and tomatoes

100ml extra virgin olive oil

2 onions, peeled and finely chopped

2 cloves of garlic, peeled and finely sliced

2 tablespoons tomato purée

1 teaspoon dried oregano

1 teaspoon caster sugar

1 × 400g tin finely chopped tinned tomatoes or passata

100g stone-in green olives, destoned

2 × 400g tins or 1 × 600g jar butter beans, drained

½ a bunch of parsley (15g), roughly chopped

½ a bunch of dill (15g), roughly chopped

200g feta, or vegan feta-style cheese, crumbled

These are loosely based on gigantes plaki – a Greek recipe for butter beans cooked with tomatoes and lots of olive oil. These are one of the things I like to cook a double batch of and have to eat for days. They are the kind of dish that's better on the second or third day. I use jarred butter beans, which are far superior, but if you can't get them, tinned will work; I find tinned less 'buttery' and not cooked as evenly. I use tins of the fine tomato pulp here or passata. If you are using chopped tinned tomatoes, whizz them up to break down any larger pieces of tomato.

SERVES 4

Caramelise the onions and garlic
Add 2 tablespoons extra virgin olive oil and 2 peeled and finely chopped onions to a large saucepan and place over a medium heat. Cook, stirring regularly, for 4–5 minutes until soft and just starting to caramelise. Add 2 peeled and finely sliced cloves of garlic and fry for another minute or so, keeping an eye on it until it is lightly golden.

Add the tomato purée
Add 2 tablespoons tomato purée, 1 teaspoon dried oregano, 1 teaspoon caster sugar, a big pinch of sea salt and a few grinds of freshly ground black pepper to the onions and garlic and stir together to cook the tomato purée into the oil for a minute or two.

Add the oil and tomatoes
Add the remainder of the olive oil (70ml) and a 400g tin of finely chopped tomatoes or passata. Bring to a simmer, then turn down the heat and allow to bubble, stirring occasionally, until the tomato sauce splits and you can see a layer of oil forming around the edges.

Add the olives and beans
Destone 100g stone-in green olives and add them to the pan with 2 drained 400g tins or 1 drained 600g jar of butter beans. Mix the beans and olives in and cook for 5 minutes over a medium heat until the beans are coated in the tomato sauce. Roughly chop half a bunch of parsley and half a bunch of dill and stir half of each into the beans.

Put everything together
Spoon big piles of the beans into bowls and top with 200g crumbled feta, more extra virgin olive oil, and the rest of the chopped dill and parsley.

If you want to cook your own beans
Soak 200g dried butter beans in cold water, ideally overnight but for at least 4 hours. Drain and place in a large heavy-based pan with a litre of water, 100ml extra virgin olive oil, 1 teaspoon sea salt, a few bashed cloves of unpeeled garlic and a few sprigs of hardy herbs (rosemary, thyme, bay all work). Bring the beans to the boil and cook over a high heat for 5 minutes, then reduce the heat to a simmer and cook for 1–2 hours, skimming away any scum that rises to the surface. Cook until the beans are just turning soft, and can be squashed with your fingers.

Tortilla Español with herbs and shallots

2 large onions, peeled, halved
  and thinly sliced
400ml extra virgin olive oil,
  plus 2 tablespoons
6 medium waxy potatoes (650g),
  peeled and cut into 3mm-
  thick sliccs
8 medium organic eggs
1 small shallot, peeled and
  finely diced
1 tablespoon red wine vinegar
1 stick of celery, finely sliced
a small bunch of parsley (25g),
  leaves picked

Tortilla is one of my favourite things in the world to eat. A Spanish friend, Carolina, used to make it for us. She'd make a huge panful and we'd eat it for dinner warm and then cold the next day with vinegary tomato salad or in bocadillos. To me a tortilla is the perfect olive oil recipe, as frying the potatoes and onions in a generous amount of oil is key. The oil can be strained and kept for your next tortilla or any other savoury dish. A special mention here to my friend Kitty, who lent me her tortilla knowledge.

SERVES 4

Cook the onions
Peel, halve and thinly slice 2 large onions. You want the slices to be equally thin, so they all cook at the same time. In a small, non-stick round pan (about 24cm) heat 400ml of your best extra virgin olive oil on a medium-high heat. Add the sliced onions and cook, stirring every so often, for 5 minutes until they are soft and slightly golden. Remove the onions from the oil with a slotted spoon to a mixing bowl and set aside.

Cook the potatoes
Cut 6 medium waxy peeled potatoes into thin 3mm-thick slices, again making sure they are the same size so they cook evenly. Add them to the same hot oil and cook for 8–10 minutes, until they are soft and a knife goes through with no resistance. Drain the potatoes, keeping the oil in a heatproof bowl or jug for later. Add the potatoes to the bowl with the onions. No need to wash the pan as you will use it later.

Whisk and add the eggs
Lightly whisk 8 medium organic eggs in a small bowl, then pour them over the warm potatoes and onions and stir gently to bring everything together. Season well with a good pinch of flaky sea salt, then cover with a plate that snugly fits over the bowl to rest for 10–15 minutes. This is a really important stage, as it makes everything thicken up, meld together and cook evenly.

Cook the tortilla
Once the mixture is rested, heat the same pan on a medium heat with 2 tablespoons of the oil you used earlier. Pour the egg mix into the pan and turn the heat down to the lowest setting for 1–2 minutes. Run a spatula around the edges a few times to make sure it's not sticking, then leave to cook for around 4–6 minutes until you can see that the bottom and edges are setting.

Flip the tortilla
Give the pan a shake to make sure the bottom hasn't stuck, then place a plate that's larger than the pan over the tortilla, cover your hand with a tea towel and carefully but confidently and quickly flip the tortilla on to the plate.

Slide the tortilla back into the pan, tucking in its edges with a spatula to get the characteristic rounded shape. Continue to cook over a low heat for a further 4–6 minutes until just set around the edges but still a little soft in the middle. Slide the tortilla out on to a plate, then leave to cool while you make the salad.

Make the parsley salad
Put 1 small finely diced shallot in a bowl with 1 tablespoon red wine vinegar and 2 tablespoons olive oil and mix until the shallot is coated. Add 1 finely sliced stick of celery and the leaves from 25g parsley, toss together once more and pile on the tortilla.

Crispy-bottomed traybake pizza

1 teaspoon (7g) active dry yeast
2 teaspoons runny honey
700g strong bread flour
½ tablespoon sea salt (about 12g)
40ml extra virgin olive oil,
   plus more for greasing and
   finishing
2 cloves of garlic, peeled and
   crushed
1 × 400g tin good-quality finely
   chopped tomatoes (I use
   Polpo ones)
1 ball of mozzarella, torn
a bunch of basil, leaves picked,
   stalks finely chopped

Plus the toppings you love –
   these are mine:
1 green chilli, finely sliced
50g Parmesan cheese, grated
2 tablespoons stone-in green
   olives, destoned and torn
1 tablespoon capers

I made this a few weeks before having my son Esca. I spent the days before he was born writing this book, and in the evenings I watched food TV. One night in particular I was a few episodes deep in the *Chef's Table* pizza – after which all I could think about was making bouncy Roman-style pizza with choose your own adventure toppings.

There is a lot to say here. First of all I make a very wet, no-knead dough, so while this recipe needs some time it's very hands off. It's the only kind of pizza I would try to make in a domestic oven, which I don't think gets quite hot enough for thin Neapolitan-style pizza.

The crispy bottom of the dough is what makes this kind of oven-baked pizza so good, so don't scrimp on the oil. Lots of oil between the dough and the hot tray is what's going to give you that golden crispy bottom.

I've given you two routes for the dough, similar to the focaccia on page 156 – one that is an overnight prove (for maximum flavour in the dough) and one that you can make at lunchtime for your dinner.

When it comes to toppings, I keep things pretty simple and truly believe the best pizza is a Margarita. I've also given some of my other favourite options – but this is pizza, which I know is personal, so feel free to put on it whatever you love best. Just don't overload it.

SERVES 6–8

Make the dough
Whether you are doing an overnight prove or a shorter prove, stir together 525ml lukewarm water with 1 teaspoon (7g) active dry yeast and 2 teaspoons runny honey. In a large bowl, mix 700g strong bread flour with ½ tablespoon sea salt, then add the yeast and honey

mixture and 40ml extra virgin olive oil. Stir to combine using a spatula or dough scraper until there are no floury pockets in the dough. The dough will still look scrappy and scruffy at this stage and that's what you want. Scrape your hands and the sides of the bowl clean and cover with a tea towel.

First prove of the dough
For an overnight prove put the covered bowl into the fridge until you are ready to work with it. It should have at least doubled in size by the morning. For a shorter prove, knead the dough for 4 minutes until smooth, then leave at room temperature (away from draughts or cold spots) for 1–2 hours, or until doubled in size.

Second prove
If you have proved your dough overnight, get it out of the fridge and allow to come to room temperature. Once it has reached room temperature or, if doing the shorter prove, doubled in size, pour 4 tablespoons oil on to a 4cm deep 35 × 35cm roasting tray. Using your hands or a dough scraper gently transfer the dough into the tray. Drizzle then use your hands to rub another 2 tablespoons olive oil over the dough. Gently stretch it to the edge of the tray. Leave it to rest for half an hour to 45 minutes until it's puffed up to about double the size.

Make the quick tomato sauce
While the dough is having its last prove, heat a glug of olive oil in a frying pan. Once the oil is warm, but not too hot, add 2 peeled and crushed cloves of garlic and cook on a medium heat until the room

Continued over...

Olive Oil

smells of garlic and the edges are just beginning to brown. Add a 400g tin of good-quality finely chopped tomatoes and a good pinch of salt and cook on a medium heat for 6–8 minutes, until the tomatoes have broken down and the sauce has thickened and sweetened. Turn off the heat.

Preheat the oven and shape the pizza
Preheat the oven to 220°C/200°C fan. After the dough has had its final rest, dimple the dough once more with the pads of your fingertips. You want the dough to be a bit flatter and less aerated than a focaccia, so don't be afraid to remove any big air bubbles here.

Top the pizza
Spread all of the tomato sauce on to the dough, leaving a border around the edges, then scatter a ball of thinly torn mozzarella over it. Then add your toppings. My forever pizza is topped with capers, destoned, torn green olives, finely sliced green chilli and a good grating of Parmesan, but top yours with what you love. Remember this is a big pizza so you can divide it up in half or quarters and finish each one differently.

Bake the pizza
Drizzle the pizza with another 1–2 tablespoons of extra virgin olive oil, then bake in the oven for 30 minutes until golden and bubbling.

Favourite pizza topping combinations:

Classic
Tomato sauce, mozzarella and – once it's out of the oven – basil.

Lemon bianco
No tomato, just mozzarella or ricotta, thinly sliced red onion, thinly sliced lemon and capers.

Potato and taleggio bianco
No tomato, just very finely sliced potato, a few rosemary needles, dotted with taleggio.

Greens and ricotta
Tomato sauce, greens scrunched with salt and olive oil, ricotta, lemon zest, lots of grated Parmesan when it comes out of the oven.

Smoky mole-spiced confit tomatoes

1 tablespoon cumin seeds
1 tablespoon coriander seeds
350ml extra virgin olive oil
1–2 tablespoons chipotle paste
   or chipotle in adobo
1 tablespoon unsweetened cocoa
   powder
1 unwaxed lime
900g tomatoes, a mixture of
   sizes, shapes and colours, on
   the vine if possible
1 whole head of garlic, halved
   horizontally across the
   middle

As these tomatoes cook they fill your kitchen with the most insane smell. Sweet and tomatoey with the back note of warm heat from chipotle and cocoa, these tomatoes are a flavour party so they are an amazing thing to build a meal around. I've given you a few suggestions on ways to eat them as they are too good to be limited to one. But however you serve them I suggest you make the jalapeño yoghurt, as it goes so well with the deeply savoury tomatoes.

How much chipotle you add to the tomatoes will depend on how spicy you like your food and also how hot your chipotle in adobo or chipotle paste is. Different brands vary.

SERVES 4–6 DEPENDING ON HOW YOU SERVE THEM

Preheat the oven and toast the spices
Preheat the oven to 160°C/140°C fan. While the oven is heating up, put 1 tablespoon cumin seeds and 1 table-spoon coriander seeds in a deep 30cm × 20cm roasting tin large enough to hold all the tomatoes and roast in the oven for a few minutes until they smell toasted.

Flavour the oil
Measure out 350ml extra virgin olive oil and mix in 1–2 tablespoons chipotle paste or chipotle in adobo (depending on its spiciness and your love of heat), 1 tablespoon unsweetened cocoa powder and a big pinch of flaky sea salt. Peel 2 strips of zest from 1 unwaxed lime using a veg peeler and add this to the oil.

Put everything in the tin
Prepare 900g tomatoes by cutting any large tomatoes in half across the middle but leave the stalks or vines on. Add to the roasting tin with the spices, making sure any tomatoes you have

cut in half are facing cut side up. Halve 1 whole head of garlic horizontally across the middle, and nestle it into the tomatoes. Pour over the chipotle oil, making sure it comes two-thirds of the way up the large tomatoes. Place the tin in the preheated oven and roast for 2 hours.

How to eat and serve the tomatoes:
There are several different ways to enjoy these tomatoes. However you serve them, make sure you squeeze the roasted garlic out of its skin and spoon over lots of the spiced oil. Any oil left after you have eaten the tomatoes can be poured into a jar and kept in the fridge for a couple of weeks.

Make the jalapeño yoghurt
My favourite way to eat these is with this yoghurt, with the contrast of cool and hot, fresh and rich. Put 200ml natural yoghurt into a small bowl, grate in the remaining unwaxed lime zest and squeeze in its juice, then mix well. Add 1 table-spoon pickled jalapeños, the picked and chopped leaves from 15g coriander and a pinch of flaky sea salt. Mix together, then top with the last tablespoon of pickled jalapeños.

Make a rice bowl
Serve the tomatoes and squeezed-out garlic on top of deep bowls full of rice tossed with lime and butter (see page 194). Add some sliced avocado, coriander, the jalapeño yoghurt and finish with a good drizzle of oil over everything.

Make a mole tomato sauce
Remove the stalks from the tomatoes and squeeze out the garlic from its papery skins, then blitz the

Continued over...

tomatoes with 8 tablespoons of the oil
for a rich, smooth tomato sauce. Stir
through pasta, or cook veg or beans
in it.

Add black beans
When the tomatoes are cooked,
strain most of the oil from the
roasting tin, squeeze the garlic out
of its skin and remove any tomato
stalks. Add 2 × 400g tins of drained
black beans to the roasting tin, spoon
and scrunch everything together,
then return to the oven for another
10 minutes to warm through. Serve
with warm corn tortillas and the
jalapeño yoghurt.

Make mole tomato tacos
Add a little salt and pepper to
seasonal vegetables (I like courgettes
or squash) and roast until golden.
Toss with the mole tomatoes then
return to the oven to warm the
tomatoes. Pile on to tacos with
chopped white onion, sour cream and
coriander. Finish with lots of lime.

Citrus olive oil cake with chocolate icing

2 clementines, or 1 small unwaxed orange
1 small unwaxed lemon
4 tablespoons extra virgin olive oil, plus 1 tablespoon for the ganache, and a little extra for greasing
Demerara sugar
4 organic eggs, at room temperature
250g soft light brown sugar
250g ground almonds
1 teaspoon baking powder
1 teaspoon bicarbonate of soda
100g dark chocolate, chopped
1 teaspoon honey

This cake is somewhere between Claudia Roden's classic boiled orange cake and a grown-up Jaffa Cake. The olive oil brings some buttery notes which bounce off the citrus and almonds. The icing is made with olive oil and is one of the easiest, most satisfying ganaches I have made. I like to grind whole blanched almonds for this cake; to do that just blitz the whole almonds to a fine powder. Shop-bought ground almonds will work fine though.

SERVES 10–12

Cook the citrus
Wash 2 clementines and 1 small unwaxed lemon, then put them into a large saucepan and cover with water. Bring to the boil, cover the pot and simmer for about an hour until very soft, then remove from the pan and leave to cool.

Preheat the oven and prepare the tin
Preheat the oven to 200°C/180°C fan and line the bottom of a 23cm round, loose-bottomed cake tin with baking paper. Drizzle the paper with olive oil, then sprinkle with a little Demerara sugar, tilting the tin so it coats all of the sides.

Blitz the citrus
Once the clementines and lemon are cool enough to handle, cut them open and remove and discard the pips. If you want to, weigh the fruit to check you have about 300g. Add 4 tablespoons extra virgin olive oil to the fruit and blitz to a smooth purée either in a food processor or with a hand-held blender.

Make the cake batter
In a stand mixer or using a hand-held whisk, beat 4 organic eggs with 250g soft light brown sugar for a minute or two, until pale and fluffy. Add the citrus purée, 250g ground almonds, 1 teaspoon baking powder, 1 teaspoon bicarbonate of soda and a pinch of salt and mix again until light and smooth.

Bake the cake
Pour the batter into the prepared tin. Bake in the middle of the oven for 50 minutes–1 hour, or until a skewer comes out clean, then leave to cool in the tin.

Make the chocolate and olive oil ganache
Put 100g chopped dark chocolate, 1 tablespoon extra virgin olive oil and 1 teaspoon honey in a heatproof bowl over a barely simmering pan of water (a bain marie) and place on a low heat. Warm gently until the chocolate has melted and the mixture is smooth. Set aside for 20 minutes or until cool. The ganache will harden once it cools, so you will want to ice the cake while the ganache is still just warm.

Finish the cake
Once the cake has cooled completely in its tin, take it out, put it on a serving plate and drizzle the top of the cake with the ganache. Slice and serve with the rest of the ganache.

Olive Oil

Double ginger cake with lemon crème fraîche

250g plain flour
2 teaspoons ground ginger
½ teaspoon ground cinnamon
1 teaspoon baking powder
1 teaspoon bicarbonate of soda
200g dark brown muscovado
  sugar
125ml olive oil
5 balls stem ginger (about 75g) in
  syrup, roughly chopped, and
  the syrup from the jar
3 large free-range or organic
  eggs
200ml whole milk or oat milk
2 tablespoons Demerara sugar
200g crème fraîche
1 tablespoon ginger syrup
zest of 1 unwaxed lemon and
  1 tablespoon juice
1 tablespoon extra virgin
  olive oil

I find it hard to love any cake more than ginger cake. This cake has two hits of ginger to make it fiery. The ginger works so well with the treacle darkness of the muscovado. Olive oil makes the most perfect sponge texture and then shows up again in a sharp lemon crème fraîche, which gives this whole thing a school dinner pudding feeling in the best, freshest possible way.

SERVES 8

Preheat the oven and prepare the tin
Preheat the oven to 180°C/160°C fan. Line the base and sides of a square 23 × 23cm cake tin with baking paper.

Mix the dry ingredients
Whisk 250g plain flour, 2 teaspoons ground ginger, ½ teaspoon ground cinnamon, 1 teaspoon baking powder, 1 teaspoon bicarbonate of soda and a good pinch of sea salt together in a large mixing bowl. Make sure there are no lumps of baking powder.

Mix the wet ingredients
In a small, deep saucepan over a moderate heat, warm 200g dark brown muscovado sugar and 125ml olive oil until the sugar has melted a little. Add 3 balls of roughly chopped stem ginger to the pan. Break 3 large free-range or organic eggs into a mixing bowl, add 200ml whole milk or oat milk and the sugar, oil and ginger mixture and mix well.

Mix dry into wet
Add the dry ingredients to the wet and mix gently but quickly until no flour is visible.

Bake the cake
Pour the batter into the tin, sprinkle over 2 tablespoons Demerara sugar and bake for about 35–40 minutes,

until it is slightly puffed and spongy to the touch. Leave to cool a little in the tin.

Make the lemon crème fraîche
Mix 200g crème fraîche with 1 tablespoon ginger syrup, 1 tablespoon lemon juice, 1 tablespoon extra virgin olive oil and stir to mix well.

Serve the cake
Once the cake is cool enough to handle, remove it from the tin and cut into 8 squares. Divide the crème fraîche between 8 bowls, put a slice of cake into each bowl, top with a drizzle of extra virgin olive oil and more chopped stem ginger and some lemon zest.

Vinegar

Sharpness in a bottle from orange to black. Pickles, sweet and sour. Malt for fish and chips. White wine for herby vinaigrette. Cider with mustard for boiled potatoes. Rice wine, gentle, for splashing on sushi rice. Herby with lovage for summer tomatoes. Blood orange for chicory salad. Black vinegar for dipping dumplings. Red wine for pink pickled onions. I have more bottles of vinegar than I need – a shelf full so I can choose the perfect match. Though really I only need one or two. Not just for dressings and pickling but for baking, roasting, dipping, curry, for balance.

On Vinegar

To me, acid is the most important and forgotten aspect of cooking. It's a highlight, a top note that brings a plate of food together. Vinegar is an always available, cheap and easy way to add a hit of acidity. It has a lower acidity level than lemon and lime, but it doesn't have the natural sweetness of citrus, and so it tastes sharper.

Vinegar is something I find myself craving, and I keep as many vinegars on hand as I do oils. An essential collection of vinegars to me would be white wine or cider, a red wine vinegar and a rice wine vinegar. With these vinegars, you can do everything.

We are used to using vinegar for dressings and seasoning, but I think vinegar is underrated as an ingredient. I will add acid to my food during cooking and at the end to balance. Adding vinegar to roasted squash, for example, seasons the squash with acidity from within, and the vinegar mellows as it cooks.

The way I use vinegar most is to quickly pickle an element of my dinner in the time it takes me to cook everything else. From finely sliced onions to grated carrot and beetroot or thinly sliced cucumber, these quick pickles are made with the vinegar that suits what I am eating best. Always with a pinch of salt and sometimes one of sugar, and often with an added herb or spice, these are a boosting final element to lots of my simple dinners.

Pickles – by that I mean gherkins and cornichons and their brine – feature heavily in this chapter too. They bring vinegary acidity as well as crunch to so much of what I cook.

Sour, Acid, Sharp, Fruity

Types

- Pasteurised vinegar is treated with heat to neutralise the bacterial culture, known as 'the mother'. Unpasteurised vinegar has the mother inside the bottle, which is the equivalent of a sourdough starter, so the unpasteurised vinegar is usually cloudy with bits.

- Balsamic
Made from grapes that are cooked before they are fermented. Dark with a syrupy flavour – the best is made in Italy's Modena and Reggio Emilia DOCG regions.

- Wine (red and white)
Made from wine – you can buy specific types: chianti, Champagne, chardonnay, etc. The sharpness and flavour vary wildly. I use this for dressings, pickles and some cooking – think red wine vinegar for braised red cabbage.

- Sherry
Made from sherry within a designated region in Spain. Rich, nutty and caramelly in flavour with a colour to match.

- Malt
Malt-flavoured with a toasty note – quite punchy, for chips and to cut through fatty foods.

- Rice
Sweet and silky, toasty, unobtrusive sourness, for rice, noodles, dressings, when you want gentle acidity.

- Cider
Sharp and fruity with a punch, I buy it unpasteurised, so it's cloudy. Used for dressings, cooking and even apple pie. Also for drinking with fizzy water or hot water, honey and lemon.

- Infused vinegars
Infusing one of these base vinegars with other ingredients gives amazing variations in flavour.

From cherries to sorrel, lovage to blood orange.

Goes well with

Vinegar cuts through fatty flavours

boiled potatoes	mustard
chicory	pickling veg
chips	rice
cucumber	roast potatoes
dairy	salad dressing
dumplings	tomato

Favourite uses

- A basic brine for pickled veg
- A sharp salad dressing
- Agrodolce leeks or squash – a hint of sweet and a hit of sour
- Pickled rhubarb and fruit
- My pickled cabbage soup
- A dipping sauce for fritters and dumplings
- Stirred through vegetables before roasting
- With sparkling water as an aperitif
- In warm water as a tonic

Storage and tips

Vinegar keeps for years thanks to its high acidity level. Keep it with the top on in a cool, dark cupboard if possible.
If your vinegar is unpasteurised, sediment might settle at the bottom. Shake it back in or strain it if that's a problem, but the sediment is thought to retain the nutrients too.

Favourite brands and where to buy

- I buy most of my vinegars from my friend Andy of The Vinegar Shed, especially his homemade infused ones – he's leading a well-overdue vinegar revolution. His lovage-infused vinegar is my go-to.

- Brindisa's Valdespino sherry vinegar is hard to beat; I've not found a better one yet.

Homemade vinegar and quick pickles

750ml good-quality British cider
150ml raw apple cider vinegar
    (with the mother)

Mix the vinegar
Put 750ml cider and 150ml raw apple
cider vinegar in a clean, large (at
least 1-litre capacity) non-reactive
container. Shake and swirl the
container to mix everything evenly,
then loosely cover the container with
a piece of muslin, a double sheet of
kitchen towel or cheesecloth and set
aside in a cool dark place.

Taste the vinegar every couple of
weeks until it's reached an acidity
you like. The cider will evaporate
over time, but you should still have at
least 500ml vinegar and 150ml left to
start another vinegar fermentation.
Transfer your 500ml finished vinegar
to a sterilised bottle and store in a
cool dark place.

HOMEMADE HERB VINEGAR
MAKES 200ML

200ml raw apple cider vinegar
a bunch (30g) any soft herbs (tarragon,
    chervil and lovage work well)

Make the vinegar
Put 200ml apple cider vinegar and 30g
soft herbs into a small, clean jar. For a
singular flavour, use just one herb, or
you could also use a mixture that you
have spare after cooking. I like to add
odds and ends of soft herbs to a jar of
vinegar in the kitchen to create
something complex and unique.

Mature the vinegar
Close the jar with a lid and set aside
for a couple of days and up to a
month, depending on how intense

you want your herb flavour. If you
can't make your own apple cider
vinegar, shop-bought raw vinegar
will work well.

QUICK PICKLES

This method of quick pickling is
great for using up those last few
vegetables in the salad drawer.
Depending on the aromatics and
the size of the veg you're using, your
pickling liquor can be used warm or
cold. Try these scattered over salads,
tossed through grains or alongside
some hummus and flatbreads for a
super-simple starter to any meal.

500g veg of your choice (radishes,
    beetroot, cauliflower, cabbage,
    carrots)
250ml white wine vinegar
150ml water
1 tablespoon fine salt
1 tablespoon golden caster sugar
1 tablespoon whole spices (coriander
    seed, fennel seed, mustard seed,
    star anise)

Prepare your vegetables
Cut 500g vegetables according
to how tender they are, and how
much cooking they would normally
require. For example, radishes could
be left whole but hardier vegetables
like cauliflower or carrots will need
to be sliced thinner.

Make the pickle liquor
In a small saucepan, put 250ml white
wine vinegar and 150ml water,
followed by 1 tablespoon sea salt and
1 tablespoon golden caster sugar.
Bring to the boil and stir until the
salt and sugar are dissolved, then add
1 tablespoon whole spices of your
choice and remove from the heat.

Jar your pickles
Fill two sterilised 500ml jars with
your chosen cut vegetables. If
the vegetables are hardier, or cut
in large pieces, pour the pickle
liquor over them while it's still a
little warm. This will soften them
slightly and help the vinegar in
the pickle liquor permeate into
them. For more tender and delicate
vegetables, allow the liquor to
completely cool and then cover
them, sealing the jars as you do
so. These will keep happily in a
cool dark place for up to 3 months.
Once open, store in the fridge and
consume within a week.

Chilli vinegar noodles with sesame tofu

a small piece of ginger (10g), grated
4 tablespoons sriracha or chilli sauce
3 tablespoons maple syrup
4 tablespoons rice wine vinegar
3 tablespoons soy sauce or tamari
½ a white or sweetheart cabbage, very finely sliced
250g firm tofu, cut into long, thin pieces (about 1cm × 3cm)
2 tablespoons neutral oil (such as groundnut or vegetable)
2 tablespoons sesame seeds
200g egg or udon noodles
½ a bunch of coriander (15g)

This is a pantry-staple noodle dish. It's made often in our house, sometimes even more simply, without the tofu. The rice wine vinegar dressing makes these simple noodles a more-than-the-sum-of-its-parts dinner. You can easily double this to serve 4.

SERVES 2

Make the dressing
Grate a 10g piece of ginger into a small bowl and add 4 tablespoons sriracha or chilli sauce, 2 tablespoons maple syrup, 4 tablespoons rice wine vinegar and 2 tablespoons soy sauce or tamari. Taste and add more soy if you like it salty.

Dress the cabbage
Scoop half a finely sliced white or sweetheart cabbage into a mixing bowl, add 2 tablespoons of the dressing and scrunch everything together with your hands so it's all evenly coated. Set aside.

Slice and cook the tofu
Slice 250g firm tofu into long, thin pieces (about 1cm × 3cm). Heat a large frying pan over a medium heat, add 2 tablespoons neutral oil and fry the tofu until golden on all sides. Add 2 tablespoons sesame seeds to toast for 30 seconds, then take the pan off the heat. Add 1 tablespoon of soy and stir for a minute before adding a tablespoon of maple syrup.

Cook and dress the noodles
Cook 200g udon noodles for a minute less than the packet instructions. Drain, keeping a little of the water. Tip them into the tofu pan, add the remaining dressing and a splash of the noodle water and put back over a medium heat for a minute or two until everything is coated in the vinegary sauce.

Serve the noodles
Divide the noodles and tofu between 2 bowls and top with the cabbage salad and the leaves from ½ a bunch of coriander.

Ajo blanco

220g blanched almonds
100g good-quality bread, stale
  (I use sourdough)
2–4 cloves of garlic, peeled
  (depending on your love of
  garlic – I use 2)
1 small cucumber (150g), peeled
  and roughly chopped
100g green grapes
600ml ice-cold water
200ml extra virgin olive oil,
  plus more to finish
3 tablespoons sherry vinegar
½ a bunch of dill (10g) or fennel
  fronds, finely chopped

I first tried this soup in a very hot kitchen during my first summer as a chef. It was made by one of my all-time favourite cooks, Steve Pooley. There are few people who have taught me more about cooking and the unbridled joy of eating. This soup is just that – a joy. Refreshing and richly satisfying all at once, with a perfect balance of mellow creaminess from the almonds, punch from the sherry vinegar-soaked bread and sweetness from the grapes. This needs to be served super-cold, so if it's not as chilled as you think it should be, add a couple of ice cubes.

If you don't have sherry vinegar, red wine vinegar will work in its place, though you might need a little less.

SERVES 4

Toast the almonds
Put 220g blanched almonds into a frying pan and place over a low heat. Shake for a few minutes, allowing the almonds to toast very slightly; you want the very palest tinge, to accentuate the taste of the nut. Tip most on to a plate and leave to cool. Toast the rest until nutty and brown. Keep the well-toasted ones separate.

Soak the bread
Tear 100g good-quality stale bread into a large bowl and cover with 100ml cold water. Leave it to soak for 10 minutes.

Blend the ajo blanco
Once the almonds are cool and the bread has soaked, discard the remaining soaking water. Put the bread into a food processor or blender, add the lightly toasted almonds, 2–4 peeled cloves of garlic, 1 peeled and roughly chopped small cucumber and 75g green grapes. Add a little of the 600ml iced water and whizz until smooth.

Add the oil
Now with the motor running slowly add the rest of the iced water, 200ml extra virgin olive oil and 3 tablespoons sherry vinegar and blitz until really smooth. If you have a powerful blender your soup may be smooth enough to eat without sieving. If not, use the back of a ladle to press the soup through a sieve into a bowl, forcing out every last drop of liquid.

Season and chill
Season your soup with a little salt and pepper, then taste and add more seasoning, vinegar or oil until it tastes good to you. Cover and chill in the fridge for at least 2 hours, along with 4 soup bowls.

Serve the ajo blanco
Chop the well-toasted almonds into little shards and slice 25g green grapes. Once cooled, divide the soup between the bowls, drizzle with a little good olive oil and top with the almonds, grapes, ½ a bunch of finely chopped dill or some fennel fronds and a few ice cubes if you want it super-cool.

Courgettes agrodolce with sticky onions

5 tablespoons extra virgin olive
  oil, plus a little extra to serve
4 small or 2 regular courgettes
  (500g), cut into 1.5cm-thick
  rounds
1 red onion, peeled and thinly
  sliced
4 tablespoons red wine vinegar
1 tablespoon golden caster sugar
1 teaspoon dried chilli flakes,
  plus extra to serve
1 clove of garlic, peeled and
  thinly sliced
½ a bunch of mint (15g), leaves
  picked
250g ricotta

Agrodolce means sweet and sour in Italian. In Italy there are so many ways of using this contrast of flavours to bring out the most in ingredients. Here I've used courgettes, but this technique would work for aubergine, thinly sliced butternut squash or fennel. The hit of vinegar which might feel angry on its own is offset with a little bit of sugar, which mellows the acidity and rounds off the flavour. I've written this recipe to serve 2 people but it can easily be doubled, though you will need to fry the courgettes in a few batches.

SERVES 2 AS A MAIN, 4 AS A SIDE

Fry the courgettes
Heat a frying pan over a medium-high heat and add 5 tablespoons extra virgin olive oil. Season 500g courgettes cut into 1.5cm-thick rounds with sea salt and fry them for 3–4 minutes on each side or until blistering and golden brown, then remove with a slotted spoon on to a plate.

Cook the onion and add the agrodolce
Add 1 thinly sliced red onion to the same pan and lower the heat. Fry for 10 minutes until soft, then add 4 tablespoons red wine vinegar, 1 tablespoon golden caster sugar and 1 teaspoon dried chilli flakes and return the courgette pieces to the pan. Cook for a few minutes, then taste and season and divide the courgettes and onion between two plates.

Season and finish
Sprinkle over 1 peeled and thinly sliced clove of garlic and a few more dried chilli flakes, tear over the leaves from half a bunch of mint and drizzle with a little olive oil. Season 250g of ricotta with salt and pepper and spoon it next to the courgettes.

Cheese and pickle roast potatoes with chilli-dressed leaves

1kg new potatoes, scrubbed clean
10 cornichons (35g), roughly chopped, plus 100ml of the brine from the jar
100ml extra virgin olive oil
3 fresh red chillies
juice of 1 unwaxed lemon
100g Comté cheese or vegan mature Cheddar-style cheese
1 head of radicchio or other bitter lettuce

A tray of these for dinner is just about the best thing I can think of to eat. Squashed crisp-edged potatoes, tossed and baked in pickle brine to give them a subtle but important chip-shop-vinegar feeling. Once hot and crisped, the potatoes are topped with cornichons and cheese and finished with a chilli and bitter lettuce salad, though the potatoes are also good just on their own.

Pickle brine is often thrown away but it is highly seasoned gold. It is acidic, a little salty and usually a little sweet, so it instantly adds depth like a splash of vinegar would but in a more mellow way.

SERVES 4

Preheat the oven and parboil the potatoes
Preheat the oven to 200°C/180°C fan. Bring a large pan of salted water to the boil, add 1kg scrubbed new potatoes and cook for 10–20 minutes, depending on their size, until they are just cooked. Drain and leave the potatoes to steam dry in a colander.

Season and roast the potatoes
Tip the potatoes into a roasting tin, toss them with 50ml cornichon brine, 2 tablespoons olive oil and salt and pepper, then roast for 15 minutes. Remove the tin from the oven and, using a potato masher, squish the potatoes until they crack and expose some of the soft, fluffy insides. Pour over another 2 tablespoons olive oil and return to the oven for another 30–40 minutes, turning the potatoes halfway, until golden and crispy.

Make the chilli dressing
Prick 3 fresh red chillies with the tip of a sharp knife – this stops them exploding when they are cooked. Using a pair of metal tongs, hold the chillies one at a time over a gas flame until they're blackened and blistered all over. If you don't have a gas hob you can do this in a dry frying pan. Once they are all blistered, put them in a small bowl, cover and leave for 15 minutes. This way they will steam in their own heat and the skins will peel off easily. Once cool enough to handle, peel the chillies, open them up and scrape out all the seeds. Discard the seeds and finely chop the flesh. Put in a mixing bowl with the remaining olive oil (70ml) and the juice of 1 unwaxed lemon and mix well. Season to taste with sea salt and black pepper.

Finish the potatoes and dress the leaves
Once the potatoes are golden and crisp, add 50ml of cornichon brine while the potatoes are still hot, then toss with 10 roughly chopped cornichons and a generous grating of Comté or vegan Cheddar. Tear 1 head of radicchio into bite-sized pieces, season with salt and toss in the chilli dressing.

White bean and pickle stew

50g unsalted butter or vegan
  butter
2 tablespoons olive oil
2 medium onions, peeled and
  finely sliced
2 × 400g tins or 1 × 600g jar
  cannellini beans, drained
1 litre hot vegetable stock (made
  with 1 teaspoon vegetable
  stock powder or ½ a stock
  cube)
½ a head (125g) cavolo nero,
  de-stemmed and leaves
  roughly chopped
12 cornichons, chopped, plus
  4 tablespoons of their
  pickling brine
½ a bunch of dill or parsley
  (10g), roughly chopped
Parmesan or vegan Parmesan-
  style cheese, grated, to finish
4 tablespoons crème fraîche
  or oat crème fraîche

I put pickles on pretty much anything. During my second pregnancy I panicked on getting near to the bottom of my last jar of Marks & Spencer's mustard seed gherkins. Most of the time pickles, gherkins and cornichons are eaten cold, to make the most of their crunch and acidity. But they keep their crunch when added to soups and stews, bringing texture and a hit of sour interest. Here they sit next to onions, beans and greens and a smattering of dill to make a quick stew that tastes much more layered and complicated than it is to make.

SERVES 4

Cook the onions
Heat 50g unsalted butter and 2 table-spoons olive oil in a deep sauté pan or wide saucepan over a medium heat. Add 2 peeled and finely sliced medium onions and cook for 10 minutes until golden and beginning to crisp. Take out half of the onions and put to one side.

Add the beans
Add two 400g drained tins, or 600g jarred, cannellini beans to the pan with 1 litre hot vegetable stock. Season with salt and pepper and use the back of a spoon to squash about half the beans to make the stew creamy. Bring to a simmer over a medium heat and cook for 15 minutes, until the beans are hot and starting to break down.

Add the greens
De-stem 125g cavolo nero. The best way to do this is to pinch a thumb and finger across the stem at the base, then run them along the stem, separating the leaves from the stem. Save the stems for a vegetable stock another day, or compost them, then roughly chop the leaves into bite-

sized pieces, add to the stew with half (6) the chopped cornichons and 4 tablespoons of pickling brine and cook for 5–7 minutes until the greens are soft. Taste and season with salt and pepper, adding more brine if needed.

Finish the stew
Once the greens are soft, spoon the stew into bowls, top with the reserved onions, the other half (6) of the chopped cornichons, ½ a bunch of dill or parsley, some more olive oil, some grated Parmesan or vegan Parmesan-style cheese and a spoonful of crème fraîche.

Cynthia's quick aubergine moju

2 medium aubergines, cut into
  2cm-thick slices
3 tablespoons neutral oil
100ml apple cider or coconut
  vinegar
2.5cm piece of ginger, peeled
  and roughly chopped
4 cloves of garlic, peeled and
  roughly chopped
2 whole cloves
5 whole cardamoms, bashed and
  seeds removed
2.5cm piece of cinnamon stick
2 teaspoons mustard seeds
1 stalk of lemongrass, roughly
  chopped
10cm piece of pandan leaf,
  roughly chopped (optional)
1 teaspoon chilli powder
2 medium red onions, peeled
  and finely sliced
4 green chillies, split down the
  middle
10–12 fresh curry leaves
3½ teaspoons sugar
to serve, rice, rotis and, if you
  like, some dal

Cynthia Shanmugalingam wrote one of my favourite books of the year: *Rambutan*, a collection of Sri Lankan recipes and stories from Cynthia and her family and friends. It's a book as rich in stories as it is in sambal. Cynthia has been kind enough to share her recipe for moju. When I read her book, I was struck by the role vinegar plays in Sri Lankan cooking. This recipe feels like a pickled curry. It's moreish and brilliant and uses vinegar in a way and with flavours I've never considered.

Cynthia tells me, 'Mojus are a kind of vinegary pickle, a wildly flavourful combination of sweet-and-sour, with cloves, cardamom, cinnamon, lemongrass, curry leaves and, if you can get it, pandan leaf.' She says that the vinegar draws out the bitterness from the mustard seeds, leaving a punchy, fragrant flavour. In Sri Lanka, aubergine moju is traditionally made of soft, deep-fried aubergine, but this is Cynthia's easier recipe where the aubergine is roasted. She eats this with rice and perhaps a simple dal curry, or smeared inside a cheese toastie.

SERVES 2 AS A SIDE, MORE AS A
SIDE/PICKLE

Roast the aubergines
Preheat the oven to 240°C/220°C fan. In a large bowl, mix 2 medium aubergines cut into 2cm-thick slices with ½ teaspoon salt and a couple of tablespoons neutral oil. Then lay out the slices on a baking tray so they are flat next to each other and roast for 30–45 minutes, until golden brown on both sides and cooked through. Remove and set aside to cool.

Make the spice paste
While the aubergines cook, make the spice paste. Blitz 100ml apple cider or coconut vinegar, 2.5cm roughly chopped ginger, 4 roughly chopped cloves of garlic, 2 whole cloves, the seeds from 5 bashed cardamom pods, 2.5cm piece of cinnamon stick, 2 teaspoons mustard seeds, 1 roughly chopped stalk of lemongrass, 1 teaspoon chilli powder and, if you are using it, a roughly chopped 10cm-piece of pandan leaf, together in a food processor to form a paste.

Cook the onions and chillies
Place a medium-sized saucepan or wok over a medium-high heat and add a tablespoon of neutral oil, 2 peeled and finely sliced medium red onions, 4 green chillies, split down the middle, and 10–12 fresh curry leaves, and cook for about 1–2 minutes until the curry leaves are bright green and the onions are beginning to brown.

Add the spice paste and serve
Add the spice paste and 3½ teaspoons sugar to the onions in the pan and cook for 2–3 minutes, until the paste begins to colour. Add the roasted aubergines, and stir gently to coat in the mixture. Taste and add more salt if you think it needs it. Serve warm or at room temperature with rotis or rice and dal.

Sweet pickled apple pie

175g cold unsalted butter, cut
    into small cubes
120g Demerara sugar
300g plain flour, plus extra for
    dusting
1 free-range or organic egg
5 tablespoons apple cider
    vinegar
1.25kg apples (an equal mix of
    tart Bramleys and crisp,
    sweet varieties like Gala,
    Jonagold or Discovery)
    (about 8 apples)
1 tablespoon cornflour
½ cinnamon stick, ground
1 teaspoon green cardamom
    pods, husks discarded, seeds
    removed and ground
2 tablespoons milk of your
    choice
crème fraîche or double cream,
    to serve

I back this apple pie as the best I've ever eaten. The appley cider vinegar brings a tartness to the apples which is so welcome against a just sweet pastry and a crunchy Demerara top. The vinegar also makes its way into the pastry to help ensure it's super short and buttery.

SERVES 8

Make the pastry
Put 175g cold, cubed unsalted butter, 50g Demerara sugar and 300g plain flour into a food processor and blitz until you have an even crumb-like texture. Next, separate 1 free-range or organic egg and keep the white for later. Add the yolk to the food processor with 1 tablespoon apple cider vinegar and 1 tablespoon iced water, then pulse until the pastry just comes together; you don't want to overwork it. If you don't have a food processor, you can do this with your hands, using a small knife to cut the butter into the flour then switching to your hands to bring it together.

Chill the pastry
Tip the pastry out and divide into two pieces, roughly two-thirds for the base of the pie and a third for the top. Shape each piece into a flat disc, wrap them separately in clean tea towels and rest in the fridge for 1 hour.

Make the pickled apple filling
Peel, core and slice 1.25kg apples into 1cm-thick slices. Add them to a bowl with 4 tablespoons apple cider vinegar, 1 tablespoon cornflour and 50g Demerara, along with ½ ground cinnamon stick and the ground seeds from 1 teaspoon cardamom pods. Toss to coat all the apples evenly, then leave to sit until the pastry has had its hour chilling.

Make the pie
Take the pastry out of the fridge and dust your work surface and a rolling pin lightly with flour. Roll the larger piece of pastry into a circle 5cm larger than your pie tin. Roll the pastry on to your rolling pin, then unroll it on to the pie tin. Use the back of your hand or a scrap more pastry to persuade it into the edges of the tin. Allow the excess pastry to hang over the edges. Spoon the pickled apples into the middle of the tin, leaving any excess liquid behind.

Top the pie and preheat the oven
Roll out the smaller disc of pastry until it is 2.5mm thick and a couple of centimetres larger than your pie tin. Brush the edges of the second disc with 2 tablespoons milk, then use the same rolling pin technique to lay the lid over the top, draping it over the apples. Use a sharp knife to trim off any excess pastry, then use your fingers or a fork to crimp or seal the edges. Chill the pie for 30 minutes while you preheat the oven to 210°C/190°C fan and preheat a baking tray.

Finish the pie
Beat the reserved egg white, brush it on to the pastry lid, scatter over 20g Demerara, then place the pie on the preheated baking tray and bake for 30 minutes, turning it around halfway. After 30 minutes turn the oven down to 180°C/160°C fan and bake for a further 20–30 minutes until the pastry is a deep golden colour. Leave to cool for 20–30 minutes then serve with crème fraîche or double cream.

Mustard

Sharp, hot, pungent, peppery. Two jars of seeds, a punchy powder in the spice drawer, four pots and a squeezy bottle stacked in my fridge door. From amber to blonde. Smooth and spoonable Dijon. Wholegrain, dotted brown and ochre. Fiery English as bright as a dandelion. A pot of smoked mustard. And American in a canary-yellow bottle, sweet but sharp. For sandwiches. For dressings. For mayonnaise and aioli. For warm potatoes. A jar lasts as long as the spices in the cupboard. A spoonful gives flavour in excess. Abounding. To be used carefully but bravely. To coat calm white vegetables in a remoulade, to top a flatbread, to be the punch in a salsa verde. Unmatched.

On Mustard

A tiny teaspoon of mustard adds an unreasonable amount of flavour. I use it in so much of my cooking. It can be a subtle, warm note or an upfront sit-up-and-pay-attention jolt of flavour. However you use it, it's such an easy way to get flavour into food quickly.

Brown and black seeds are hotter than the white/yellow ones. How hot a particular mustard tastes is dependent on the type of seed used, as well as what it's blended with.

This chapter focuses on mustard as a jarred condiment made from the seeds, as well as on whole seeds and powdered mustard. You can also buy mustard oil, widely used in India.

Mustard and ketchup are the perfect combination. Mustard brings heat and a little bitterness to the sweet, sour umami of ketchup. Add a pickle and you are very close to perfect.

When we think of mustard, we don't often think of texture, but if you have ever made your own mayonnaise, think of the role it plays in helping the oil begin to emulsify. And as well as heat or pepperiness, it also adds acid from the vinegar it is made with. Hence it goes so well with honey, which adds the sweetness it lacks.

Sharp, Hot, Pungent, Peppery

Types

- Dijon
  A classic French mustard made from brown mustard seeds, white wine and vinegar. On the hotter side.

- Wholegrain
  Made with yellow and brown mustard seeds, and sometimes with other spices added too. Pungent and aromatic.

- English
  Hot and unmistakably bright yellow, made from brown and sometimes yellow seeds. You can buy it jarred or powdered.

- American yellow
  Made from yellow mustard seeds and turmeric for colour, this is a smooth and mild mustard.

- Honey mustard
  As it sounds, wholegrain blended with honey for a sweeter taste, lovely in mashed potato.

- Mustard powder
  A bright-yellow powder with a punchy hot kick, made by drying and grinding black and white mustard seeds.

- Seeds
  Black, brown, white/yellow, use these whole. Buy them in small amounts and use within a couple of months, as the oils in them can go bitter quickly.

Goes well with

apple	honey
butter	leek
cabbage	lentil
cheese	mayonnaise
chilli	miso
coconut	mushroom
dill	olive oil
egg	potato
green bean	radish
greens	white bean

Favourite uses

Jarred/squeezy

- A cheese toastie
- A classic vinaigrette
- Beaten into eggs for an omelette
- On hot dogs and burgers with pickles
- In salsa verde
- In potato salad
- Slathered on sandwiches
- With mushrooms on toast

Seeds

- Tempered with curry leaves to finish a curry
- With coconut milk
- Fried until they pop and stirred into mash

Storage

Keep unopened jars in a cool, dark spot. Once open, I keep it in the fridge, but thanks to the acid in it you can keep it at room temperature.

Favourite brands/where to buy

For Dijon I usually buy Maille, the iconic French brand; for wholegrain, I like big jars of Pommery. I always have a jar of smoked Dijon from Halen Môn on hand too. For English, I go classic Colman's, or Tracklements also make a fiery one I love. I also have a squeezy bottle of French's American and Johnny's Senap, Hot and Sweet Swedish Mustard.

Homemade mustard

6 tablespoons black mustard
    seeds
6 tablespoons yellow mustard
    seeds
1 tablespoon fine sea salt
½ cup (120ml) verjus (or another
    ¼ cup vinegar and
    ¼ cup apple juice)
¼ cup (60ml) raw organic apple
    cider vinegar
¼ cup (60ml) apple juice

Once you've got your head around the principles of making mustard, it is actually pretty easy. Making your own means you can create one that's suited to your tastes, whether it be fiery and smooth for toasted sandwiches or textured and sweet for dressing bitter winter salads.

In its simplest form mustard is just two ingredients: mustard seeds and a liquid. Yellow mustard seeds are the mildest, brown mustard seeds are warmer still and black pack the most punch. A blend gives you a wonderful balance of heat and aroma.

Most mustards use vinegar as their base liquid, along with a little salt. In southern Germany beer may be used in place of vinegar and in Dijon it's common to see verjus (unripe, unfermented grape juice) used.

The cooking method also alters the final character of your mustard. Mixing or blending the ingredients cold (or at room temperature) retains the fiery character of the seeds, whereas adding heat dulls the fire of the seeds for a more mellow mustard.

If you can get verjus then it's such a great ingredient to use here, but if not, just double up on the cider vinegar and apple juice. You will need a 300ml sterilised jar to store the mustard.

MAKES APPROXIMATELY 300G

Grind the mustard seeds
In a blender or pestle and mortar, pound or pulse together 6 table-spoons black mustard seeds and 6 tablespoons yellow mustard seeds to the consistency you like: a powder for a smooth Dijon-style mustard, or rough and coarse for something more rustic like a wholegrain mustard.

Add the salt
Put the ground or bashed mustard seeds in a bowl with 1 tablespoon fine sea salt and mix well to combine.

Heat the liquid
Here you need to make a decision on how punchy or mellow you want your mustard to be. Heating your liquid will mellow the heat of the mustard. It's nice to experiment with different batches. If you decide to heat the liquid, put ½ cup verjus (or another ¼ cup vinegar and ¼ cup apple juice), ¼ cup raw organic apple cider vinegar and ¼ cup apple juice in a small pan and warm but don't boil.

Add the liquid to the seeds
Add the warm liquid to the mustard seeds and salt and mix well to combine.

Steep and store
Put the mustard into a glass bowl or jar, cover and set aside for 24 hours or up to a week. The mustard's flavour deepens over time and as the seeds absorb the liquid it will thicken slightly too. Taste it each day until it has a consistency and flavour you're happy with, then transfer to a sterilised glass jar and store in the fridge for up to 6 months (I've used mine for much longer though).

Mustard egg mayo with pickles

6 large free-range or organic eggs
4 good ripe tomatoes, sliced
a dash of red wine or cider
    vinegar
6 tablespoons good-quality or
    homemade mayonnaise
    (see method)
1 heaped teaspoon Dijon mustard,
    plus more for the bread
½ teaspoon English mustard,
    plus more for the bread
6 cornichons, roughly chopped
½ a bunch of soft herbs (15g),
    finely chopped – I like a
    mixture of chives and tarragon
4 slices of good bread (I use a
    poppy-seed sourdough),
    about 400g
good olive oil
1 Little Gem lettuce, finely
    shredded

This is a staple lunch at home, something I crave every couple of weeks. I am not into the more traditional finely chopped egg mayo. I like it to have generous bits of fudgy yolked egg, crunchy bits of cornichons and lots of mustard.

The key here is the balance, so make sure you add more mustard, pickles, lemon and salt and pepper to taste. It's your lunch.

I have given a quick mayonnaise recipe here if you want to make your own, but jarred is fine.

SERVES 4 (BUT EASILY HALVED FOR 2)

Cook the eggs
Bring a small deep pan of water to the boil, then add 6 large organic eggs and simmer gently for 7 minutes (do a minute less for medium eggs). The eggs will be set but still a little fudgy in the middle.

Peel the eggs
Drain the eggs then put them back in the pan. Shake the pan gently to break the eggshells, then fill the pan with cold water and leave the eggs to sit in the cold water for a couple of minutes. This helps the shells detach from the egg whites, making them easier to peel.

Season the tomatoes
Slice 4 good ripe tomatoes, season generously with salt and sprinkle over a dash of red wine or cider vinegar.

Make the egg mayonnaise
Once cold, peel the eggs, chop into rough quarters and slices and put in a bowl with 6 tablespoons mayonnaise, 1 heaped teaspoon Dijon mustard, ½ teaspoon English mustard, 6 roughly chopped cornichons and ½ a bunch of finely chopped soft herbs. Gently stir together, trying not to break up the eggs too much.

Pile it on toast
Toast 4 slices of good bread, then rub with olive oil and a little salt. Add a thin slick of mustard to each slice of toast – Dijon or English. Finely shred 1 Little Gem and pile it on the toast. Lay the seasoned tomatoes over the top of the lettuce, then pile on the egg mayonnaise. Finish with the last of the herbs and more olive oil, salt and pepper.

To make your own mayonnaise:
Put a wet cloth on your work surface and rest a mixing bowl on top. Add an egg yolk to the bowl with 1 teaspoon Dijon mustard and 2 tablespoons lemon juice. Whisk this together for a minute until it becomes pale and thick. If the egg yolk is not whisked enough before you add the oil, it won't emulsify. Next start adding 175ml groundnut or vegetable oil a little at a time in a slow and fine stream. Keep adding the groundnut oil, then do the same with 75ml mild olive oil in the same steady stream until you have a thick, glossy mayonnaise. Once you have added all the oil, add some sea salt and some more lemon juice.

What to do if your mayonnaise splits:
Don't panic! Either add 1 teaspoon at a time of freshly boiled water, whisking until it comes back to a silky mayonnaise. Or whisk another egg yolk in a separate bowl and slowly whisk this into the split mayonnaise, one teaspoon at a time, until smooth.

Leeks and peas with spiced mustard butter

10 leeks, washed, trimmed and
    cut into 5cm-wide pieces
150g salted butter or good
    extra virgin olive oil
zest and juice of 1 unwaxed
    lemon
2 teaspoons mustard powder
1 teaspoon yellow mustard seeds
1 teaspoon coriander seeds,
    bashed
300g frozen garden peas
toasted sourdough or flatbreads,
    to serve
thick Greek yoghurt, oat
    yoghurt or soft goat's cheese,
    to serve

Leeks and mustard are a prime flavour match. I find it hard to cook leeks without adding a spoonful of mustard somewhere along the way. Here the leeks are half-braised and half-roasted with the lift of some vivid mustard powder, which brings a fierce but welcome punchy hit, and mustard seeds which bring texture as well as a more mellow pop of heat. Adding peas at the end brings sweetness which rounds out the mustard.

SERVES 4

Prepare the leeks
Preheat the oven to 200°C/180°C fan. Wash and trim 10 leeks, removing any large leafy bits and the thicker outer layer. Cut them into 5cm-wide pieces and stand them upright in a deep tray or thick pot, so they are all tightly packed together.

Dress and bake the leeks
Mix 100ml boiling water and 1 teaspoon salt in a small jug then pour this over the leeks. Dot 75g salted butter on top, season with freshly ground black pepper, cover with foil and place in the oven for 40–50 minutes until they are really soft.

Make the mustard-seed butter
In a small pan, melt 75g salted butter with the zest of 1 unwaxed lemon, 2 teaspoons mustard powder and 1 teaspoon yellow mustard seeds. Add 1 teaspoon bashed coriander seeds to the pan, heat until fragrant, then set aside.

Add the peas
Remove the leeks from the oven and gently stir 300g frozen garden peas into the buttery leek liquid. Place the foil back on top and set aside for 5 minutes for the peas to cook in the steam. They should stay bright green.

Serve the leeks
Squeeze the lemon juice over the leeks and peas and re-melt the butter so it's slightly foaming. Serve the leeks with toast, a big dollop of yoghurt or soft goat's cheese and the butter poured over the top.

Mustard

Roast spring vegetables with mustard cheese sauce

a bunch of purple sprouting or
    Tenderstem broccoli (200g)
1 bunch of asparagus
150g fresh, unpodded peas
4 tablespoons olive oil
1 tablespoon fennel seeds
a few sprigs of thyme (5g),
    leaves picked
300g crème fraîche or oat
    crème fraîche
50ml whole milk or oat milk
175g mature Cheddar or vegan
    Cheddar-style cheese, grated
2 tablespoons Dijon mustard
10g unsalted butter or vegan
    block
½ a bunch of parsley (15g),
    leaves picked
½ a bunch of sage (15g),
    leaves picked
½ a bunch of tarragon (15g),
    leaves picked
extra virgin olive oil, for
    drizzling

This is a plate of everything that I find comforting. Roast broccoli with its crispy roasted flowery ends, and roasted spring peas and asparagus with a cheesy mustard sauce that brings it all together. The mustard lifts the flavour and puts a bit of punch into the plate of comfort. Some roast herbs add texture and fresh dimension.

SERVES 4

Prepare the vegetables
Preheat the oven to 240°C/220°C fan. Cut 200g purple sprouting or Tenderstem broccoli into florets, then trim any tough bits from the stalk and slice the stalk into 1–2cm-thick pieces. Trim the tough ends from 1 bunch of asparagus.

Roast the vegetables
Put the broccoli, asparagus and 150g of unpodded peas into a large roasting tray with 3 tablespoons olive oil, 1 tablespoon fennel seeds and the leaves from a few sprigs of thyme. Season with sea salt and freshly ground black pepper, then toss together so the vegetables are all evenly coated. Roast in the oven for 30 minutes, turning halfway through.

Make the sauce
Meanwhile, put 300g crème fraîche and 50ml milk in a small saucepan and bring to a low simmer over a medium heat. Turn off the heat, add 175g grated Cheddar, 2 tablespoons Dijon mustard and 10g unsalted butter and stir until the cheese is melted and you have a cheesy, mustardy sauce.

Roast the herbs
Remove the broccoli and asparagus from the oven and set aside to cool slightly. On a low-sided/flat baking tray, mix the leaves from ½ a bunch each of parsley, sage and tarragon with 1 tablespoon of olive oil, then spread them out on the tray so they are all in one even layer, with no leaves overlapping. Bake in the oven for 2–3 minutes, until the herbs have crisped up but are still green. Keep a close eye on them as they can overcook and turn brown very quickly.

Bring everything together
Spoon the cheese sauce on to the base of a large serving platter or on 4 plates, top with the roast vegetables, the crispy herbs and a drizzle of extra virgin olive oil. Serve with bread for mopping up the sauce.

Mustard

Warm lemon and double mustard potato salad

1.2kg waxy new potatoes
a bunch of spring onions or
    2 small leeks, washed,
    trimmed and finely sliced
1 unwaxed lemon, half finely
    chopped
4 tablespoons extra virgin olive
    oil, plus extra for frying
1 teaspoon runny honey or
    maple syrup
1 tablespoon apple cider vinegar
    or white wine vinegar
1 tablespoon Dijon mustard
2 tablespoons wholegrain
    mustard
4 sticks of celery, thinly sliced
    on the diagonal, leaves
    reserved
a small bunch of radishes,
    trimmed and thinly sliced
a bunch of dill (25g), roughly
    chopped

I think that potato salad is my favourite way to eat mustard. This easy version uses two mustards, wholegrain and Dijon, countered by some lemon and lots of freshness and crunch from celery, radishes and herbs. I eat it at room temperature in the summer and just warm in the winter. The key here is dressing the just-drained potatoes while they are still warm, allowing the mustard vinaigrette to flavour them all the way through.

SERVES 4–6

Cook the potatoes
Boil 1.2kg waxy new potatoes in a pan of well-salted boiling water for 15–20 minutes until they are tender and easily pierced with a knife. Drain in a colander and allow them to steam dry for a couple of minutes.

Prepare the spring onions and lemon
Wash and finely slice a bunch of spring onions or 2 small leeks. Cut half of an unwaxed lemon into thin slices, removing the pips as you go, then pile the slices on top of each other and chop finely so you have small pieces of lemon, skin and all.

Caramelise the spring onions and lemon
Heat a little olive oil in a frying pan over a medium heat and add the chopped spring onions or leeks and cook for 2–3 minutes until beginning to brown. Add the lemon pieces and cook for another 5 minutes, allowing them to char at the edges. Turn the heat off but leave the spring onions and lemon in the pan.

Make the dressing
In a mixing bowl large enough to fit all your potatoes, mix together 1 teaspoon honey or maple syrup, 1 tablespoon apple cider vinegar,

1 tablespoon Dijon mustard, 2 tablespoons wholegrain mustard, 4 tablespoons extra virgin olive oil and the juice from half a lemon.

Drain and bash the potatoes
Once the potatoes are cool enough to handle, use your hands or a potato masher to gently break their skins (you don't want to mash them). Add them to the bowl of dressing while still warm and toss together. Dressing the potatoes while still warm allows them to absorb the flavour better.

Finish the salad
Once the potatoes have cooled to room temperature, add 4 sticks of celery, thinly sliced on the diagonal, and a bunch of trimmed and sliced radishes to the bowl, with the lemon and spring onion mixture, a bunch of roughly chopped dill and the celery leaves. Mix again gently, breaking things up a little more. Taste and season well with sea salt and black pepper. Add more olive oil, salt or vinegar if you think they are needed until the flavours are well balanced.

Store the salad
The salad will keep for up to 4 days in an airtight container in the fridge; let it come to room temperature before eating.

Mustard

Mustard seed and curry leaf snacking nuts

400g unsalted nuts – I used
cashews but unsalted
macadamia, pecans, almonds
or peanuts would work
1 tablespoon groundnut,
vegetable or coconut oil
1 teaspoon flaky sea salt
a handful of fresh curry leaves
– about 30
3 tablespoons mustard seeds
(I use a mixture of black and
yellow)
1 tablespoon mustard powder
1 teaspoon black pepper, freshly
ground
1 unwaxed lime

These to me are the perfect thing to
have with a drink. With a decent hit
of mustard seeds and the punch of
mustard powder, freshness from lime
and the impossible-to-put-into-words
flavour of curry leaves. If you want
the spices to stick to the nuts more,
you could toss the warm nuts in a
tablespoon of honey or maple syrup
once out of the oven. This will also
add a little sweetness. I like mine as
they are. These last a couple of weeks
if you snack on them slowly, but if
you are making them for a party then
double up.

MAKES 450G TO SERVE 4–6 AS A SNACK

Toss the nuts with the spices
Preheat the oven to 180°C/160°C fan.
Put 400g nuts on a lined baking tray
with 1 tablespoon groundnut oil
and 1 teaspoon flaky sea salt and toss
to coat.

Roast the nuts
Roast in the oven for 10 minutes,
stirring a few times, until they are
golden and toasted. After 10 minutes,
when golden, scatter over 30 fresh
curry leaves, 3 tablespoons mustard
seeds and 1 tablespoon mustard
powder and shake the tray so the nuts
are all evenly coated. Return to the
oven to roast for another 5 minutes.

Finish the nuts
Remove and season with 1 teaspoon
freshly ground black pepper, leave
to cool a little, then grate over the
zest of 1 unwaxed lime. Allow to
cool completely, then transfer to an
airtight container where they will
keep for a couple of weeks.

Jammy onion and salsa verde flatbreads

4 onions, peeled, halved and
 sliced about 1mm thick
6 tablespoons olive oil
2 tablespoons butter (optional)
400g plain flour
1 teaspoon baking powder
2 tablespoons capers, roughly
 chopped if large, plus
 2 tablespoons brine from
 the jar
a bunch of parsley (30g)
a bunch of basil (30g)
½ a bunch of mint (10g)
1 tablespoon Dijon mustard
1 tablespoon red wine vinegar
8 big green pitted olives,
 roughly chopped
2 tablespoons extra virgin
 olive oil
250g ricotta or vegan soft cheese

Mustard to me is the heart of a good salsa verde, bringing together the green hit of herbs and the saltiness of the capers and cornichons. Salsa verde is all about balance between salty capers, sharp cornichons, fragrant mint, basil and parsley and some acid from vinegar rounded out with the heat of some Dijon mustard. This version uses more mustard than usual, as I wanted it to be front and centre against the blank canvas of the flatbread and ricotta. If you don't have time to make the flatbread this is nearly as good on toasted sourdough.

SERVES 4

Prep and cook the jammy onions
Slice 4 onions as thinly as you can, ideally on a mandoline. Put the onions into a large frying pan with 4 tablespoons olive oil and a pinch of flaky sea salt. Stir to evenly coat the onions in the oil, then slowly cook them on a medium-low heat for 25–30 minutes until they are really, really soft.

Turn the heat up
Now turn the heat up a little and, if you are using it, add 2 tablespoons butter, then stir for a few minutes until the onions are starting to caramelise. Take off the heat, set aside in a bowl and wipe out your pan with kitchen paper.

Make the flatbread dough
In a mixing bowl whisk 400g plain flour with 1 teaspoon baking powder and a good pinch of sea salt. Mix 2 tablespoons caper brine with 150ml warm water and add it, little by little, to the flour, bringing the mixture together with your hands until you have a rough dough.

Knead and roll the flatbreads
Add 2 tablespoons light olive oil to the dough, gently knead in the bowl for a minute, then tip out on to a clean surface and knead for another minute until you have a soft ball of dough. If it's too sticky or dry, add a little more flour or water as needed. Cover with a damp tea towel until you're ready to cook.

Make the salsa verde
Roughly chop most of a bunch of both parsley and basil, and ½ a bunch of mint, leaving a few leaves whole for later. Add to a bowl with 1 tablespoon Dijon mustard, 1 tablespoon red wine vinegar, 2 tablespoons capers and 8 roughly chopped green olives. Mix well, then drizzle in 2 tablespoons extra virgin olive oil. Taste and add a little more salt, olive oil or vinegar as needed. You are looking for a spoonable herby sauce.

Cook the flatbreads
Divide the dough into 4, then roll each piece into a rough circle with a rolling pin or stretch the dough into rounds with your hands. Heat the frying pan you used for your onions to a medium heat and add the flatbreads one by one, cooking for about 2–3 minutes on each side until lightly golden and slightly puffed up. Remove and wrap in a clean tea towel to keep warm while you cook the rest.

Put everything together
Drain 250g ricotta, then tip it onto a small plate. Drizzle with a little extra virgin olive oil and season with salt and pepper. Scoop some of the ricotta on to the warm flatbread with a good layer of the jammy onions and top with the salsa verde and the herb leaves you saved earlier.

Mustard, mushroom and walnut flammekueche

100g crème fraîche or vegan
    crème fraîche
1 tablespoon wholegrain mustard
1 tablespoon and 1 teaspoon
    Dijon mustard
1 teaspoon runny honey
zest of ½ an unwaxed lemon
½ teaspoon fennel seeds,
    bashed
100g Parmesan (I use a
    vegetarian one) or vegan
    Parmesan-style cheese,
    freshly grated
150g greens of your choice
    (I like chard or cavolo nero)
3 tablespoons olive or rapeseed
    oil, plus extra for frying
150g mixed mushrooms
    (I use a mixture of oyster,
    shiitake and wild)
200g plain flour, plus extra
    for dusting
a few sprigs of thyme (15g),
    leaves picked
50g toasted walnuts,
    finely chopped

This is a version of flammekueche, often dubbed 'German pizza', and the inspiration for it comes from my dear friend and writer Anja Dunk. Here you make an instant dough with no rising agent, which makes it easy, quick and foolproof. The topping uses an upfront hit of wholegrain and Dijon mustard both in the crème fraîche and tossed through the mushrooms before they bake, which give them majorly satisfying crisp edges.

SERVES 2 GENEROUSLY, OR 4 AS PART OF A MEAL

Make the mustard filling
Put 100g crème fraîche into a medium mixing bowl with 1 tablespoon wholegrain mustard, 1 tablespoon Dijon mustard, 1 teaspoon runny honey, the zest of ½ an unwaxed lemon, ½ a teaspoon bashed fennel seeds, and 50g freshly grated Parmesan. Put to one side.

Cook the greens
Peel the leaves from the stems of 150g greens and finely chop the stems. Heat a frying pan over a medium heat and add some olive oil. Once hot, add the stems and cook for 2–3 minutes. Roughly chop the leaves then add these too, cooking them for 4–5 minutes until wilted and all the moisture has evaporated. Set aside to cool.

Prepare the mushrooms
Use a brush or a piece of kitchen paper to remove any dirt from 150g mixed mushrooms, then tear them into bite-sized pieces, varying the size and shape. Put the mushrooms in a bowl with 1 teaspoon of Dijon mustard and stir gently so they are all coated in the mustard.

Preheat the oven and make the dough
Preheat the oven to 220°C/200°C fan and put a large baking tray into the oven. Put 200g plain flour, the leaves from a few sprigs of thyme and a big pinch of sea salt into a large mixing bowl with 3 tablespoons olive or rapeseed oil and 80ml cold water. Mix together with your hands to form a dough. Put the dough on to a floured surface and roll into a roughly A4-sized rectangle. Take the tray out of the oven and transfer the dough to the tray.

Assemble the flammekueche
Working quickly, spread the dough with the crème fraîche mixture, top with 50g chopped toasted walnuts, the wilted greens and finally the mustardy mushrooms, then grate over 50g of cheese.

Bake the tart
Bake for 15–18 minutes until the edges are deep golden and the filling bubbling. Cool on the baking tray for a few minutes, then carefully slide on to a wire rack to cool. Serve at room temperature (or hot from the oven if you like!) with a bright green salad like the one on page 30.

Jeremy Lee's rémoulade

2 organic egg yolks

1 teaspoon organic cider vinegar

2 heaped teaspoons Dijon mustard

a few drops of Tabasco

200ml groundnut or vegetable oil

50ml extra virgin olive oil

juice of 1 unwaxed lemon

1 heart of leafy celery, thinly sliced

300g celeriac, peeled and cut into fine strips

1 kohlrabi, peeled and cut into fine strips

2–3 apples

1 level teaspoon English mustard

50–75g freshly grated horseradish

some salad leaves (Jeremy uses 50g baby spinach, 50g land cress and 50g leafy rocket)

a bunch of flat-leaf parsley (30g), leaves picked and chopped

Jeremy Lee is one of my favourite cooks. When I started writing about mustard, he was for some reason never far from my thoughts. Jeremy does British food better than anyone, and mustard shows up in so many of his recipes. So when I was thinking of iconic mustard recipes, this rémoulade was non-negotiable. Thanks for sharing it with me, Jeremy.

Jeremy describes this as a feisty salad that pairs well with sharp cheese and many other things. He believes wholeheartedly in making plenty of mayonnaise for when urges for a sandwich mount. For this salad, use half the recipe for mayonnaise and keep the rest in a sealed jar in the fridge.

If you can't find kohlrabi then you could replace it with more apple, or a firm pear or a bunch of radishes. This recipe requires a good bit of chopping, so a mandoline or julienne peeler (very cheap) or food processor with a slicing blade can come in handy.

SERVES 6

Make the mayonnaise
Beat 2 organic egg yolks with 1 teaspoon organic cider vinegar, a pinch of sea salt, a teaspoon of Dijon mustard and a drop or three of Tabasco. Add 200ml groundnut or vegetable oil drop by drop, whisking thoroughly. Continue until the sauce thickens, then add the oil a spoonful at a time. Slowly add 50ml olive oil and drops of lemon juice and taste for seasoning. Cover and refrigerate.

Slice the veg and apples
Thinly slice 1 celery heart. Peel 300g celeriac and 1 kohlrabi, then slice thinly and cut into fine strips. Slice 2–3 apples thinly and cut into fine strips, tossing them in the juice of half a lemon as you go to stop

the slices browning. If chopping this much veg sounds a chore you could use a julienne peeler or a mandoline.

Dress the rémoulade
Place all the vegetable and apple strips in a large bowl with 1 teaspoon of Dijon mustard, 1 level teaspoon English mustard, 50–75g freshly grated horseradish and a big pinch of freshly ground black pepper. Mix well. Add half the mayonnaise, then some salad leaves and the chopped leaves from a bunch of flat-leaf parsley. Mix deftly and serve.

Vegetarian flavour swaps

There are some flavours and ingredients that, as a vegetarian, I still miss: how easily anchovies build the umami base of a tomato sauce, the crispness a lardon brings or the deep savouriness of Parmesan. Over the years, I have come up with ways to echo some of these flavours. Most of these swaps come out of cooking recipes I used to love as an omnivore, and trying to make them as delicious without meat, fish and sometimes dairy. I am not saying these are the same or exact flavour matches, but they are ways to build flavour and texture that echoes and equals.

Often, we imagine it's the headline ingredients, like prawns or pancetta, that give us the unmistakable sense of a dish like paella or carbonara. More often than not, though, it's one of the 'supporting actors' – like the saffron in a paella – and the way the dish is cooked that will actually be the signature flavour and texture.

Chorizo
Smoked paprika

One ingredient I hear people say they miss a lot when they eat more plants is chorizo. Using smoked paprika in your food, where you might have used chorizo before, is a great swap. Try it in baked eggs, or in a stew or soup. Smoked paprika comes in sweet (less hot) and hot (as it sounds), which I use the most, as well as 'agridulce' or bittersweet (a little pleasant bitterness). Smoked paprika adds a great depth and rounded flavour from the top notes of chilli and the base notes of smoke. My favourite smoked paprika is La Chinata or Santo Domingo.

Smoked meat
Smoked salt/water

The smoked and cured meats that I used to cook with, things like lardons, pancetta and prosciutto, add fattiness and a smoky flavour with very little effort. But I have found that by using smoked salt or smoked water (which is just water that has been put in a smoker), you can achieve the same rounded woody smokiness, which really helps replicate that flavour. A good example is a version of a carbonara that I make. I use root veg, or tofu, cooked in a pan until crisp using lots of olive oil, which echoes the fat in the meat, then I add smoked salt or smoked water to give them a smoky flavour, which is such a great interruption to the creamy carbonara. The best smoked salt and water is from Halen Môn.

Lardons
Crispy capers

As well as using lardons for flavouring, I also cooked with them for their texture. A handful of golden lardons sprinkled on to a salad, for instance, could really lift the level of crisp-edged crunch. My new answer? Crispy capers.

Essentially, these are capers that you have fried hard and fast in olive oil. They open into a kind of flower. They're super salty like lardons, and they have a texture all of their own. I sprinkle them on top of pasta, quiches, tarts or even just a traybake of vegetables to add that pleasing texture and saltiness.

Anchovies
Capers

Anchovies are one thing that I used a lot in cooking, though I was never a huge fan of anchovies on their own. I often replace anchovies in my recipes with capers, from pasta to pizza, and way beyond. The intense saltiness of a caper replicates that of an anchovy. I realised I mainly used anchovies as a seasoning, cooking them down with chilli, olive oil and garlic for a quick sauce for pasta. The idea here is that the anchovy breaks down and just becomes a kind of sauce or seasoning. If you finely chop your capers and use them in the same way in a pasta sauce, you'll get that deep umami saltiness. For this, I think the larger capers in vinegar or salt (soaked and washed before using if salted) are best.

Parmesan cheese
Old Winchester

Parmesan cheese uses animal rennet, so it's not vegetarian. Any cheese that calls itself Parmesan, which has protected origin status, has to be made in this way with rennet. So if you're vegetarian and want to avoid this, it's important to look for a 'Parmesan-style' cheese in the supermarket – they're not allowed to call it 'Parmesan'. However, these cheeses often don't have the same pleasing crystally structure that is the reason I love Parmesan so much. So I prefer a cheese called Old Winchester for this reason. It's a British cheese that is both butterscotch-sweet and deeply umami, and, like Parmesan,

it has those moreish crystals. And, being British, it means it hasn't travelled as far.

Umami richness
Miso

Miso isn't a specific swap, but it's something I use often to add that umami depth that comes from meat or meat stock. If I'm making a vegetable stock and I want it to be deep, dark and full-bodied, I will add some red miso or dark miso. If I want to make something that has a lighter, brighter stock, more in the chicken stock territory, then I might start with a bit of white miso, more caramel in colour, with a rounded flavour that's a bit gentler and less salty.

Depth
Star anise

One spice I find myself using a lot in my cooking since becoming vegetarian is star anise. It has a deep, rounded flavour with a sort of aniseed note. I find it really helpful for adding to things like Vietnamese pho, massaman curry, stocks and soups, as well as marinades for vegetables or tofu. Try adding a couple of star anise to a squash soup.

Sea flavours
Seaweed

Adding seaweed to your food brings a fresh, clean taste of the sea without using any fish. For something like sushi rice, I often top it with crumbled-up crispy seaweed sheets or furikake seasoning, or use dried kombu to make a quick stock or add depth to an existing broth.

Bacon
Smoked tofu

I'm not going to pretend that smoked tofu tastes exactly like bacon, because it doesn't. There are many types of vegan bacon, but I've never met one that I liked and was not super

processed. Where I may have had bacon in a sandwich before, I now use smoked tofu. I slice it thinly and fry it in a hot pan with some oil until crisp on each side. Then I mix a little maple syrup with smoked paprika and drizzle this on to the hot slices, then turn off the heat and toss, making sure it's evenly coated. I'll give the slices a few more seconds on each side and then put them into my sandwich. Great for a vegan BLT or crumbled on top of a salad.

Deep savouriness
Marmite

Marmite is cheap, nutritious and very useful. A spoonful of Marmite can add a deep flavour that it might take hours of cooking to produce another way. I often add Marmite to my stews and gravies. It's one of the things that I might add towards the end of cooking. If I've got a gravy, for instance, that I feel is lacking in flavour, if it needs that umami hit and some more depth, then a little bit of Marmite – just a quarter or half a teaspoon – will add a rich colour and also that distinctive flavour but in a much mellower form.

Rounded depth
Saffron

Saffron has a reputation for being really expensive, and by weight it is expensive, but to get that rounded, sunshiny flavour you only need to use a tiny bit. Bloom the saffron in hot water – essentially soaking the threads in hot water until they release the golden saffron colour and flavour. Saffron is used a lot in many different cultures. It's obviously a key ingredient in paella, so if you were making a vegetarian paella (see page 182), the saffron would still give you the same signals as a fish paella, but without any of the fish or seafood. It's also used a lot in Persian cooking: adding a little bit of bloomed saffron to some yoghurt served next to some barbecued veg transports me to my Iranian friends' houses, a real decadent flavour that is hard to put your finger on.

How to cook flexibly

1

What is the anchor?

Ingredient cooking method, cuisine?

A ————————————————→
Craving spice — dal

B ————————————————→
I have potatoes to use up

2

How will I cook it?

Fry, braise, char, grill, roast, keep it raw. How will that affect the flavour?

————————————————→
Fry, simmer, temper

————————————————→
Tortilla Español

3

Main and supporting flavours?

Is the main ingredient going to carry the dish? What does it need to back it up?

————————————————→
No, the lentils need some help, so I will add spices, tomato, coconut

————————————————→
Yes, this is a simple dish — potatoes, onions, olive oil, salt

It can be useful to think about cooking in the same terms as music. When I listen to a song, I hear the song, as a whole, without much nuance. I don't have musical instincts and have not spent time training my ear. When my brother (a musician) listens to the same song, he hears something totally different.

When it comes to food, I know I have an instinctive understanding of it, and I have spent the last twenty years honing that understanding. Just like music, you need to know the basics – a few principles, scales and standards – before you can improvise. I am hoping this framework will get you to ask the right questions when you cook and give you the confidence to cook without a recipe and build your own dishes, just as a musician might build the layers in a song.

7

How will I balance it?

A ————————————————→
Serve with plain rice/breads for contrast, and yoghurt for temperature contrast and richness, chutney for sweetness

B ————————————————→
Hot and cold contrast from the tortilla and the salad, sweetness from onions, butteriness and pepperiness from olive oil

4

How and when will I add salt?

Which ingredients are already salty? When would it make sense to season each element?

Season the onions at the start, taste and season as I go at each stage

Season the onions and potatoes well as they cook, the eggs when they are whisked

5

How will I add acidity?

Are there naturally acidic ingredients? How and when will I add acid?

I will add tinned tomatoes and finish with lemon juice

No natural acidity in a tortilla — add acid with lemon-dressed herb and shallot salad

6

How will I layer flavour?

By cooking the onions until sweet, then adding spices at the beginning, and more spice in a temper at the end

By frying onions and then the potatoes in olive oil, by browning the egg on the outside, adding the salad for acidity

8

How will I add texture?

A temper of spices at the end, yoghurt for creaminess, crisped roti or chappatis

Softness inside, crispness from browning on outside, crunch from the salad

9

Does it need something to finish?

Yoghurt, chutney, herbs

The herb and shallot salad

10

Taste / Adjust / Taste / Adjust

Here you could add more lemon juice or salt, more tempered spice if it was lacking, herbs for freshness, yoghurt to reduce heat

To check the seasoning before cooking the whole tortilla you could fry off a little of the mixture and taste and adjust

Tomatoes

Tinned, paste and passata. Reliable tins and tubes. Bringing summer when it's not. Sun-scorched ripe tomatoes, pressed and packed into tins and jars. Intense paste, cooked, milled then dried, in the sun if you are lucky, for a deep hit of tomato. Tomatoes for us when they have long since left the vines. An intense tomato flavour that a fresh tomato could not give. Extra acidity from the tins or passata which makes the tomato sauce I always want to eat – a clove of garlic smashed whole and sizzled in olive oil, a tin of tomatoes splattered in, and a pinch of salt, makes something much more, so loved. Beyond their million other uses, I would love a tin of tomatoes for this alone.

On Tomatoes

This chapter centres on preserved tomatoes, not fresh. I eat fresh tomatoes for most of the year – colourful British ones in the summer and the hardier, saltier Italian and Spanish winter varieties in the winter. But nothing comes close to the ease of a tin or the squeeze of a tube.

Tinned tomatoes and passata are almost always the tomatoes I use for cooking, even in tomato season. To me, once cooked, they have a perfect balance of acidity and sweetness. It is harder to get that sharp acidity from a fresh tomato. And the paste or purée is so deeply flavoured that you only need a tablespoon or two; its raw edges softened by a minute or two cooked and stirred in the pan.

Tomatoes are rich in citric acid, so they have a lot of natural acidity as well as sweetness.

Sweet, Rich, Silky, Umami

- Tinned, chopped or plum
Peeled, from tomatoes with few
seeds; acidic, jammy when cooked.
I use these for almost everything.
Whole DOP San Marzano are
the best.

- Tinned cherry tomatoes
Often much more flavourful than
fresh cherry tomatoes – they usually
include skin and seeds. I use these
for cooked salsas, pasta sauce and
for when I want more of a feeling of
fresh tomato from a tin.

- Purée
Intensely rich, sweet, sticky – I use
this when I want an intense savoury
hit of tomato without adding too
much liquid.

- Passata
Fruity, bright – cooked and sieved
tomatoes. I use these for a thinner
sauce for pizza or for a soup or stew
where I need more liquid.

Goes well with

allspice	ginger
aubergine	lemon
avocado	lime
black bean	mint
basil	miso
caper	mustard
chilli	olive
cheese	oregano
cinnamon	parmesan
coriander	peanut
corn	potato
cucumber	rosemary
egg	tamarind
garlic	watermelon

Favourite uses

Tinned
- My kind of puttanesca with capers,
olives and parsley
- Spaghetti and (veg) meatballs
- Red curry
- Store cupboard chickpea stew with
preserved lemon and herbs

- Shakshuka
- Quick tomato soup

Paste
- To flavour baked rice
- To bolster the base of a soup, stew
or curry
- To make a dry, flavourful sauce
for pasta
- To add to ratatouille or baked
vegetables for a boost of flavour

Passata
- For pizza sauce
- In soup

Storage

Store somewhere cool and dry, and,
once open, in the fridge for up to
a week.

A squeeze of lemon is said to
remove the metallic taste from a
tin of tomatoes.

Favourite brands/where to buy

Most supermarkets sell decent tinned
tomatoes, passata and paste. Buy the
best your budget allows.

I buy whole tomatoes and chop
with scissors in the tin. To me, the
whole plum tomatoes are usually
better quality. Whole Italian plum
seem to be the most reliably good.

Paolo Petrilli organic peeled
tomatoes are expensive jarred
tomatoes (they use them at the River
Cafe for a reason).

Bomba tomato paste is worth a
mention for deep savouriness too
– made with extra strength triple
concentrated tomato paste, full-
bodied red wine and tasty soffrito,
meaning it's good for vegans.

Easy Wins

Oven-dried tomatoes

2kg tomatoes
olive oil
2 tablespoons flaky sea salt
spices: a teaspoon of ground
    fennel, cumin or coriander
    seeds are my favourite
    (all optional)

I could have written a recipe here for homemade tinned tomatoes, which I have made once, and while it was satisfying, I have not done it again, which says it all. You can buy very good tinned tomatoes, so I do. This tomato recipe, though, is a game-changer. It makes tomatoes their most tomatoey – the very best version of themselves. It's very easy and gives you an intense oven-dried tomato that you won't be able to buy in a shop. This recipe asks you to leave the oven on (low) for a couple of hours, so I suggest making a decent batch to make it worthwhile.

MAKES ABOUT 2 MEDIUM JARFULS

Prepare your tomatoes
Heat your oven to 100°C/80°C fan. Wash the tomatoes, then slice them in half, cutting away any bits of core as you go. Place the tomatoes cut side up on a baking tray.

Season your tomatoes
Brush or drizzle the top of each tomato with olive oil, then liberally but evenly scatter over sea salt. If you are adding spice, sprinkle this evenly over the tomatoes too.

Bake the tomatoes
Bake the tomatoes in the warm oven for 4–6 hours until they have shrunk to about a third of the size they were when they were fresh. You want them to be dried out but still a little juicy.

Store
Allow the tomatoes to cool completely before putting them into jars or airtight containers. They will keep in the fridge like this for a week or so. To keep them for longer, store them under oil – spoon the tomatoes into sterilised jars, then cover with oil and keep in the fridge for up to 2 months.

Ways to use your tomatoes:
- Great with any kind of eggs, particularly egg mayonnaise
- Good tossed in a salad with herbs and a mustardy vinaigrette
- Excellent in a sandwich of any kind. I like crispy smoked tofu, lettuce and these tomatoes, BLT style
- Great in a toasted sandwich
- Good in a tart or quiche where normal tomatoes would have too much liquid

Any way Puy lentils with tomato sauce

300g Puy lentils, washed
4 cloves of garlic, 2 peeled and
    whole, 2 finely sliced
1 small tomato, or a plum
    tomato from a tin
a few sprigs of thyme or oregano
2 bay leaves
1 tablespoon vegetable stock
    powder, or ½ a stock cube
olive oil
1 red onion, peeled and finely
    chopped
1 × 400g tin good-quality
    chopped tomatoes
a pinch of golden caster sugar
a splash of red wine vinegar
½ a bunch of tarragon (10g),
    leaves picked and roughly
    chopped
4 tablespoons good-quality
    crème fraîche

Lentils pair so well with tomatoes. Both the lentils and the tomato sauce here are basics which I love to cook and often form part of my kitchen routine. Eaten together, they are even better.

Puy lentils lend themselves amazingly to quick cooking – they don't need soaking, they cook in 30 minutes and they're hearty, delicious and creamy. Adding a tomato and a few cloves of garlic to the pan as the lentils cook imparts great flavour.

SERVES 4

Cook the lentils
Put 300g washed Puy lentils into a saucepan with 2 peeled cloves of garlic, 1 small whole tomato, a few sprigs of thyme or oregano, 2 bay leaves and 1 tablespoon vegetable stock powder or ½ a stock cube. Cover with a litre of hot water, place on a medium heat, bring to a simmer, then turn the heat down. Blip away for 25–30 minutes, until the lentils are soft and the water has almost evaporated. If they are looking too dry, top up with a little more boiling water from the kettle.

Make the tomato sauce
While the lentils are cooking, make the tomato sauce. To a small pan, add a good glug of olive oil and 1 peeled and finely chopped red onion and cook for 10 minutes, or until soft and sweet. Add 2 thinly sliced cloves of garlic and cook until browning at the edges, then add a 400g tin of good-quality chopped tomatoes and about 200ml or half a tomato tin of water, a pinch of golden caster sugar and a good pinch of sea salt. Cook for 15 minutes until sweet and thick. Add 3 tablespoons olive oil and keep warm.

By now the lentils should be cooked and most of the water should have evaporated, so scoop out the tomato and the garlic and put them into a bowl. Once cool enough to handle, pop the garlic cloves out of their skins and use a fork to mash them to a paste. Peel the cooked tomato and mash it with the garlic, too. Stir this paste back through the lentils. Taste, season with salt and pepper, then dress with a generous glug of olive oil and a splash of red wine vinegar.

To serve, ladle the lentils into bowls and top with a couple of spoonfuls of the tomato sauce. Roughly chop ½ a bunch of tarragon leaves and fold through 4 tablespoons good-quality crème fraîche, then add spoonfuls of the herby mixture to the top of each bowl. Finish with a good drizzle of olive oil and some black pepper.

Tomatoes

Black bean nasi goreng

250g cooked brown basmati rice
4 shallots, peeled and finely
 chopped
2 sticks of celery, finely chopped
3 tablespoons groundnut oil
5 cloves of garlic, peeled and
 finely chopped
2 red chillies, 1 finely chopped
a bunch of coriander (30g),
 stalks and leaves finely
 chopped
2 small cucumbers or ½ a large
 one, thickly sliced
2 tablespoons rice wine vinegar
½ teaspoon runny honey or
 sugar
2 tablespoons plus ½ teaspoon
 toasted sesame oil
2 tablespoons plus 1 teaspoon
 soy sauce
2 tablespoons tomato purée
1 tablespoon miso paste (I use
 red or brown rice miso)
3 tablespoons kecap manis, or a
 mixture of soy and honey
1 × 400g tin black beans,
 drained
4 free-range or organic eggs
 (optional)
a bunch of spring onions,
 trimmed and finely sliced
2 unwaxed limes to serve

Dear friends David and Naomi live down the street from me. Naomi was once a ballerina and is now a yoga teacher, and David is a writer. David also loves to cook. Not many people invite me for dinner – one of the few downsides of cooking for a living. David and Naomi do, and one night David made this. Black bean rice inspired by nasi goreng. A wholly untraditional take, but a very good one. The key here is the depth the tomato purée (and a little miso), fried off until it's browned and sweet, brings to the rice as well as the frankly inspired addition of black beans, which give a deep umami hum. It's topped with a spring onion-fried egg and some quick pickled cucumber. That night I could not have imagined anything I would have rather eaten.

SERVES 4

Do you need to cook some rice?
If you don't have cooked rice to use up, cook 250g brown basmati rice according to the packet instructions.

Fry the veg and aromatics
Finely chop 4 peeled shallots and 2 sticks of celery and sweat in a tablespoon of groundnut oil for about 10 minutes, or as long as you've got, until soft and sweet. Add 5 cloves of garlic, peeled and finely chopped, 1 finely chopped red chilli and the finely chopped stalks from a small bunch of coriander and fry for a couple more minutes.

Make the cucumber pickle
Meanwhile, thickly slice 2 small cucumbers or ½ a large cucumber and finely chop another red chilli. Put it all into a little bowl and add 2 tablespoons rice wine vinegar, ½ teaspoon each of runny honey and

toasted sesame oil and 1 teaspoon soy sauce. Stir through half of the chopped leaves from a bunch of coriander.

Add the flavourings
Add 2 tablespoons tomato purée and 1 tablespoon miso paste (I use red or brown rice miso) to the pan and cook for 5 minutes before adding 2 tablespoons toasted sesame oil, 3 tablespoons kecap manis and 2 tablespoons soy sauce. Then add a 400g tin of drained black beans and cook for a few more minutes. Tip into a bowl.

Fry the rice
Put the pan back over the heat and add another couple of tablespoons of groundnut oil. Once hot, add 250g cooked brown basmati rice and cook for a few minutes until it is beginning to crisp at the edges and is piping hot. Tip in the black bean mixture, stir in well and cook for another couple of minutes.

Fry the eggs
If you are cooking the eggs, heat another large frying pan and add a couple of tablespoons of groundnut oil. Once hot, add a bunch of trimmed and finely sliced spring onions, then crack in 4 eggs and cook until the edges are crisp but the yolk is still soft.

To finishs
Serve the nasi goreng piled into bowls with the spring onion-fried egg, cucumber pickle and the rest of the bunch of chopped coriander and wedges of lime.

Traybake lemon dal with pickled green chillies

1 tablespoon coriander seeds
2 teaspoons cumin seeds
2 × 400g tins plum tomatoes
2 tablespoons ghee or other
    cooking oil
2 unwaxed lemons
a thumb-sized piece of ginger,
    peeled
8 cloves of garlic, peeled and
    finely sliced
2 green chillies, sliced
2 teaspoons golden caster sugar
50ml white wine vinegar
1 teaspoon sea salt
a bunch of coriander (30g),
    chopped
1 teaspoon ground turmeric
a cinnamon stick
1 tablespoon Kashmiri chilli
    powder (or ½ teaspoon if
    using other chilli powders)
1 tablespoon yellow mustard
    seeds
300g split red lentils
1 × 400ml tin coconut milk
800ml hot vegetable stock
250g paneer or firm tofu
warm rice, parathas or roti,
    yoghurt and chutney to serve

Dal is a staple of our weeknight cooking. It's the dinner I never get bored of. I have a few favourites I make on rotation: coconut, lemon and now this traybaked tomato one. This dal is made in the oven, so it's very hands-off. The tinned tomatoes are roasted first to give a deeper hit of tomato flavour. Serve this with a pot of rice, some parathas, some salted yoghurt and chutney.

SERVES 4

Crush the tomatoes
Preheat the oven to 220°C/200°C fan.
    Add 1 tablespoon coriander seeds and 2 teaspoons cumin seeds to a high-sided baking tray and toast in the oven for 2–4 minutes until fragrant, then remove and tip into a pestle and mortar and crush before returning to the tray. Drain 2 × 400g tins of tomatoes and add to the tray. Use a potato masher or the back of a large spoon/fork to crush the tomatoes to release their juice and flatten them a little, and spread them evenly over the tray.

Add the flavourings and roast
Add 2 tablespoons ghee or oil, then grate in the zest of 1 unwaxed lemon and 1 thumb of ginger and add 8 thinly sliced cloves of garlic. Toss the tomatoes in the spices and roast for 30 minutes until sticky and intensified in flavour.

Make the quick pickle
Put 2 sliced green chillies, 2 teaspoons golden caster sugar, 50ml white wine vinegar and a teaspoon of salt into a small bowl and mix well. Add the zest of a second unwaxed lemon. Stir through a bunch of chopped coriander, stems and all. Put in the fridge to keep cool.

Add the spices and lentils
Once the tomatoes have had their time, remove them from the oven and stir in 1 teaspoon ground turmeric, a cinnamon stick, 1 tablespoon Kashmiri chilli powder and 1 tablespoon yellow mustard seeds. Add 300g split red lentils and pour over a 400ml tin of coconut milk and 800ml hot vegetable stock. Cover tightly with foil and return to the oven for another 40 minutes.

Add the paneer
After 40 minutes, carefully take the tray out of the oven and remove the foil. Stir the dal, then season well with sea salt. Tear 250g paneer or firm tofu over the top of the dal and squeeze over the juice of the 2 zested lemons. Return to the oven for a further 15 minutes or until the edges of the paneer are beginning to turn golden, the dal is creamy and the lentils are soft.

Finish with the chilli and serve
Serve with rice, parathas, yoghurt and chutney and the pickled chilli and coriander mixture. Will keep in the fridge for up to 7 days.

Orzo, feta and tomato traybake

4 red onions, peeled and cut
  into thin wedges
1 red chilli
1 red pepper, deseeded and
  chopped
1 head of garlic, cut across the
  middle
olive oil
1 × 400g tin plum tomatoes
1 teaspoon nigella seeds
1 teaspoon coriander seeds,
  crushed
250g orzo
200g feta or vegan feta-style
  cheese
½ a bunch of coriander (15g),
  leaves picked
½ a bunch of parsley (15g),
  leaves picked
2 tablespoons toasted pine nuts

Along with rigatoni, spaghettini and casarecce, orzo is one of my most-used kinds of pasta. Special mention also goes to rachette (tennis racket-shaped pasta my kids love). Orzo has such a pleasing texture with an olive oil-rich tomato sauce. This is a frequently cooked dinner all made in a tray. Roasted onions go sweet and jammy, then tinned tomatoes are added and roasted until their flavour intensifies, more jammy, sticky flavour builds up and then, when the orzo and liquid are added, all the flavour is swept up off the tray and a broken-up slab of feta tops it all. It's a very hands-off, pleasing dinner.

SERVES 4

Roast the onions and peppers
Preheat the oven to 220°C/200°C fan. Put 4 peeled red onions cut into thin wedges into a large deep-sided baking tray (roughly 30cm × 40cm) with 1 whole red chilli, 1 red pepper, deseeded and chopped, and 1 head of garlic cut across the middle. Drizzle over a splash of olive oil. Roast in the hot oven for 20 minutes until the onions are cooked and the edges of the peppers are beginning to char.

Add the tomatoes and spices
Drain a 400g tin of plum tomatoes and keep the juice. After the onions and peppers have been cooking for 20 minutes, put the tomatoes into the tray with 1 teaspoon nigella seeds and 1 teaspoon coriander seeds, crushed, then put the lot back into the oven for another 20 minutes so the tomatoes can roast and intensify.

Break up the tomatoes and squeeze out the garlic
Take the tray out of the oven and use the back of a wooden spoon or a potato masher to break up the tomatoes. Take the garlic out and squeeze it from its papery skins into the tray – discard the skins.

Add the orzo and liquid
Put the tomato liquid from the can into a measuring jug then add freshly boiled water until you have 800ml of liquid. Add to the tray with 250g orzo and dot the top with 200g feta or vegan feta-style cheese, then return it to the oven for 15 minutes, stirring it all halfway, until the orzo is cooked.

Add the herbs and serve
Take it out of the oven and shower with the picked coriander and parsley leaves and the pine nuts as well as a drizzle of olive oil, and eat right away as the pasta will continue to cook as it sits.

Coconut and tomato laksa

1–3 small Thai red chillies, depending on how hot you like it

6 cloves of garlic, peeled

2 shallots, peeled and chopped into a few chunks

a thumb-sized piece of ginger, peeled and chopped into 3

15 raw cashew nuts (40g)

1 tablespoon sambal oelek or other chilli sauce

2 tablespoons coconut oil or other cooking oil

2 tablespoons tomato purée

200g dried flat rice noodles

1 × 400ml tin coconut milk

3 unwaxed limes

4 lime leaves

½ a bunch of coriander (15g) (reserve a few sprigs for garnish)

½ a bunch of mint (15g) (reserve a few sprigs for garnish)

200g silken tofu, cut into cubes

1 tablespoon coriander seeds

ADD SEASONAL VEGETABLES

Spring – 2 handfuls of freshly podded peas, a bunch of asparagus, thinly sliced, and a few sliced spring onions

Summer – 2 handfuls of halved cherry tomatoes, 2 handfuls of halved sugar snaps (120g)

Autumn – a small sweet potato, peeled and very finely sliced, and 2 handfuls of shredded kale

Winter – 2 carrots, peeled into thin ribbons with a speed peeler, and a bunch of purple-sprouting broccoli, stalks cut into thin rounds and florets halved

Tomato purée feels old-fashioned, retro and reliable. While it might not have the draw of a tall jar of passata or a pleasingly designed tin of tomatoes, a tube of tomato purée holds promise. This laksa-style soup shows it off in all its glory – the dish gains so much depth from a tablespoon or so. Here that deep, savoury tomato is mixed with aromatics, and once it hits the creamy coconut milk, well-rounded, multi-layered flavour is created in not much time at all. I use the term 'laksa' so you know to expect richness, spice and coconut. This recipe is far from a traditional laksa, which has so many variations all over South East Asia, for which I encourage you to seek out chefs like Lara Lee or Mandy Yin. The paste can be made and frozen in ice-cube trays for a very quick version if that's your kind of thing. I have suggested some seasonal variations for vegetables here so you can make this all year round.

SERVES 4

Make the laksa paste
Blend 1–3 small Thai red chillies, 6 cloves of garlic, 2 chopped shallots, a chopped thumb of ginger and 40g raw cashews in a blender or food processor until smooth. Add 1 tablespoon sambal oelek, 2 table-spoons coconut oil and 2 tablespoons tomato purée and blend until smooth.

Cook the rice noodles
Fill a pan with water and bring to a boil. Once boiling, remove from the heat, add 200g dried flat rice noodles and soak them for 6–10 minutes, until tender but still chewy. Drain the noodles and rinse well under cold water, then toss in a little oil to stop them sticking.

Make the soup
Fill and boil your kettle. While the noodles soak, heat a large saucepan over a medium heat, add the laksa paste and fry for a couple of minutes to cook the tomato purée and the spices. Once the paste has darkened in colour a little, add a 400ml tin of coconut milk along with a tin-full (400ml) of boiling water. Add the juice of 2 unwaxed limes, 4 lime leaves, most of ½ a bunch each of coriander and mint and season to taste with sea salt.

Add the vegetables
Add your chosen veg to the pan and simmer until tender. This may take longer for some of the winter vegetables than for the spring and summer vegetables.

Serve the laksa
Divide the cooked noodles between 4 bowls, then divide 200g cubed silken tofu among them. Evenly add the vegetables, then the laksa broth. Finish with the remaining mint, coriander and wedges from the remaining lime.

Linguine with mushroom and herb polpette

3 tablespoons capers
zest and juice of 1 unwaxed lemon
100ml extra virgin olive oil
8 cloves of garlic, peeled
2 × 400g tins cherry tomatoes
200g mushrooms (I use chestnut
   mushrooms)
2 onions, peeled and roughly
   chopped
200g smoked tofu
2 tablespoons olive oil
a sprig of rosemary, leaves finely
   chopped
10 sage leaves, finely chopped
50g fresh breadcrumbs
1 × 400g tin black beans, drained
   (240g black beans once
   drained)
50g pine nuts
125g ball of mozzarella, grated
50g sundried tomatoes, finely
   chopped
500g linguine
a bunch of basil, leaves separated
Parmesan cheese

Linguine and meatballs, vegetarian ones, are Dylan's favourite. As hard as I tried, Dylan still preferred the shop-bought 'meat' balls to the ones I made. Until now. I agree with him that there are few better ways to use a tin of tomatoes than in a big platter of tomato linguine twisted around little savoury polpette. These are rich with umami mushrooms, black beans and smoked tofu and have the pleasing bounce which I think Dylan loves so much. I make double the amount of these and freeze a batch.

SERVES 4

Make the tomato sauce
Put 3 tablespoons capers and the zest and juice of 1 unwaxed lemon into a food processor and blitz until you have a smooth paste. Add 100ml extra virgin olive oil to a large saucepan, add 4 peeled and sliced cloves of garlic and fry over a medium heat until just turning golden. Spoon in the caper mix and fry for a minute, then add 2 × 400g tins cherry tomatoes. Season generously with salt and pepper and leave to simmer away.

Make the meatball mix
Put 200g mushrooms, 2 peeled and roughly chopped onions and 4 peeled cloves of garlic into the food processor and blitz until you have a roughly chopped mixture. Add 200g smoked tofu and pulse to incorporate. In a large frying pan add 2 tablespoons olive oil and place over a high heat. Tip in the veg mix and fry for 10 minutes, stirring often until all the veg is dry and a little golden. Add a sprig of finely chopped rosemary, 10 finely chopped sage leaves and 50g breadcrumbs and continue to fry for another 5 minutes.

Finish and shape the meatballs
Tip the vegetable mixture into a mixing bowl to cool. Blitz 1 × 400g tin of drained black beans and 50g pine nuts until you have a textured paste. Add the black bean mixture to the cooled veg with 125g grated mozzarella and 50g chopped sundried tomatoes. Using clean hands give it all a really good scrunch until it clings together. Shape into 30 roughly 30g balls and put on a plate and into the fridge for 10 minutes.

To fry the meatballs
Heat your biggest frying pan over a medium heat and add 4 tablespoons olive oil. Once hot, fry the polpette for 4–5 minutes on each side until golden brown. You may have to do this in batches. You could also roast them for 20–25 minutes at 200°C/180°C fan.

To bake the meatballs
Preheat the oven to 200°C/180°C fan and put the polpette on to a baking tray and drizzle generously with oil and toss to coat. Bake in the hot oven for 25 minutes until golden and crisp.

Cook the pasta
Bring a large pan of water up to a rolling boil. Season the water generously with salt, add 500g linguine and cook until al dente.

Mix the pasta and sauce
Toss the pasta and meatballs into the tomato sauce and add most of a bunch of basil, reserving a handful for serving. Tip on a platter and top with the rest of the basil and a grating of Parmesan if you like.

Nadya's tepsi with amba tomatoes

2 medium aubergines (about 300g
    each), cut into 1cm-thick slices
olive oil
3 medium potatoes, peeled and
    sliced ½cm thick
3 onions, peeled and sliced
    ½cm thick
100g tomato purée
2 green peppers, deseeded and
    cut into 1cm-thick slices
3 tablespoons tamarind paste,
    or juice of 1 unwaxed lemon
150ml hot good-quality vegetable
    stock
400g tomatoes, sliced ½cm thick
    (I used a mixture of colours
    and sizes)
½ a bunch of parsley (15g),
    leaves picked
2 tablespoons amba
juice of ½ an unwaxed lemon
pickled turnips (optional)
100g salted yoghurt

Sometimes people come into your life at the perfect moment. Nadya Mousawi did. Nadya is a doula and came to us in the hazy days when Esca was small and helped me navigate having a tiny baby again. She made us food, helped me feed him, chatted through my worries. It's how all mums should be supported (which I could write much much more about). This tepsi was a favourite thing Nadya made. It's from Iraq, where Nadya is from. For this and so many other things, I am so grateful, Nadya.

Here, tomato purée joins up with sour/sweet tamarind to make a flavour blanket which coats layers of aubergine, peppers and potatoes in a moreish sweet and sour bake. It gets better as the days go by and will sit unbaked in the fridge for a couple of days. Nadya eats it with rice and yoghurt and Iraqi pickled turnips, so we do too.

SERVES 4–6

Roast the aubergine
You will need a medium baking dish, roughly the size of a sheet of A4 paper. Preheat the oven to 240°C/220°C fan. Salt 2 medium aubergines, cut into 1cm-thick slices and toss to season, then drizzle a good amount of olive oil on both sides and roast them on a baking tray for 30 minutes until soft and golden. Turn the oven down to 180°C /160°C fan.

Cook the potatoes
Cook 3 medium potatoes, peeled and sliced ½cm thick, in boiling salted water for about 8 minutes until cooked through, then drain and allow to steam dry.

Cook the onions
Meanwhile, heat a glug of olive oil in a frying pan and cook 3 onions, peeled and sliced ½cm thick with a little salt until soft and sweet. Add 1 tablespoon tomato purée and a splash of water to cover the onions in a thick tomatoey sauce. Once it bubbles, take the pan off the heat and spread the onions evenly on to the bottom of your baking dish and season. This is your first layer.

Cook the green peppers
Put the frying pan back over a medium heat, add a little olive oil and once hot add 2 green peppers, cut into 1cm-thick slices, and cook until charred and soft. Layer them on top of the onions and season with salt, then wipe the pan clean.

Sauté the cooked potatoes
Put the frying pan back on the heat again, add a good amount of olive oil and then add the drained potatoes and fry until golden (in batches if needed). Once golden, layer the potatoes on top of the peppers and season really well with salt.

Add the aubergine layer
Take the aubergines out of the oven, lay on them top of the potatoes and season.

Make the tamarind mix
In a jug mix the remaining tomato purée with 3 tablespoons tamarind paste or the juice of a whole lemon and 150ml hot stock. Pour the mixture over the tepsi, then top with 400g tomatoes sliced ½cm thick, salt and pepper and a generous drizzle of olive oil. Then bake for 45 minutes until bubbling and charred.

Make the parsley salad
Mix the leaves from ½ a bunch of parsley with a little lemon juice and serve with the amba, pickles and 100g salted yoghurt.

Spiced tomato soup with lemon and herb flatbreads

5 tablespoons olive oil

3 onions, peeled and finely chopped

4 sticks of celery, finely chopped

2 carrots, peeled and finely chopped

6 cloves of garlic, peeled and finely chopped

1 tablespoon cumin seeds

1 tablespoon coriander seeds

2–4 tablespoons harissa paste (depending on heat)

2 × 400g tins cherry tomatoes

800ml hot vegetable stock (made with 1 teaspoon bouillon powder or ½ a stock cube)

200g mature Cheddar or vegan Cheddar-style cheese, grated

50g feta or vegan feta-style cheese

2 preserved lemons, skin roughly chopped

50g pickled green chillies, roughly chopped

a bunch of parsley (30g), chopped

½ a bunch of mint (15g), chopped

½ a bunch of dill (15g), chopped

4 large fluffy Turkish flatbreads

4 tablespoons za'atar

There are two soups I make for our family when the reserves are low and cupboards are bare: a quick frozen pea and coconut soup from my second book and a version of this soup. I think it's a bit of magic that a delicious soup can come from nothing more than a few simple vegetables, a little spice and a couple of tins of tomatoes. I use tinned cherry tomatoes as I like the sweetness they bring, but a couple of tins of plum tomatoes would work well too. The soup starts with a base of onion, garlic, carrot and celery, but you could also use leek, fennel or shallots too. The crowning glory of this soup is the lemon and herb flatbreads. They come together just like a cheese toastie. I come back to them again and again.

SERVES 4

Start the soup
Add 3 tablespoons olive oil to a medium saucepan along with 3 peeled and finely chopped onions, 4 finely chopped sticks of celery, 2 peeled and finely chopped carrots, and 6 peeled and finely chopped cloves of garlic and fry the lot over a medium-low heat for 15–20 minutes, stirring every so often, until soft and sweet but not browned. You will need to adjust the heat as you go and perhaps add a little more oil or even a splash of water if it's beginning to catch.

Add the spices
Once the vegetables have softened, add 1 tablespoon cumin seeds, 1 tablespoon coriander seeds, and 2–4 tablespoons harissa paste and stir to toast for a minute. Add 2 × 400g tins of cherry tomatoes and their juice, then 800ml hot vegetable stock. Reduce to a simmer and cook for 20 minutes, stirring often.

Make the flatbread filling
Grate 200g Cheddar cheese into a mixing bowl, then crumble in 50g feta cheese. Add 2 roughly chopped preserved lemons and 50g chopped pickled green chillies. Mix in the chopped leaves from a bunch of parsley and from ½ a bunch each of mint and dill. Taste and season with salt and pepper if needed.

Bake the flatbreads
Preheat the oven to 240°C/220°C fan. Place the flatbreads on a baking tray and drizzle one side with oil and a little za'atar. Flip the flatbreads over on to the unoiled side, pile the filling on to one of the flatbreads and spread evenly, then sprinkle over some more za'atar. Place the other flatbread to sandwich the filling – oiled side up – then place in the oven for 10 minutes so the cheese melts and the flatbread toasts.

Blend the soup
While the flatbreads are in the oven, use a hand-held blender to blend the tomato mixture until you have a creamy soup. Keep it warm on a low heat. Taste and season with more salt if needed.

Serve the soup and flatbreads
Take the flatbreads out of the oven, slide on to a large chopping board and carefully slice up and serve alongside the soup.

Mersedeh's mirza ghasemi

3 large aubergines or 5 medium
    aubergines
3 tablespoons olive oil
1 medium onion, peeled and
    finely chopped
2 cloves of garlic, peeled and
    finely chopped or grated
1 teaspoon ground turmeric
1 × 400g tin chopped tomatoes
3 tablespoons tomato purée
1 teaspoon maple syrup or sugar
2 large free-range or organic
    eggs (beaten), plus more if
    eating as a main course
chopped chives and crushed
    walnuts, to finish
flatbreads to serve

This is a recipe from my lifelong friend Mersedeh Prewer. Our friendship has seen us through all the ups and downs, but up or down, our friendship has always centred around what's for dinner.

This is a rich dip I've eaten at Mer's table, made with tomatoes and tomato purée and smoked aubergine. The unusual thing (for me) is that eggs are stirred through at the end to enrich it. It's so good scooped with flatbread and next to a pile of herbs and some feta. It's not just eaten as a dip to start a meal but is also great as a main dish with rice.

SERVES 6

Char the aubergines
Cook 3 large or 5 medium aubergines whole over an open flame (gas hob or barbecue) until blackened and the flesh has softened. You can also do this under the grill, set to medium-high, in your oven. The idea here is to get a smoky flavour into the final dish.

Cool and peel the aubergines
Allow the aubergines to cool, then peel them or cut them in half and scoop out the flesh, discarding the skins.

Cook the onion
Put a lidded frying pan over a medium-low heat, add 3 tablespoons olive oil and 1 medium onion, peeled and finely chopped, and a pinch of sea salt. Cook the onion for 10 minutes until it is soft and sweet and starting to brown, then add 2 finely chopped or grated cloves of garlic and cook for another 2–3 minutes, making sure the garlic does not burn. Then stir in 1 teaspoon ground turmeric.

Add the tomatoes
Add a 400g tin of chopped tomatoes and cook until the tomatoes have softened and broken down. Stir in the aubergine flesh and mash the mixture gently. Add 3 tablespoons tomato purée, 3 tablespoons water, 1 teaspoon maple syrup or sugar, then season and cook for about 10 minutes, stirring gently now and then.

Add the eggs
Make a few holes in the mixture and add 2 beaten eggs. Once the eggs start to turn pale yellow and firm a little, stir them in until evenly distributed through the aubergine mixture. Let the mixture simmer gently on a low heat and with a lid on the pan for a further 10 minutes.

Finish with herbs
Serve warm but not piping hot, with a drizzle of olive oil and a sprinkling of chopped chives and crushed walnuts, alongside more fresh herbs, feta and flatbread.

Paneer rolls with quick tomato chutney

2 tablespoons ghee or vegetable oil

2 red onions, cut into eighths

1 green or red pepper, deseeded and cut into long strips

a 250g block of paneer or firm tofu, cut into 2cm pieces

6 tablespoons quick tomato chutney

4 parathas (I use the frozen ones)

a small bunch of coriander, leaves picked

wedges from 1 unwaxed lime

FOR THE QUICK TOMATO CHUTNEY

1 teaspoon cumin seeds

½ teaspoon dried chilli flakes

1 tablespoon olive oil

1 red onion, peeled and finely chopped

2 cloves of garlic, peeled and finely chopped

1 small thumb-sized piece of ginger, grated (15g)

1 green chilli, sliced lengthways

1 × 400g tin chopped tomatoes

20g caster sugar

100ml red wine vinegar

juice of 1 unwaxed lime

One lunchtime as I was putting this book together, I was craving both the bounce of paneer and the sharp sweetness of a tomato chutney. Half an hour later I was eating these in a quick break from writing. The chutney is quick, keenly spiced and comes from a tin of tomatoes. What is left can be kept in a jar in the fridge for a week or so. What's key in this recipe is coating and quickly cooking the paneer in the chutney. The perky sweetness of the tomato is such a good contrast to the milky paneer (and also works very well with firm tofu). I used ready-made parathas here, but roti or chapatis would work too.

MAKES 4

Cook the onions and peppers
Put a large frying pan over a medium heat and add a little oil or ghee. Add 2 red onions, cut into eighths, and 1 green or red pepper, deseeded and cut into long strips. Turn up the heat and cook for 5 minutes until charred at the edges and softening. Tip the onions and peppers on to a plate.

Add the paneer/tofu
Put the empty pan back on the heat, add a little more oil or ghee, turn up the heat and add 250g paneer or tofu, cut into rough 2cm pieces. Cook for 4–5 minutes, turning every couple of minutes, until hot, crisp and browned all over. Add the onions and peppers back to the pan.

Coat the paneer in the chutney
Take off the heat and add 2 tablespoons of the tomato chutney and stir to coat. Put to one side to cool slightly.

Cook your paratha
Toast your parathas in a pan until warm. If using the frozen ones, follow the instructions on the packet.

Make your rolls
Pile the sticky paneer into the warm parathas, top with a tablespoon of the chutney and a few sprigs of coriander and a squeeze of lime. Add a little yoghurt too if you like. Serve warm with a napkin.

For the chutney:
Toast the spices
Put 1 teaspoon cumin seeds and ½ teaspoon dried chilli flakes in a dry frying pan and toast for a couple of minutes, then crush in a pestle and mortar.

Cook the aromatics
Put the frying pan back over the heat, add a little olive oil and 1 finely chopped red onion, 2 cloves of finely chopped garlic, and 1 small thumb of grated ginger, then fry for about 10 minutes until soft.

Add the liquid
Add a 400g tin of chopped tomatoes, the toasted cumin and chilli flakes, 20g sugar and 100ml red wine vinegar.

Simmer the chutney
Bring to the boil, then reduce the heat and simmer for 25 minutes, squashing the tomatoes with the back of a spoon as they soften, until the chutney is sweet and sticky.

Add the lime
Take the pan off the heat and squeeze in the juice of 1 unwaxed lime.

Capers

I buy four jars at a time. The tiny ones are my favourite; rarely a day passes without their briny, salty acidity. Vinegary buds, so full of flavour they pop in your mouth. Little hits of acid that make meals better. So small they have no right to be so flavourful. Fry them in hot oil and they open out into deep-green flowers, still sour but crispy. We ate them at our wedding, fried into bloom on top of a tomato tart. Scatter them into mayonnaise with herbs and cornichons, fold them into caponata with olives and parsley, bake them into focaccia with their brine. Sizzle them in browning butter to spoon over mashed potato. Allow them to crisp next to roast potatoes. Make margaritas with the brine. And ice cream, caper chocolate cream.

On Capers

Capers are a constant in my kitchen. To me, they are the perfect balance between salty and acidic. They bring salt, acidity and umami, with a perky, almost mustardy, note. They ask little of me and sit in my fridge for months.

I think they are unmatched in vegetarian cooking in the way they can create a rounded savoury, umami base of flavour, and they stand in for anchovies in my cooking.

Do not pour away the brine. It's a perfectly salty-sour flavour hit that can be used to add a seasoning, giving the dish a nip and a lift. It's also incredible in margaritas (page 173).

Fried, these little flowers transform into crunchy savoury flavour bombs. I use these fried capers anywhere that their salty crunch is welcome. I lean towards the small jarred nonpareille capers in vinegar, as they are so easy to use. I love how easy they are to use straight from the jar.

You can't argue that the flavour of salted capers is the best. All my chef friends use them. The salt seems to preserve their flavour better.

Types

Capers are the small flower buds of the Capparis, or caper, bush that grows in the Mediterranean. Capers are the immature, unripe green flower buds. You can eat the fruits of the same plant, which we know as caper berries. They're picked by hand, often on a small scale. New buds develop on the bush every day, so the capers are harvested daily.

There are lots of varieties – in size order starting with the smallest: nonpareille, surfines, capucines, capotes, nocella, fines and grusas.

I mostly buy larger capote, nocella or fines capers – all larger types of caper, which I tend to chop a bit before using – and the tiny lilliput or nonpareille capers, which I eat whole.

- Brined in salted water
  The most common

- In vinegar
  With an extra kick: my favourite

- Salted
  Salt is said to keep their flavour best; the salt should still be white when you buy them

Goes well with

beetroot	lemon
cauliflower	olive
chocolate	parsley
cucumber	pickles
dill	potato
egg	tomato

Favourite uses

- Puttanesca pasta
- Crisped in oil to top pretty much anything
- In salsa verde
- In tartare sauce
- To scatter into a tray of roast potatoes for the last 10 minutes
- Always on pizza

Storage

Brined or vinegared capers need to be covered in their pickling liquid when stored or they will dry out and quickly lose their flavour. You can top up a jar with white wine vinegar and a little water. I keep them in the fridge once open.

Salted capers last for years if kept in an airtight container. To use salted capers, they must first be soaked in cold water to mellow the saltiness, then drained. I like to soak mine for at least an hour. If they are particularly salty, you can change the soaking water once during soaking.

What to buy

If I am buying from a supermarket, I opt for the small lilliput or nonpareille (which translates from French as 'has no equal') caper, which I find plumper and I like the smaller size.

Buy them on holiday in Italy, Spain, France or Greece – often they will be cheaper and handpicked locally.

Nasturtium capers

300g nasturtium seeds
15g fine sea salt
500ml white wine vinegar

Nasturtiums are a wholly edible plant, providing peppery leaves at the last turn of spring, vibrant edible flowers through the warmer months and seed pods at the end of summer. Often termed 'poor man's capers'. Punchier and more peppery than a classic caper, they can be then used throughout the year as a direct replacement.

MAKES A 1-LITRE JAR

Steep the nasturtium seeds
Steep 300g nasturtium seeds in plenty of cold water for a moment to clean them. Drain and blot dry on kitchen paper. Tip the cleaned, drained seeds into a 1-litre sterilised jar.

Make the brine
Put 15g fine salt and 500ml white wine vinegar in a medium saucepan and bring to the boil. As soon as it boils, remove from the heat and pour directly over the nasturtium seeds. Seal the jar and store it in the fridge, where it will keep indefinitely. The seeds will be ready to use after a couple of months.

Use the vinegar
Once you have used all the nasturtium 'capers' you'll be left with nasturtium vinegar. Keep it in the fridge and use it in dressings and braises. A little of it is amazing poured over super-sweet fruit.

Wild garlic capers

(Photograph opposite)

300g wild garlic seed heads
6g fine sea salt
500ml apple cider vinegar

Like nasturtiums, wild garlic can be used in a lot of ways in the kitchen. Just before the plants retreat to the woodland floor the seed heads remain, standing proud. Preserving these seed pods requires a little time, but they bring an entirely new dimension to cooking with capers.

MAKES A 1-LITRE JAR

Pick the wild garlic pods
Harvest 300g seed heads from the top of the wild garlic flower stems, trying to pick heads with as few white flowers left on them as possible. In a large bowl or bucket, steep the seed heads in plenty of cold water to rinse and remove all dirt and remaining white flowers. Drain and repeat the process once more.

Salt the wild garlic heads
Pat the seed heads dry and add to a large bowl, weighing them as you do so.

Add the salt and scrunch it in until everything is thoroughly mixed.

Store in their salt
Put the salted seed heads into a sterilised jar and store in the fridge, shaking the jar every few days, for a month.

Add the vinegar
After leaving the heads for a month, put 500ml apple cider vinegar in a medium saucepan, bring to the boil, then set aside. Rinse the seed heads under cold running water for a moment, then put into a new sterilised jar of the same size they were salted in. Pour over the vinegar while it is still piping hot and seal the jar. Store in the fridge indefinitely and use in place of normal capers for a subtly garlic-y addition.

Focaccia with lemon, capers and fennel seeds

2 teaspoons runny honey

3.5g/½ sachet or 7g/1 sachet
   active dry yeast

700g plain flour

½ tablespoon sea salt (about 12g)

40ml extra virgin olive oil,
   plus more for greasing and
   finishing

40g capers, plus 2 tablespoons
   brine from the caper jar

1 tablespoon fennel seeds

the peel of 1 unwaxed lemon,
   pared with a vegetable peeler

½ small bunch of oregano,
   leaves picked

flaked sea salt, for finishing

This recipe is inspired by my brilliant friend Samin Nosrat, who uses a brine to season her focaccia, evenly salting the dough to make it all the more delicious. Here I put capers on top and use the brine they sit in to season the focaccia. You can make this two ways: either with an overnight prove, or with a shorter 2–3 hour prove.

To store the focaccia, wrap it in baking paper then keep it in an airtight bag or container. Gently toast or reheat before serving.

MAKES 1 LARGE FOCACCIA FOR 8–10

Make the dough
Whether you are doing an overnight prove or a shorter prove, mix 525ml lukewarm water with 2 teaspoons runny honey then add ½ teaspoon active dry yeast for overnight, or 1 teaspoon yeast for a shorter, 2-hour prove and stir to dissolve. In a large bowl, mix 700g plain flour and ½ tablespoon sea salt, then add the yeast and honey mixture and 40ml extra virgin olive oil. Stir to combine everything and bring it together to a rough dough, and, using a spatula or dough scraper, scrape your hands and the sides of the bowl clean, then cover the bowl with a tea towel.

Prove the dough
For an overnight prove, leave at room temperature for 12–14 hours, until at least doubled in size. For a shorter prove leave for 2–3 hours, or until doubled in size.

Transfer the dough
Once your dough has doubled in size, pour 3 tablespoons extra virgin olive oil on to a 20cm × 30cm, 4cm-deep roasting tray. Carefully transfer the dough into the tray – use a dough scraper to help you. Rub 2 tablespoons olive oil over the dough and gently stretch it to the edge of the tray. Leave it to rest for half an hour, pulling it back to the edges again if need be.

Add the topping
Mix together 40g capers and 1 tablespoon fennel seeds and evenly sprinkle them over the dough with a pinch of flaked sea salt.

Dimple and brine the dough
Oil your fingers lightly again and, forming a claw with your fingers, dimple the dough all over, creating irregular and deep dimples. Pour over the caper brine, trying to spread it as evenly as you can. This brine will season the focaccia to begin with. Leave to rest for another half an hour.

Preheat the oven and bake the focaccia
Preheat the oven to 220°C/200°C fan. After the dough has had its final rest, run your fingers back over it in the same claw-like fashion to make sure the toppings are at one with the dough. Bake for 25–30 minutes on the middle shelf, until golden-brown. Add the peel of 1 unwaxed lemon, ½ a bunch of picked oregano leaves, a little more oil and flaked sea salt, then move the focaccia to the top shelf and bake for a further 5–7 minutes.

Remove from the oven and drizzle over 2 tablespoons more oil. Leave to cool for 5–10 minutes, before lifting it out of the tin.

Other toppings I love are jarred artichokes, cherry tomatoes, red grapes, bay leaves, rosemary, thyme, red or green chilli, pickled chillies, half a thinly sliced onion or jalapeños.

Cauliflower caponata

1kg cauliflower, broken into
    roughly 4cm florets
3 red onions (350g), peeled and
    cut into eighths
3 sticks of celery, cut into 2cm
    pieces
extra virgin olive oil
3 tablespoons white wine
    vinegar
2 × 400g tins plum tomatoes
100g stone-in green or black
    olives, stones removed
    (I use a mixture of both)
3 tablespoons capers
50g raisins
½ a bunch of parsley (20g),
    leaves picked
warm bread, to serve

Caponata is a masterclass in balancing sweet, sour and salty. It's most often made with aubergine, which you have to fry in lots of olive oil first, making it less of a weeknight situation. This buttery cauliflower version is all done in the oven and to me it's just as good as the aubergine version. It has the texture of a stew and can be eaten warm as an antipasto, as is most common in Italy, or on toast or tossed through pasta.

SERVES 4

Preheat the oven and roast the cauliflower
Preheat the oven to 220°C/200°C fan. Put a cauliflower, broken into roughly 4cm florets, 3 red onions, peeled and cut into eighths, and 3 sticks of celery, cut into 2cm pieces, into a large, high-sided baking tray with 1 tablespoon extra virgin olive oil, 2 tablespoons white wine vinegar and a little sea salt and pepper. Toss to coat, then roast for 25 minutes, until everything is slightly charred and starting to soften. Turn the oven down to 200°C/180°C fan.

Add the rest
Add 2 × 400g tins of plum tomatoes, breaking them in your hands as you do so, along with 100g stone-in green or black olives (stones removed), 3 tablespoons capers and 50g raisins. Give everything a good mix, mashing slightly with a fork, and return to the oven for 40 minutes, or until everything is soft and sticky.

Finish with the vinegar and oil
Once ready, and while the mix is still piping hot, add another tablespoon of vinegar, toss through a handful of parsley leaves and serve. Finish with a very generous dousing of extra virgin olive oil to bring it all together.

Courgette and salsa verde gratin

a few sprigs of oregano or
  marjoram (5g)
½ a bunch of mint (15g)
½ a bunch of parsley (15g)
150ml extra virgin olive oil
2 small cloves of garlic, peeled
3 tablespoons capers, drained
  (rinsed and soaked if salt-
  packed)
zest and juice of 1 unwaxed
  lemon
1kg courgettes, cut into 5mm-
  thick discs
200g fresh breadcrumbs, from
  good bread
50g unsalted butter (or vegan
  butter) or more olive oil
2 banana shallots (about 100g),
  peeled and finely sliced
1 green chilli or jalapeño,
  deseeded and finely chopped
120g nutty cheese, like Gruyère
  or Emmental, or 100g vegan
  Cheddar-style cheese,
  coarsely grated

This recipe is loosely based on one
I have been making for years
from the *Sunday Suppers at Lucques*
restaurant cookbook. Capers
are front and centre here, tossed
through the gratin and providing the
backbone to the salsa verde. This is a
light gratin, with lemon, capers, mint
and parsley the main events rather
than the heavy cheese or cream a lot
of gratins go in for. I make this with
a lemony-dressed peppery salad.

SERVES 4

Make the salsa verde
Using a mortar and pestle (or a food
processor if you prefer), pound or
blitz 5g oregano, 5g mint and 5g
parsley leaves to a paste. You may
have to do this in batches if your
pestle and mortar is small. Add 50ml
extra virgin olive oil and mix or blitz
it in. Tip the mixture into a bowl.
Pound 1 clove of garlic with a little
salt and add it to the herb oil. Gently
pound or pulse 2 tablespoons capers
until they're partially crushed, and
add them to the herby garlic mixture.
Stir in 100ml extra virgin oil, a
grinding of black pepper and the zest
and juice of 1 unwaxed lemon. Taste
and adjust for acidity and salt.

Prepare the courgettes
Heat the oven to 200°C/180°C fan.
Toss 1kg courgettes, cut into 5mm-
thick discs, in a colander with a good
pinch of sea salt and let them sit for
10 minutes over a bowl to catch any
juices (there won't be loads of liquid).

Prepare the brown butter breadcrumbs
Place 200g breadcrumbs in a
heatproof bowl. Heat a small pan
over a medium heat for 1 minute.
Melt 50g unsalted butter until it
begins to turn light brown and starts

to smell nutty, then pour it over
the breadcrumbs and mix well.

Make the gratin
Tip out any liquid from the mixing
bowl under the courgettes and
put the courgettes into it. Finely
slice 1 clove of garlic and add it
to the courgettes with 2 shallots,
1 deseeded and finely chopped
green chilli, 4 tablespoons of the
salsa verde and a good grind of
pepper. Toss to mix everything and
add 120g coarsely grated Gruyère
or vegan cheese and half of the
breadcrumbs. Taste for seasoning.
The raw garlic will taste strong but
will mellow as it cooks. Toss the
remaining tablespoon of capers
with the rest of the butter-coated
breadcrumbs.

Bake the gratin
Place the courgette mixture in
a 26–30cm round gratin dish,
ovenproof pan or something
similar. Scatter the remaining
caper breadcrumbs over the top
and bake for 40–45 minutes, or
until the courgettes are soft and
the top is golden and crisp.

Serve the gratin
Serve with the remaining salsa
verde spooned over the top. I like
mine with a lemon-dressed green
salad, and if I'm hungry some boiled
or roasted buttered new potatoes.

Pantry pasta with capers and lemons

50g shelled unsalted pistachios

2 banana shallots, peeled and
thinly sliced

4 cloves of garlic, peeled and
thinly sliced

100ml olive oil

1 unwaxed lemon

3 tablespoons capers

400g pasta, like linguine

½ a bunch of flat-leaf parsley
(15g), finely chopped

grated Parmesan cheese or
vegan Parmesan-style cheese,
to serve

Like all the best recipes, this comes from the store cupboard, with the exception of a bit of parsley, which can be left out if you don't have any. Here, a good hit of capers, sticky shallots, lemon and pistachios come together to make a quick sauce that gives you all the flavours. Pasta water is key to getting the lemony–capery sauce creamy and sticking to the pasta, so make sure you don't miss out keeping it back – it's the most important ingredient in this recipe.

SERVES 4

Cook the pistachios and shallots
Heat a large frying pan over a medium heat and add 50g shelled pistachios. Toast them, tossing regularly, until golden brown and fragrant. Allow to cool for a moment, then transfer to a pestle and mortar and roughly bash. Set aside for serving. Peel and finely slice 2 shallots and 4 cloves of garlic. Return the frying pan to a medium–low heat and add 100ml olive oil. Add the shallots and garlic and cook for 8–10 minutes, or until golden at the edges.

Chop the lemon
Cut 1 unwaxed lemon in half, removing the pips, then slice and finely chop one half, peel and all, discarding the pithy end. Keep the other half of the lemon for squeezing over later.

Finish the sauce
Add 3 tablespoons capers and the finely chopped lemon to the shallots and garlic in the frying pan and cook for another couple of minutes until you have a thick paste, then turn off the heat. This can be done ahead.

Cook the pasta
Put a large pot of very well salted water on to boil. Add 400g pasta to the boiling water and cook for a couple of minutes less than the packet instructions – you want it not quite al dente. Drain, keeping a mugful of pasta water to finish the sauce.

Finish the sauce
Add the drained pasta to the shallot pan along with about half a mug of pasta water and cook, turning the pasta with tongs or a spoon, until the caper, shallot and lemon mixture has come together into a thick sauce, adding a dash more pasta water if needed. Add the juice of the remaining half lemon and ½ a bunch of finely chopped flat-leaf parsley and toss again. Serve in bowls with a scattering of toasted pistachios and grated Parmesan.

Brown butter potatoes with lime tartare sauce

1kg small floury or new
  potatoes, scrubbed clean
100g salted butter (or 100ml
  olive oil)
6 tablespoons capers, plus
  2 tablespoons caper brine
1 large free-range egg yolk
2 tablespoons Dijon mustard
150ml olive oil
100g sour cream
zest and juice of 1 unwaxed lime
a small bunch of dill or fennel
  fronds, to serve

These have quickly become my desert-island potato. And, coming from a major potato enthusiast, that's something. The capers are added for the last bit of roasting with the potatoes, which adds a super-savoury crispy little pop of saltiness. Capers are used again in a lime and sour cream tartare sauce. For me, this is a complete dinner with a zippy green salad, perhaps some lemon-dressed chickpeas or white beans.

SERVES 4–6

Parboil the potatoes
Bring a large pan of salted water to the boil, add 1kg small potatoes, then bring back to the boil and simmer for 10–20 minutes, depending on the size of your potatoes, until they are just cooked. Drain and leave the potatoes to steam dry in a colander.

Brown the butter
Preheat the oven to 200°C/180°C fan. Put the potato pan back on the hob and add 100g salted butter. Cook over a medium heat until it turns nutty brown and smells toasty. If you are vegan, use a good olive oil in place of the butter and skip the browning stage; it will still be delicious, and you could add a toasty note with some smoked salt.

Roast the potatoes
Take the butter pan off the heat, put the potatoes in a 25cm × 30cm roasting tray and pour over the brown butter. Season generously with salt and pepper and toss everything in the tray. Roast for 25 minutes. Take the potatoes out of the oven and use a potato masher to crush the potatoes into the base of the pan, making a flat surface for crisping up. Scatter over 4 tablespoons capers and bake for another 25 minutes until golden and crisp.

Make the lime tartare sauce
Meanwhile make your tartare sauce. Put 1 large free-range egg yolk and 2 tablespoons Dijon mustard in a bowl and mix well. Gradually whisk in 150ml olive oil. Loosen with 2 tablespoons caper brine and 100g sour cream. Finely chop 2 tablespoons capers and add to the sauce along with the zest and juice of 1 unwaxed lime.

Serve the crispy brown butter potatoes with the tartare sauce and with dill or fennel fronds torn over.

Pumpkin cecina with caper-lime chutney

200g gram flour
400g butternut squash, peeled
 and grated
zest and juice of 1 unwaxed lime
2 tablespoons olive oil, plus
 extra for greasing
1 red onion, peeled and finely
 chopped
4 cloves of garlic, peeled and
 sliced
a few sprigs of oregano (5g),
 leaves picked and finely
 chopped
2 jalapeños or fat green chillies,
 finely sliced
4 tablespoons capers
50g stone-in green olives,
 destoned and roughly
 chopped
400g tomatoes (vine or cherry),
 roughly chopped or halved
1 tablespoon light brown soft
 sugar
150g soft cheese – drained
 ricotta or feta
a few handfuls of peppery salad
 leaves, to serve

This recipe comes from a few places. Cecina is a Tuscan chickpea flour flatbread similar to socca, farinata or panisse. It comes together quickly and it's a super-affordable vegetarian dinner. I add squash to mine but other root veg like sweet potato, celeriac or salted and squeezed-out grated courgette would work too. The chutney is inspired by Mexican Veracruz sauce, which uses capers and olives for punch and is great to scoop up with the cecina.

SERVES 4

Make the squash cecina
Mix 200g gram flour with 400ml cold water in a bowl, mix in 400g grated squash, the zest of 1 unwaxed lime and a pinch of sea salt and let the mixture sit for an hour.

Make the Veracruz-style chutney
Heat a large pan over a medium heat, drizzle 1 tablespoon of olive oil into the pan, then add 1 peeled and finely chopped red onion and cook for 10 minutes until soft and sweet. Add 4 peeled and sliced cloves of garlic and cook for a further 3 minutes. Add the finely chopped leaves from a few sprigs of oregano and 2 finely sliced green chillies and cook for another minute or so. Add 4 tablespoons capers, 50g destoned and roughly chopped green olives and 400g chopped tomatoes, along with 1 tablespoon light brown soft sugar and the juice of 1 unwaxed lime, and cook for 10–15 minutes over a medium-high heat until the tomatoes have broken down and the chutney is sticky.

Cook the squash cecina
Preheat the oven to 220°C/200°C fan. Once the oven is hot, oil a 25cm × 30cm high-sided baking tray with 2 tablespoons olive oil and put back

in the oven for 5 minutes. Carefully remove the oiled tray from the oven, add the cecina batter and bake for 35–45 minutes, turning it in the oven halfway through (to ensure it cooks evenly), until set and golden brown around the edges.

Finish with the chutney and cheese
Remove the cecina from the oven and let it cool for a few minutes before loosening from the tray. Once cool enough to cut, chop into large pieces and top with 150g soft cheese, the chutney and a few handfuls of salad leaves.

Corn on the cob with caper and herb crumbs

4 corn on the cob in their husks
2 tablespoons olive oil
100g fresh breadcrumbs
4 tablespoons capers, roughly
    chopped, plus 1 tablespoon
    of caper brine
1 red or green chilli, deseeded
    and finely chopped
100g crème fraîche or sour cream
1 unwaxed lime
50g Parmesan or pecorino
    cheese, finely grated
½ a bunch of chives (10g), finely
    chopped

This recipe comes from my love of Mexican elote corn – crema and mayo-smothered corn topped with chilli and cotija cheese. This takes that idea down a different flavour route with capers, chives, lime and green chilli. A coating of crème fraîche, then caper-y breadcrumbs, then cheese and chives makes this my perfect corn. It also works as a salad if you cut the corn from the cobs, dress the kernels in the lime crème fraîche, then top with the caper breadcrumbs and cheese.

SERVES 4

Cook the corn
De-husk 4 cobs of corn, removing all the leaves and strings. You can then cook the corn one of two ways. To boil it, add the cobs to a deep pan of salted boiling water and cook for 10–12 minutes until tender. To griddle or barbecue it, blanch the cobs in boiling salted water for 5 minutes, then cook on a smoking hot griddle pan or barbecue until charred all over.

Fry the breadcrumbs
While the corn is cooking, heat 2 tablespoons olive oil in a large frying pan then add 100g breadcrumbs, 4 tablespoons capers, roughly chopped, and 1 deseeded and finely chopped red or green chilli. Cook the breadcrumbs for about 5–8 minutes, or until they are golden and toasted. Allow to cool.

Make the dressing
Mix 100g crème fraîche or sour cream with the zest and juice of ½ an unwaxed lime and 1 tablespoon caper brine, then put to one side.

Dress the corn
Once cool enough to handle, put the corn on to a plate, dress with the crème fraîche mixture and the remaining lime zest, then use the back of a spoon to cover the cobs all over. Next roll the cobs in the caper-spiked breadcrumbs, but don't worry if you don't get a perfect covering. Finally, scatter over 50g finely grated Parmesan or pecorino and top with ½ a bunch of finely chopped chives and the remaining lime half cut into wedges.

Capers

Kitty's caper and chocolate ice cream

1 heaped tablespoon salted
    capers (about 15g)
200ml double cream
500ml whole milk
20g cocoa powder
5 organic egg yolks
140g caster sugar
80g good-quality dark milk
    chocolate, broken into pieces

On a trip to Italy I'd heard about a caper and chocolate ice cream and as wild as it sounds I imagined the salty depth that the capers would bring to a rich chocolate ice cream. So I asked my friend Kitty Travers of La Grotta Ices if she had a recipe, which of course she did. Kitty makes my favourite ice cream, mostly using in-season fruits. It's like she has climbed inside my head and come up with all the flavours I would love. This caper and chocolate one is up there with her best. Like all real ice cream, it does take a little time and an ice-cream machine, but you won't be sad you made the effort.

MAKES 1 LITRE ICE CREAM

Soak the capers
Soak 1 heaped tablespoon salted capers in a good amount of cold water for at least 1 hour.

Heat the cream and milk
Heat 200ml double cream, 500ml whole milk and 20g cocoa powder in a large heavy-based saucepan until it comes to a simmer, then turn down very low to bubble away for 8–10 minutes, whisking constantly to combine and cook the cocoa. Turn off the heat.

Add the eggs to make the custard
Put 5 organic egg yolks and 140g caster sugar into a mixing bowl and whisk together. Add a ladleful of the hot milk mixture and whisk it into the eggs. Then add the egg mixture to the rest of the hot milk and put the pan back on a medium-low heat and cook, stirring all the time, until it coats the back of a spoon. Take off the heat.

Add the chocolate and capers
Break 80g good-quality dark milk chocolate into pieces. Pour the custard into a blender and while it's still hot add the chocolate pieces and blend to melt them into the custard. Drain the capers and squeeze out any excess liquid. Add the capers to the mixture in the blender and blend in well.

Refrigerate and churn
Refrigerate the custard overnight. Put the whole blender jug into the fridge, if it fits, as you will blend it again before churning. The next morning blend the mixture again, then put it in an ice-cream machine and churn it according to the instructions.

Freeze
Transfer to a lidded container and freeze for 4 hours before serving. Take it out of the fridge a few minutes before you want to eat it to make it scoopable.

Caper brine margarita

zest and juice of 2 large
    unwaxed limes (you need
    60ml of juice)
½ teaspoon fine red chilli
    powder
5g flaky sea salt (½ teaspoon)
10ml caper brine, plus extra for
    the rim
120ml best-quality mezcal or
    tequila
30ml agave syrup

When it comes to drinks I am a sour and salty person. This margarita uses caper brine that would otherwise be thrown away, bringing to the table what olive brine might to a martini. In fact I've made a dirty martini with caper brine and it was great, but this is better.

MAKES 2 MARGARITAS

Make the chilli-lime mixture for the glass
Put the zest of 2 large unwaxed limes into a bowl with ½ teaspoon fine red chilli powder and 5g flaky sea salt. If you like, put your glasses in the freezer to frost up. (I like thin tumblers or coupes).

Rim the glasses
Put the chilli-lime salt mixture on a plate. Pour a couple of tablespoons of caper brine onto another plate. Dip the rims of two glasses into the caper brine, then into the chilli-lime mixture.

Make the margarita
Put some ice into a cocktail shaker or other similar container with a lid. Add 120ml best-quality mezcal or tequila, 30ml agave syrup, 60ml lime juice and 10ml caper brine and shake until the shaker is frosty and cold. Load your rimmed glasses with ice and divide the margarita mix between them.

Chilli
and Harissa

From searing heat to gentle hum. Chilli is the warming heart. A spike of heat. I love mellow, rounded heat, so I use dried and preserved chillies. Whole raisiny ancho to spoonable spiced harissa and smoky chipotle in adobo. The chillies I have in my spice cupboard and this book are the few I can buy with ease. There are many more, and they all belong to cultures that are not my own. I use them with wonder, respect and reverence. A spoonful of harissa adds deep embedded flavour that fills the room. Smoked paprika brings a fruit-like roundedness that makes it the spice I reach for most. Chipotle in adobo brings smokiness to an aubergine parmigiana. Ancho brings mild, raisiny-sweet smokiness to tacos, salsa and chimichurri.

On Chilli and Harissa

Chilli gives heat; a warming sensation in your mouth. This warming feeling is not actually your mouth heating up but something called chemesthesis – your mouth's response to irritation. When we eat something spicy, from a hot chilli to a peppercorn, our sensory receptors get irritated and that gives the sensation we get from 'hot' or spicy food. Chilli heat is measured in Scovilles and ranges from a mild red pepper to chillies that will blow your socks off.

In Mexico alone, there are close to a hundred varieties of chilli. In the UK, we use very few varieties. When it comes to dried chilli, which is my focus in this chapter, I would wager that a lot of houses might have some chilli powder and some dried chilli flakes. And if that is what you have, then you can use a small amount of either in any of these recipes. They might not have the same depth of flavour, but your recipe will still taste good.

Heat, Smoky, Sweet, Earthy

Types

There are hundreds of types of dried chillies, but in this chapter I focus on the ones that I buy fairly easily and that get used a lot in my kitchen.

Dried chillies and spices

- Chipotle – a ripe smoke-dried jalapeño chilli used in Mexico.

- Ancho – mild, sweet-tasting. They have a fruity, earthy flavour.

- Pasilla – translates as 'little raisin', a wrinkly medium-hot chilli.

- Arbol – have an intense, clean heat and a nutty, grassy flavour.

- Smoked paprika – smoky, finely ground chilli, which you can buy in dulce (sweet), hot (picante) and agridulce (bittersweet).

- Turkish chilli or pul biber – a bright reddish chilli from Turkey, that's used like the Eastern equivalent of black pepper. It has a sweeter, more friendly chilli flavour. I use it when I'm cooking for kids.

Jarred chilli and chilli pastes

- Harissa – a North African red chilli paste made from chilli, garlic, olive oil, citrus and warm spices.

- Chipotle in adobo – smoky chillies cooked in a vinegary tomato sauce ready for cooking.

Goes well with

almond	lime
avocado	mango
aubergine	mint
broccoli	orange
cauliflower	peanut
chickpea	pepper
chocolate	pineapple
coconut	potato
coriander	pasta

Favourite uses

Dried chillies
- Chilli flakes – with cinnamon and fennel seeds on squash for roasting

- Chilli flakes – on top of thick yoghurt with salt and lemon, or see page 340

- Chilli flakes – sizzled in oil with slices of garlic, then tossed through pasta

- Pul biber – sprinkled on hummus with olive oil and sumac

Harissa
- Spooned into a stew of chickpeas, kale and lemon

- Swirled into yoghurt for spooning on soups/stews and flatbreads

Chipotle in adobo
- Spooned into a tin of black beans with some sizzled garlic

Storage and tips

Buy chillies in small quantities and replace them often, as they will lose their potency over time. Pastes can be stored in the fridge.

Pastes like harissa and chipotle will keep in the fridge for months once opened.

Favourite brands

For harissa, La Miri from Tunisia is my current favourite. For whole dried chillies, the Cool Chile Company have a good selection. And I love Daphnis and Chloe's chilli flakes.

Ancho chilli harissa

6 dried ancho chillies
1 tablespoon cumin seeds
1 tablespoon coriander seeds
6 cloves of garlic, peeled
2 roasted red peppers in brine, drained
200ml olive oil, plus a little extra
1 tablespoon red wine vinegar

Harissa is one of my most used ingredients. I don't think anything can beat it on the flavour it gives for not much cost or effort. It's so low-maintenance as an ingredient; a jar will sit happily for ages in your pantry unopened and then for months in the fridge without spoiling. It is a sure-fire way of making something taste like you have spent a lot more time cooking than you actually have. This is a mellow harissa that uses sweet, smoky anchos and roasted red peppers.

MAKES 1 × 500G JAR

Toast the chillies and spices
Put 6 dried ancho chillies into a piping hot frying pan and toast until fragrant. Set aside to cool slightly while you toast 1 tablespoon cumin seeds and 1 tablespoon coriander seeds in the same hot pan. When fragrant, set aside the spices and remove the seeds and stems from the chillies.

Soak the chillies
Put the chillies into a heatproof bowl, cover with boiling water and set aside for half an hour to soften.

Blitz the harissa
Drain the chillies and put into a food processor with the cumin and coriander seeds, 6 peeled cloves of garlic, 2 drained, roasted red peppers in brine, 200ml olive oil and 1 tablespoon red wine vinegar. Pulse until you have a not-quite-smooth paste, adding a little extra oil to loosen if you like.

Jar and store
Transfer to a sterilised jar, cover with a little extra olive oil and store in a cool dark place until needed. Once opened keep in the fridge.

Quick charred corn and crispy onion salad

6 corn on the cobs, husks
    removed, or 780g frozen
    sweetcorn
a small bunch of coriander,
    chopped
zest and juice of 2 unwaxed
    limes
3 tablespoons extra virgin
    olive oil
1 teaspoon harissa paste
100g crispy onions/shallots,
    shop-bought or see recipe
    on page 268

A recipe that's more than the sum of its parts. This is great with flatbreads and perhaps some baked feta, or even in tacos with some avocado and more coriander. The harissa adds a bolt of flavour for very little effort and brings it all together.

Fresh corn is best here, but if you want to make the dish out of season, use cooked and cooled frozen or unsweetened tinned corn, then char the kernels in a dry frying pan. Work to about 130g of frozen corn per cob.

SERVES 4

Cook the corn
Heat a griddle pan to a high heat, then, when the pan is piping hot, add 6 de-husked corn cobs in batches, turning every few minutes, until charred all over and cooked through. This works really well on a barbecue too. Or you can cut the kernels from the cobs use 780g of frozen sweetcorn and char them in a dry frying pan.

Cut the kernels from the corn
Set aside to cool slightly, then, if necessary, slice off the kernels with a sharp knife. Add to a serving bowl with a small bunch of chopped coriander.

Make the dressing and serve
Put the juice and zest of 2 unwaxed limes, 3 tablespoons extra virgin olive oil and 1 teaspoon harissa paste into a bowl or jam jar, give it a good shake, then pour it over the corn and coriander. Give everything a mix, taste and season with salt, and top with 100g crispy onions or shallots and serve.

Lemon, artichoke and butter bean paella

1 litre vegetable stock

2 onions, peeled and finely chopped (keep the trimmings)

1 carrot, peeled and finely chopped (keep the trimmings)

5g saffron threads, soaked in 50ml warm water

good-quality extra virgin olive oil

1 bulb fennel, trimmed and finely chopped, any herby bits kept for later

1 red pepper, deseeded and finely chopped

2 ripe tomatoes, flesh finely chopped, seeds discarded

4 cloves of garlic, peeled and finely chopped (keep the trimmings)

1 heaped teaspoon sweet smoked paprika

100ml white wine

100ml tomato passata

300g short-grain paella rice (see recipe intro)

1 × 700g jar butter beans, drained

1 × 400g jar artichokes, chopped into bite-sized pieces

1 unwaxed lemon, cut into 8 wedges

a bunch of parsley (30g), chopped

A few things to say about paella: while recognising I am absolutely no expert, I have found it's best made in a thin-based paella-style pan over a gas flame. Failing that, whatever large shallow (to remove the liquid quickly) sauté pan you have will work, the thinner-based the better.

The rice must be short-grain so it won't dry out when toasted. I have used bomba (also known as Calasparra). I have been told that risotto rice works as well too.

DO NOT STIR. This is not a risotto. The lack of stirring is what gives you the crisp, browned, sticky, chewy layer of 'socarrat' which is the main reason I eat paella.

Don't scrimp on the olive oil – the oil and your generosity with it is what makes this.

SERVES 4–6

Heat the stock and soak the saffron
Put 1 litre vegetable stock in a pan and add all the trimmings from your veg to add some more depth to the stock. Soak 5g saffron in 50ml warm water.

Fry the vegetables
Heat about 4 tablespoons oil in your pan, add 2 peeled and finely chopped onions, 1 peeled and finely chopped carrot and 1 trimmed and finely chopped bulb of fennel and sauté for about 10 minutes until really soft and sweet and beginning to brown. Add 1 deseeded and finely chopped red pepper, 2 finely chopped ripe tomatoes, 4 peeled and finely chopped cloves of garlic and 1 heaped teaspoon smoked paprika and cook for another few minutes. Add the soaked saffron and its water, 100ml white wine and 100ml tomato passata and cook for another few minutes.

Add the rice
Add 300g short-grain paella rice to the pan and stir it well to coat, adding more oil here if you think you need it. Strain the stock. Shuffle the rice into an even layer and add about 800ml of the stock. Simmer hard, no stirring, for 10 minutes, by which time a good amount of the liquid should have been absorbed but it should still feel like there is enough for it to cook for another 10 minutes. If not, add some of the remaining stock. Remember, no stirring.

Add the butter beans and artichokes
Next, scatter over a 700g jar of drained butter beans and a 400g jar of artichokes, chopped, and cook, without stirring, for another 8–10 minutes. Again, if the rice looks too dry before it's cooked (check by trying some – it should be just al dente but not too hard or chalky), add a little more stock, but do not stir it in.

Crisp up the bottom (the socarrat)
The key to the crispy bottom is to let it cook for a while after all the liquid has been absorbed. You should hear a sizzle. Leave it for about 30 seconds then turn off the heat – you should begin to see the edges crisp. The thicker the base of the pan you have, the harder this is. If you serve and haven't got a crispy bottom, drizzle a little oil around the edge of the pan and put it back on a high heat for another few minutes. Take it off the heat and cover to allow it to rest for 10 minutes then top with lemon wedges, a bunch of chopped parsley and any fennel fronds.

Squash and smoked chilli empanadas

1kg squash (butternut or any firm squash), peeled, seeds removed and cut into 1cm cubes

2 tablespoons olive oil, plus 80ml

½ a bunch of fresh oregano (5g), leaves picked, or 1 teaspoon dried oregano

2 dried ancho chillies

500g plain flour, plus extra for dusting

160g unsalted butter or vegan butter, cold and cubed

1 red onion, peeled and very finely sliced

zest and juice of 1 unwaxed lemon

100g Cheddar or vegan Cheddar-style cheese

1–2 green chillies, finely chopped

½ a bunch of parsley (15g), chopped

1 egg, beaten, or a few tablespoons oat milk

Years ago, I spent a few brilliant months in Argentina. Money was tight, so I lived mostly on empanadas: cheap, filling, delicious. In Argentina and across South America, if you're lucky, you'll come across an empanaderia – a bakery with glass cabinets full of empanadas. It's been years since I walked through the doors of such a place, but I find myself craving the flaky pastry and chilli eaten with your hands, all of which adds up to empanadas.

I dip them in chimichurri, an Argentinian-style salsa verde which is by no means traditional with empanadas but I like it. These are filled with squash, Cheddar (again not traditional, but I like the kick), herbs and quick-pickled red onions. If you can't get your hand on the dried chillies, then 2–3 teaspoons of chipotle or ancho in adobo (jarred paste) will work in their place.

MAKES 16 EMPANADAS

Roast the squash
Preheat the oven to 220°C/200°C fan. Scatter 1kg peeled, deseeded and cubed squash on a roasting tray with 2 tablespoons olive oil, the leaves from a couple of sprigs of fresh, or ½ teaspoon dried, oregano, salt and pepper, and roast for 25–35 minutes, until soft and slightly caramelised. Set aside to cool. Turn the oven down to 210°C/190°C fan.

Soak the chillies
Put 2 dried ancho chillies into a wide-based bowl or a heatproof measuring jug with 100ml boiling water and leave to sit and soften for 5 minutes. Once soft, remove the stalks and deseed if you like things less spicy. Then finely chop 1 of the chillies and keep the other aside for the chimichurri.

Make the pastry
While the squash is cooking, make the dough. Put 500g plain flour, a good pinch of sea salt and 160g cold, cubed butter in a food processor and blitz until it resembles breadcrumbs (you can do this by hand in a bowl using the rubbing method too). Add 80ml olive oil and blitz until the mixture has the texture of sand, then add 50–100ml ice-cold water, a little at a time, until it comes together into a dough. Tip out onto a clean work surface and gently knead until it is smooth, then shape into a disc, cover with a clean tea towel and chill in the fridge for an hour.

Pickle the onion
Put 1 peeled and very finely sliced red onion and the zest and juice of 1 unwaxed lemon into a bowl, then scrunch it all together with your hands until the onion starts to turn pink. Add the chopped soaked chilli, crumble in 70g Cheddar or vegan Cheddar-style cheese, add 1–2 finely chopped green chillies, 15g chopped parsley and the remaining sprigs of fresh, or ½ teaspoon dried, oregano and season. Add the squash and mix until combined.

Make the empanadas
Line two baking trays with baking paper. Cut the pastry into two (putting half back into the fridge while you roll out the first batch of dough) and on a lightly floured surface roll it out to a thickness of a 50p piece. Use a 10cm cutter (or a bowl this width) to cut out 6 rounds (you will have 16 in total), then place a heaped tablespoon of the filling in the centre of each. Brush one side of the pastry with the

Continued over...

Chilli and Harissa

beaten egg or oat milk, then fold the other side over. Press down the edges with a fork, to stick them together neatly. Repeat this process with the other half of the pastry so you have 16 in total.

Lay the empanadas on the tray, brush the tops with egg wash or oat milk and grate over 30g Cheddar. Grind over the remaining black pepper, then bake in the oven for 25 minutes, or until golden brown. Leave to cool for a few minutes before serving with a dollop of chimichurri.

vinegar and 1 teaspoon sea salt. Stir together to form a silky, herby sauce, taste, adjust the seasoning if needed, and serve. This can be kept in a jar in the fridge for up to 1 week.

SMOKED ANCHO CHIMICHURRI

As well as being the perfect accompaniment for empanadas, chimichurri is also great as a dressing for roast veg or as a topping for a bowl of polenta or lentils.

a bunch of flat-leaf parsley (30g),
    finely chopped
½ a bunch of oregano (10g), leaves
    picked and finely chopped
1 shallot, peeled and finely chopped
2 cloves of garlic, peeled and finely
    chopped
1–2 dried ancho chillies, soaked,
    deseeded and finely chopped, or a
    good pinch of dried chilli flakes
3 tablespoons extra virgin
    olive oil
1 tablespoon red wine vinegar

MAKES 1 SMALL BOWLFUL

In a small bowl, mix a bunch of finely chopped flat-leaf parsley, ½ a bunch of finely chopped oregano leaves, 1 finely chopped shallot, 2 finely chopped cloves of garlic, 1–2 soaked, deseeded and finely chopped dried ancho chillies, 3 tablespoons extra virgin olive oil, 1 tablespoon red wine

Chilli and Harissa

Roast sweet potatoes with sticky chilli salsa

1kg sweet potatoes (about
    3 large potatoes), cut into
    2cm-thick rounds
4 tablespoons extra virgin
    olive oil
2 large red onions, peeled and
    finely chopped
1 large thumb-sized piece of
    ginger (about 50g), peeled
    and finely grated
2 vine tomatoes, roughly
    chopped
1 dried ancho chilli, soaked and
    roughly chopped
1 tablespoon red wine vinegar
1 teaspoon caster sugar or maple
    syrup
50g skin-on almonds, roughly
    chopped
150g Greek yoghurt or oat
    yoghurt
3 unwaxed limes
8 corn tortillas or tacos, to serve

Sweet potato, lime, ginger, yoghurt and smoked chilli come together to make a plate of food that feels like everything I want to eat. The onions, ginger and tomatoes make a salsa that would and does make anything better. This would work really well with squash or pumpkin too.

If you can't find dried ancho chillies, you can use a tablespoon of ancho flakes or ancho in adobo or chipotle paste.

SERVES 4

Roast the sweet potatoes
Preheat the oven to 220°C/200°C fan. Put 1kg sweet potatoes, cut into 2cm-thick rounds, into a large baking tray or 2 smaller ones, drizzle over 2 tablespoons olive oil and scatter with salt. Roast for 20 minutes, then turn the potatoes over and cook for 15 minutes until golden on both sides.

Make the salsa
Heat 1 tablespoon extra virgin olive oil in a frying pan over a medium heat, add 2 finely chopped red onions and a good pinch of sea salt and cook for 10 minutes, until soft. Add a large finely grated thumb of ginger to the pan and cook for another 5 minutes.

Finish the salsa
Add another tablespoon of olive oil to the onions, plus 2 roughly chopped vine tomatoes, 1 soaked and roughly chopped dried ancho chilli, a table-spoon red wine vinegar and a teaspoon caster sugar or maple syrup. Turn the heat down to low and cook for 20 minutes until sticky and sweet, then add 25g roughly chopped, skin-on almonds and take off the heat.

Make the lime yoghurt
Mix 150g Greek yoghurt with a good pinch of salt and the juice and zest of 1 unwaxed lime.

Put it together
Once the sweet potatoes are cooked, you are ready to serve. Spread the lime yoghurt over a plate or platter and top with the sweet potatoes and half of the salsa. Cut 2 unwaxed limes into wedges and put around the plate for squeezing over. Serve with warm tacos, the rest of the salsa and another 25g chopped skin-on almonds.

If you are only eating a bit at a time, the salsa, yoghurt and sweet potatoes are best stored separately. They will keep in the fridge for up to 4 days.

Chilli and Harissa

Chipotle aubergine parmigiana

4 large aubergines (1.4kg in total)
olive oil
1 small onion, peeled and
    finely chopped
2 cloves of garlic, peeled and
    finely sliced
2 × 400g tins good-quality
    plum tomatoes or 800g fresh
    tomatoes, peeled and roughly
    chopped
1–2 tablespoons chipotle in
    adobo (depending on your
    love of heat)
1 tablespoon red wine vinegar
a small bunch of oregano (15g),
    or 1 tablespoon of good dried
    oregano
3 balls mozzarella (375g) or 300g
    vegan mozzarella, drained
    and thinly sliced
120g Parmesan or vegan
    Parmesan-style cheese, grated
100g fresh breadcrumbs (about
    4 slices of bread)

I love parmigiana. I love its layers, its buttery aubergine, the carefree amount of olive oil. Everything. In this parmigiana the aubergine is griddled, not fried, then doused in olive oil (though you use a good amount less than if it was fried). The griddling sounds like a job but it's pretty easy to do and you can start them off while you make the sauce. I've added some smoky chipotle in adobo here, which backs up the smoky notes of the griddled aubergine and rounds it all off. It is far from traditional.

I appreciate that buying 3 balls of mozzarella or vegan mozzarella can be expensive and it's a lot of cheese. I've made this with just two balls of mozzarella, making a thinner layer of cheese, and it was still great.

SERVES 4–6

Prepare and griddle the aubergines
Top and tail 4 large aubergines, then cut them lengthways into 5mm–7mm-thick slices. Generously drizzle them with olive oil and toss to coat well. Get a cast-iron griddle pan or barbecue really hot and, working in batches, griddle the aubergines first on one side, then the other, until cooked through and charred in places – each side will take about 4 minutes, so settle in. As they are ready, lay them on a large tray or plate and, when they're still warm, sprinkle with salt and drizzle with oil.

Make the tomato sauce
While the aubergines are grilling, get your tomato sauce on. In a deep pan, fry 1 small finely chopped onion and 2 peeled and finely sliced cloves of garlic gently in a couple of tablespoons of olive oil, until soft and sweet, then add 2 × 400g tinned or 800g chopped fresh tomatoes,

1–2 tablespoons chipotle in adobo, 1 tablespoon red wine vinegar and half a small bunch of fresh, or ½ tablespoon dried, oregano. Give it a good stir, mashing up the tinned tomatoes if necessary, and simmer for 25 minutes, until rich and thick. Preheat the oven about now to 200°C/180°C fan, so it is ready at the same time as the sauce.

Layer up the parmigiana
Spread a little tomato sauce in the bottom of a roughly 30cm × 20cm ovenproof dish, then cover with a layer of the charred aubergines, overlapping the slices slightly. Cover this with another thin layer of tomato sauce – use the back of a spoon to spread it out evenly, then top with a layer of mozzarella slices from 1 ball of mozzarella and ⅓ (40g) of the grated Parmesan. Repeat with another layer of aubergine, sauce, mozzarella and Parmesan and continue the layers until all the ingredients are used up. You should end up with three layers of each.

Make the breadcrumbs
Blitz 100g fresh breadcrumbs with the other half-bunch of fresh, or the remaining ½ tablespoon dried, oregano, 2 tablespoons of olive oil and a pinch of salt and toss together. Then sprinkle over the top.

Cook the parmigiana
Bake the parmigiana in the middle of the oven for 30–35 minutes, then remove and leave to rest for at least an hour before serving. I serve mine with a lemon-dressed green salad.

Spiced potato traybake with crispy chickpeas

olive oil
1kg waxy potatoes, cut into 1cm-
    thick wedges, skin-on
2 red peppers, deseeded and cut
    into 3cm pieces
1 whole head of garlic, cut in half
    across the middle
1 tablespoon coriander seeds,
    bashed in a pestle and mortar
300g cherry tomatoes, halved, or
    1 × 400g tin cherry tomatoes,
    drained
1 × 600g jar chickpeas, drained
2 tablespoons harissa paste
1 tablespoon black mustard seeds
1 teaspoon ground turmeric
200g Greek yoghurt or oat
    yoghurt
juice of 1 unwaxed lemon
½ a bunch of coriander (15g)

All the things I want to eat on a weeknight. This is cooked in two trays so you get a tray of crisp-edged potatoes and peppers and a tray of crispy harissa chickpeas and tomatoes. It's all brought together with a spiced yoghurt. I serve this with a herb salad of coriander and parsley leaves dressed in a little lemon and salt.

SERVES 4–6

Season and bake the vegetables
Preheat the oven to 220°C/200°C fan. Put a couple of tablespoons of olive oil in a baking tray and put in the oven to warm for 5 minutes. Take the tray out and carefully add 1kg skin-on waxy potatoes cut into 1cm-thick wedges, 2 deseeded red peppers cut into 3cm pieces, 1 whole head of garlic cut in half across the middle and 1 tablespoon bashed coriander seeds. Season well with salt and pepper and roast in the oven for 40 minutes until the potatoes are beginning to turn golden.

Make the crispy harissa chickpeas
Cut 300g cherry tomatoes in half (no need to do this if you are using tinned). In another baking tray put 600g drained jarred chickpeas, 2 tablespoons harissa paste and the halved tomatoes (or 400g tin cherry tomatoes, drained). Season well with sea salt and freshly ground black pepper and roast on a shelf below the potatoes for 35 minutes at the same temperature.

Make the spiced yoghurt
Meanwhile, heat 2 tablespoons of olive oil in a small pan and add 1 tablespoon black mustard seeds. Cook until they pop, then take off the heat and stir in 1 teaspoon ground turmeric. Allow to cool, then ripple through 200g yoghurt with the juice of 1 unwaxed lemon.

Serve
When the potatoes are browned and soft and the peppers jammy and charred, finely chop 15g coriander and scatter over the chickpeas and tomatoes. Serve in bowls with the spiced yoghurt.

Koftes with spiced tomato and lime butter rice

olive oil
1 onion, peeled and finely
    chopped
6 cloves of garlic, peeled and
    finely sliced
2 small thumb-sized pieces
    of ginger (10g), peeled and
    finely grated
3 tablespoons rose harissa paste
½ a bunch of coriander (15g),
    roughly chopped
½ a bunch of parsley (15g),
    roughly chopped
450g firm tofu, crumbled
6 tablespoons gram flour
2 × 400g tins finely chopped
    tomatoes, or passata
300g (about 1½ cups) basmati rice
25g butter, ghee or coconut oil
1 teaspoon cumin seeds
zest and juice of 1 unwaxed lime

These koftes are so moreish, made from tofu, herbs and harissa, and cooked first until golden in the pan and then in tomato and harissa sauce. I serve them on top of cumin and lime butter rice. I use a cup method for perfect rice; it's much easier than weighing it.

SERVES 4

Make the koftes mixture
Put 2 tablespoons olive oil in a large frying pan on a medium-high heat and add 1 peeled and finely chopped onion. Cook until soft, sweet and golden at the edges. Add 3 peeled and finely sliced cloves of garlic, a small thumb of finely grated ginger and cook for another couple of minutes before adding 1 tablespoon rose harissa and cooking for another 2 minutes. Transfer to a bowl to cool. Once the mixture is cool, add most of the roughly chopped parsley and coriander, reserving a little for the end, 450g crumbled firm tofu and 6 tablespoons gram flour, a good pinch of sea salt and a grinding of black pepper. Blitz half the mixture with 1–2 tablespoons cold water until you have a rough paste, then mix both together.

Roll out the koftes
Divide the mixture in half, then each half into 6 pieces (so you have 12 in total) and, with slightly wet hands, roll each one into a firm oval shape.

Cook the koftes
Put 4 tablespoons olive oil into the same pan on a medium-high heat. Once hot, fry the koftes in batches for 2–3 minutes on each side, until golden brown all over, then transfer to a baking tray and put into a low oven to keep warm. Wipe the pan clean.

Make the tomato sauce
Put the same pan on a medium-high heat. Add 1 tablespoon olive oil and, once hot, add another small thumb of grated ginger and 3 cloves of finely sliced garlic, and fry, stirring, for 2 minutes. Add 2 tablespoons rose harissa and stir, then add 2 tins of finely chopped tomatoes or passata and ½ a teaspoon of sea salt. Simmer for about 10 minutes until you have a rich tomatoey sauce.

Cook the rice
Put 300g (1½ cups) basmati rice in a sieve and run it under cold water for 30 seconds, until the water is clear. Fill and boil the kettle. Get a medium saucepan with a tight-fitting lid. Melt 25g butter, ghee or coconut oil in a saucepan over a medium heat. Add the rice and 1 teaspoon cumin seeds. Cook for 2–3 minutes, stirring all the time, until the rice looks shiny. Add 3 cups or 750ml boiling water, 1 teaspoon sea salt and the juice and zest of 1 unwaxed lime. Bring to the boil and simmer for 8 minutes on a medium heat with the lid off.

Then turn off the heat, wrap the pan lid in a tea towel and put it on the pan (this will absorb excess moisture). Leave for at least 5 minutes, avoiding the temptation to peek. When you take the lid off, you should see little air holes in the light and fluffy rice, with no liquid at the bottom. Stir in more lime and butter if you like.

Add the koftes to the sauce and finish
Gently put the koftes into the tomato sauce in the pan, spoon the sauce over to coat and cook for another 2 minutes, until the koftes are warmed through. Serve the koftes with the rice and the last of the coriander and parsley.

Chilli and Harissa

Smoked chilli cornbread

140g unsalted or vegan butter
  (see intro), plus extra to serve
150ml Greek-style yoghurt or
  oat Greek yoghurt
2 large free-range or organic
  eggs
2 dried ancho chillies, soaked,
  deseeded and finely chopped
  (soaking liquid reserved)
4 spring onions, trimmed and
  finely chopped
zest of 1 unwaxed lime, finely
  grated
2 tablespoons runny honey or
  maple syrup
100g quick-cook polenta
75g plain flour
½ teaspoon fine sea salt
the kernels from 4 corn on the
  cob, or about 520g defrosted
  frozen corn
½ teaspoon baking powder
½ teaspoon bicarbonate of soda
olive oil
2 garlic cloves, peeled and finely
  sliced
2 × 400g tins black beans with
  liquid
3cm piece of cinnamon, ground
feta or vegan feta-style cheese,
  crumbled, to serve
a bunch of fresh coriander (30g),
  chopped, to serve

This brown butter cornbread is inspired by one made by Ixta Belfrage in her book *Mezcla*. This one differs a lot from Ixta's; it has ancho chillies, spring onions, lime and honey to flavour the cornbread as it cooks. The brown butter is Ixta's trick, though, giving the whole thing a satisfying deep nutty flavour.

I have only found one vegan butter (Naturli vegan block) that browns, so I'd search that out or skip the browning step altogether. I most often make this with fresh corn, but defrosted frozen corn will work too.

SERVES 8

Get ready
Preheat the oven to 220°C/200°C fan. Grease and line a 20cm cake tin.

Brown the butter
Add 140g unsalted or vegan butter to a pan over a medium heat and cook, stirring, for 5 minutes, until the butter foams, turns a deep nut brown and smells toasty. Leave to one side to cool.

Make your batter
In a large mixing bowl, mix 150ml Greek yoghurt or oat Greek yoghurt with 2 large eggs, 1 soaked, deseeded and finely chopped dried ancho chilli, 4 finely chopped spring onions, the finely grated zest of 1 unwaxed lime, 2 tablespoons honey or maple syrup, 100g quick-cook polenta, 75g plain flour and ½ a teaspoon of fine sea salt.

Prepare the corn
If using 4 fresh corn ears, cut the kernels from the husks. If using 520g kernels (defrosted if frozen), just make sure you dry them with kitchen paper. Blitz 400g kernels in a food processor until you have a rough porridge with pieces the sizes of

breadcrumbs. Keep the remaining 120g or so whole and set aside.

Finish the batter
Add the cooled brown butter, ½ teaspoon baking powder and ½ teaspoon bicarbonate of soda to the batter and mix well.

Bake the cornbread
Pour the batter into the lined tin and scatter the remaining 100g whole corn kernels on top. Bake for 40–45 minutes until cooked through and evenly golden. Leave to cool a little before serving.

Cook the black beans
Whilst the cornbread bakes, heat a little olive oil in a small saucepan. Add 2 peeled and finely sliced garlic cloves, cook for a minute, then add 2 × 400g tins black beans with their liquid, a 3cm piece of cinnamon, ground to a powder, and 1–2 tablespoons of the soaking liquid from the chillies, along with 1 soaked, deseeded and finely chopped ancho chilli. Cook for 6–8 minutes, or until thick and glossy, then set aside. Keep warm.

Serve the cornbread
Serve the cornbread in wedges with the black beans, feta and a bunch of chopped coriander. Some chopped tomatoes dressed with lime would also work well here.

Chilli and Harissa

Tahini

Tahini the colour of caramel sits on my counter next to the oils and vinegars. It's used too often to be put away. Buttery and sweet with some backup from gentle bitterness. It walks the line between sweet and savoury like nothing else. It's borrowed from a culture that's not my own, with thanks and grace. I spoon it onto fruit, yoghurt and honey with coffee to start the day. Drizzle it into focaccia sandwiches of tomato and rocket for lunch. Scoop it onto chickpea stew for dinner. It brings depth. Savouriness. It's baked into cookies and cakes, swirled into breads. I whip it and drizzle it, whisk it into a dressing for salad, for noodles. It has my heart.

On Tahini

Tahini comes from an Arabic word meaning 'to grind'. It is of course made from sesame seeds and is used from the Middle East to the Mediterranean and the Balkans. Tahini can be made from black or white sesame seeds and is usually made with hulled or shelled seeds, for a smoother, less bitter flavour. Unhulled tahini is usually a little coarser, with a more earthy taste. Use it as a spread, a dressing or a dip. Maybe it's best known for being an essential ingredient in hummus and baba ghanoush, but its uses are countless.

Its flavour profile is slightly bitter, nutty and earthy. Its fattiness means it's a really useful ingredient for marrying things together, and its rich creaminess also makes it a really useful vegan ingredient.

Rich, Silky, Sweet, Bitter

- White
  Made from white sesame seeds, much like peanut butter. How dark and toasty the tahini is depends on how well-toasted the sesame seeds are. A deeper toast will give a darker colour and a more intense flavour.

- Black
  Made with black sesame seeds. A deep, thick, black paste, it has a nuttier and deeper flavour than white, so you need less.

- Hulled vs unhulled
  Hulled sesame seeds are the ones which have had their tough outer shell removed. Tahini from hulled seeds is smoother and less bitter. Most tahini you can buy in the shops is made from hulled seeds. Unhulled tahini is usually labelled as such and has a darker, more bitter and earthy taste and is more textured.

Goes well with

blood orange	noodles
broccoli	parsley
carrot	peanut butter
cauliflower	pear
chickpeas	pomegranate
chilli	rocket
chocolate	soy
cucumber	sugar
flatbread	sweet potato
honey	tomato
kale	walnut
lemon	yoghurt

Favourite uses

- Add it to yoghurt – with a little garlic, lemon and plenty of herbs for an easy dip
- Swirl it through brownies to balance out their richness
- Make a salad dressing with olive oil, lemon, salt and tahini
- Pair it with date molasses to balance out its bitterness and drizzle over yoghurt, toast or aubergines
- Swirl it into soup or stew with a squeeze of lemon
- Mix it with chilli oil and toss through warm noodles
- Put it in a smoothie with dates, banana and oat milk
- Spread it on toast with in-season fruit
- Spoon it into a baked sweet potato
- Mix with honey and serve next to cheese

Storage

Once open, it can be stored in a cool place or a fridge for several months after opening. Like peanut butter, it will separate and will need a stir before using. It's important to stir your tahini really well before you use it, getting right to the bottom of the jar. It seems a pain, but it will mean you don't end up with half a jar of unusable claggy tahini.

Favourite brands/where to buy

Brands can differ hugely. I want my tahini smooth and rich, rather than thick and claggy. Lebanese, Israeli and Palestinian brands tend to pour well. I love Al Nakhil tahini, which I buy from the Honey & Co Deli online but can be found all over. The Al Arz brand is another favourite. Belazu's tahini is also really good and available in most supermarkets in the UK. From the US, I love Seed & Mill tahini.

Homemade tahini

300g white sesame seeds
50–75ml neutral oil (such as
  sunflower or vegetable)

Homemade tahini is hard to beat. It's actually surprisingly low-effort. Toasting the sesame seeds before blending them not only turns up the flavour, but releases a little of the seeds' oil, making the whole process easier. To make a strikingly dark version, simply swap the toasted white sesame seeds for black sesame seeds, though take care when toasting them to watch that they don't burn.

MAKES 1 MEDIUM JARFUL

Toast the seeds
The depth of colour and flavour of your tahini will depend on how much you toast your sesame seeds. I like them well toasted, taken to a deep golden-brown colour, but toast them less for a milder tahini. Toast 300g sesame seeds in a dry frying pan over a medium heat, moving them every 30 seconds so they don't catch.

Blend the seeds
Put the sesame seeds into a food processor with a pinch of salt and pulse a few times. Scrape down the sides of the processor and blitz for around a minute before scraping down the sides again. Repeat this process until the sesame seeds have broken down into a light sandy texture.

Add the oil and jar
Scrape down the sides of the processor once more, then blitz again, gradually adding 50–75ml neutral oil, such as sunflower or vegetable, until the sesame mixture is the thickness you like – I go for the consistency of double cream. Transfer to a sterilised jar, where it will keep happily for at least a month in a cool dark place. Over time the oil from the mixture will naturally move to the top of the jar.

Tahini

Honey & Co's tahini-creamed chard

200g tahini

3 tablespoons extra virgin olive oil

1 teaspoon ground cumin

4 cloves of garlic, peeled and crushed, and 3 cloves of garlic, peeled and minced

juice of ½ an unwaxed lemon

2 large bunches of Swiss chard, green, rainbow or a mix (once separated should produce 400g stalks, 400g leaves)

4 tablespoons olive oil

1–2 large onions, peeled and diced (about 200g)

1 teaspoon sea salt

2 tablespoons toasted white sesame seeds, to sprinkle over the top

Sarit Packer and Itamar Srulovich are two of my favourite people. I have passed by their deli a lot over the last few years and every time I do I leave with a full bag of supplies. Always a pot of tahini. So much so that I can't think of tahini and not think of Sarit and Itamar. I thought I could not love them more, and then they sent me this recipe. It's a lesson in how simple is often the most perfect.

They learnt about it on a trip to Boston, where they ate at Ana Sutron's Oleana, which they tell me was one of the first restaurants to bring Middle Eastern food to contemporary dining in the West.

Itamar says, 'All the food we had there was dream-worthy, but it was the simplest plate that had us pining to go back to Boston – a dish of Swiss chard with tahini that was so good, such a wonderful marriage of flavour and texture, that we couldn't get it out of our heads from the moment we got back from Boston.'

And so, as with all great recipes, this is passed from Ana to Sarit and Itamar, to me and now to you. In Oleana they serve it as a mezze, but I have taken to serving it for dinner with bread.

SERVES 4–6

Make the tahini sauce
Place 200g tahini, 3 tablespoons extra virgin olive oil, 1 teaspoon ground cumin, 1 minced clove of garlic and the juice of ½ an unwaxed lemon in a blender with a good pinch of sea salt and 150ml cold water and blitz to a smooth, airy sauce.

Prepare the chard
Tear away the leafy parts of 2 large bunches of Swiss chard and set aside. Cut all the stalks into small dice.

Cook the onions and stalks
Heat 4 tablespoons olive oil in a very large saucepan on a medium heat and add 4 peeled and crushed cloves of garlic and 1–2 large peeled and diced onions and sauté for about 8 minutes. Add the diced chard stalks and 1 teaspoon of sea salt and continue sautéing for another 10–12 minutes or until the stalks are very soft.

Add the leaves and finish
Next add 2 cloves of peeled and minced garlic and the chard leaves. You may need to add the leaves in batches and allow them to wilt before adding the next. Increase the heat to high, mix well, cover the pan and cook for about 2 minutes until the greens are wilted. Remove from the heat and mix in the tahini sauce, sprinkle with 2 tablespoons toasted sesame seeds and serve.

Tahini

Tomatoes and whipped tahini

500g good ripe tomatoes, at
    room temperature
2 tablespoons red wine vinegar
150g tahini
2 cloves of garlic, peeled
2 teaspoons Dijon mustard
a bunch of flat-leaf parsley (30g),
    leaves picked
¼ red onion, peeled and finely
    diced
3 tablespoons olive oil
2 tablespoons small capers
    (or larger ones, chopped)

This came from a craving for Ed Smith's tomato tonnato, a riff on vitello tonnato. Both are distinctly un-vegetarian but I wanted the acid-spiked creamy sauce against a salted and vinegared summer tomato. Here the creaminess comes from tahini, which partners so well with tomato. It's important that your tomatoes are at room temperature, to make the most of their flavour.

I use brined capers here, but if you are using salted capers soak them in lots of cold water for 1 hour before using.

SERVES 4

Chop and season the tomatoes
Cut 500g ripe tomatoes into slices and chunks which look good and are bite-sized. Put them in a colander over a bowl and season with a teaspoon of salt (seems a lot but it's needed) and 1 tablespoon of red wine vinegar. Leave to sit.

Whip the tahini
Put 150g tahini, 2 peeled cloves of garlic, 1 tablespoon red wine vinegar, 2 teaspoons Dijon mustard and 100ml ice-cold water into a food processor and blitz for 4–6 minutes. It will seize and stiffen at first (don't worry) but then it will lighten in colour and turn fluffy and creamy. Taste and add salt and more vinegar and mustard, if needed.

Make the parsley salsa
Meanwhile, make the salsa. Finely chop the leaves from a bunch of fresh flat-leaf parsley, then finely dice ¼ of a peeled red onion and mix with 2 tablespoons of olive oil. Season with a tablespoon or two of the reserved tomato juices (these should be salty and acidic, so add as much or as little as you like).

Put everything together
Spoon the whipped tahini on to a plate and use the back of a spoon to spread it into peaks and dips. Any leftover whipped tahini can be kept in a jar in the fridge for 3–4 days. Taste the tomatoes, adding more salt if you think it's needed. Dress them with a tablespoon of olive oil, then spoon the tomatoes over the tahini and top with 2 table-spoons small capers (or larger ones, chopped). Spoon the salsa over the tomatoes to finish.

Tahini

Butter bean, tomato and tahini cassoulet

450g ripe cherry tomatoes
1 bulb of fennel, trimmed and
    cut into thin wedges
4 cloves of garlic, peeled
olive oil
1 × 700g jar cooked butter beans
    or 2 × 400g tins
juice of ½ an unwaxed lemon
4 tablespoons tahini
3 tablespoons white sesame
    seeds
2 slices sourdough bread (150g)
a bunch of basil (30g)

This is a riff on the cassoulet recipe from my first book *A Modern Way to Eat*. It's one of the most-cooked recipes from that book, and I think it's so loved thanks to the fact it's super-easy to make but also because of its velvety butteriness. I am working with the same theme here; the tahini adds an instant richness which sits up against the tomatoes, fennel and butter beans. You will need an ovenproof pan – mine is a cast-iron one that's 30cm across.

SERVES 4

Cook the tomatoes
Preheat the oven to 240°C/220°C fan. Put 450g ripe cherry tomatoes and 1 trimmed bulb of fennel, cut into thin wedges, into an ovenproof pan. Flatten 2 peeled cloves of garlic with the blade of a knife, add those to the pan with 2 tablespoons olive oil and a good amount of salt and pepper, then stir to mix. Roast for 20 minutes, until the vegetables are soft and charred.

Mix the butter beans
Tip 1 × 700g jar or 2 × 400g tins of butter beans and their liquid into a bowl along with ½ a jar or 1 tin of water, grate in 2 cloves of garlic, then add 4 tablespoons olive oil, the juice of ½ an unwaxed lemon, 4 tablespoons tahini and 3 table-spoons white sesame seeds.

Add the butter beans and bread
When the vegetables have had their time, scoop them out of the pan, then tip the garlicky butter beans into the ovenproof pan. Tear over 2 slices of sourdough bread (150g), return the veg to the pan on top of the beans and bread, and put back in the oven and bake for another 30 minutes.

Finish
Once the butter beans look crisp and the bread golden, take them out of the oven and tear over a 30g bunch of basil. Serve with a lemon-dressed green salad or some greens.

Börek with dark molasses tahini

500g spinach, chard, spring
  greens, cavolo nero or kale
200g feta or manouri, or vegan
  feta-style cheese, crumbled
3 tablespoons toasted white
  sesame seeds, plus extra for
  sprinkling
2 sprigs of thyme, leaves picked
1 large handful of Greek (or
  regular) basil, torn
50ml olive oil (or melted butter),
  plus an extra drizzle of oil
  for the greens
250g pack fresh filo pastry
  (about 6–9 sheets,
  30cm × 40cm)
4 tablespoons tahini
1 tablespoon runny honey or
  maple syrup
1 teaspoon carob molasses
  (optional)

I spent a week a while back in Turkey in the pine forests above Göcek with my friend Nadia. We ate like queens: breakfasts of fresh cheese, scarlet tomatoes, bitter greens and dark tahini. There were little börek pastries, sweet olive oil-kissed tomatoey green beans, and courgette and cauliflower fritters, all served close enough to the Greek basil growing in the garden that you could reach out and tear it from your seat.

This börek is my attempt to make the one that Sevgi, the cook, and the all-women kitchen crew served. They served it with some molasses tahini, the discovery of my trip.

MAKES ONE BÖREK TO SERVE 6–8

Blanch the greens
Put 500g greens in a colander and pour just-boiled water over them, so that they wilt a little. (For hardier greens, like cavolo nero or kale, remove the stems, cut, put them in a lidded pan on a high heat and steam, covered, for 2 minutes, then drain.) Once cool, squeeze out as much liquid as possible, then roughly chop.

Make the filling
Transfer the chopped greens to a large bowl. Add 200g crumbled feta, 3 tablespoons toasted sesame seeds, the picked leaves from 2 sprigs of thyme, a large handful of torn basil and a drizzle of olive oil, then mix. Season well and set aside.

To make the swirled large börek
Preheat the oven to 200°C/180°C fan and heat a baking sheet lined with baking paper. Lay 3 sheets of filo on a work surface, with the longest side facing towards you, and the shorter side in front of you, as if you were reading a letter. Keep the remaining sheets covered with a damp tea towel.

Working one sheet at a time, overlap the 3 sheets, moving from left to right, by around 2–3cm, brushing oil between each layer so it seals. You should end up with a large sheet about 65cm × 45cm. Fold the sheet in half horizontally so you end up with a sheet about 22cm wide.

Lay half the greens and feta filling 2cm up from the longest edge and brush the pastry around it with oil or melted butter. Roll it up gently but tightly to create a long sausage shape, then curl it around anticlockwise from right to left, to create the start of the swirl, and place in the centre of a large baking sheet. Repeat this method twice more with the other 6 sheets, using up the remaining filling mix. Then wrap the second two shapes around the first in a circle.

Cook the börek
Brush generously with oil or melted butter and sprinkle with sesame seeds, then bake for 30–35 minutes or until golden.

Make the molasses tahini
Meanwhile, mix 4 tablespoons tahini, 1 tablespoon honey or maple syrup and 1 teaspoon carob molasses (if using), then whisk with 40ml water to loosen. Let the börek cool slightly, then drizzle with the tahini and sprinkle with more sesame seeds. Serve warm or at room temperature.

Sesame and chilli oil noodles

150g medium dried egg noodles
1 tablespoon peanut butter
2 tablespoons tahini
1 tablespoon soy sauce or tamari
1 clove of garlic, peeled and
    finely chopped
2 teaspoons toasted sesame oil
2–3 tablespoons chilli oil or
    chilli crisp
a bunch of spring onions (about 6),
    trimmed and finely sliced
4 tablespoons toasted sesame
    seeds (white, black or both)

Lucky and Joy is a Chinese-influenced restaurant local to me with brightly painted walls and food that slaps you in the face with flavour. For the last year or so I've been eating their sesame noodles most weeks. This is a quick version of cold sesame noodles I made when I was craving them but they were shut for a holiday. It uses tahini as opposed to Chinese sesame, which is not traditional in any way, but it is what I always have at home so...

SERVES 2 AS A MAIN, 4 AS A SIDE

Cook the noodles
Cook 150g medium dried egg noodles in boiling salted water for a minute less than the packet instructions, until al dente. Drain and rinse under cold water.

Make the tahini sauce
Whisk together 1 tablespoon peanut butter, 2 tablespoons tahini, 1 table-spoon soy sauce and 1 finely chopped clove of garlic. Add 2 teaspoons toasted sesame oil and between 75ml and 125ml room-temperature water (depending on the thickness of the tahini) and whisk until you have a smooth, pourable sauce about the thickness of double cream.

Toss together and serve
Toss the cold noodles in the tahini sauce and scoop into bowls, then top each with 1–2 tablespoons of chilli crisp, adding a little at a time until it's the right kind of heat for you (you can always serve extra on the table). Scatter over a trimmed and finely sliced bunch of spring onions and finish each bowl with a tablespoon of toasted sesame seeds.

Tahini

Wedge salad with tahini ranch dressing

2 cloves of garlic, peeled
2 tablespoons olive oil
100g fresh breadcrumbs
50g pitted green olives, roughly
    chopped
2 unwaxed lemons
250g Greek yoghurt or oat
    Greek yoghurt
120g tahini
1 bunch of chives (20g), chopped
1 bunch of dill (20g), chopped
2 iceberg lettuces or 8 Little Gems

This is what I want to eat all summer. The lettuce is seasoned with salt and pepper and lemon (always season your lettuce), then covered, and I mean covered, in the yoghurt tahini ranch. As with any dressing you want it to be a little too much when tasted on its own, as the crispy iceberg will water it down – tasting the dressing on a bit of lettuce will help you check if it's right.

SERVES 4

Make the breadcrumbs
First make the breadcrumbs. Smash 1 peeled clove of garlic and put it in a frying pan with 2 tablespoons olive oil. Place on a medium-low heat and allow to sizzle for 3–4 minutes until the garlic is golden brown and smells great. Add 100g breadcrumbs and cook for 3 minutes, moving them all the time, then add 50g roughly chopped pitted green olives and continue cooking for a couple of minutes until the breadcrumbs are toasted. Season with ½ teaspoon of sea salt, tip into a shallow bowl to cool and grate in the zest of 1 unwaxed lemon.

Make the tahini ranch
Put 250g Greek yoghurt or oat Greek yoghurt into a bowl with 120g tahini, grate in 1 peeled clove of garlic, add the juice of 1 unwaxed lemon and season with salt and pepper. Add ½ a bunch of chopped chives and ½ a bunch of chopped dill and stir in. Add a little cold water to thin it to a drizzleable dressing with the consistency of double cream. Taste and adjust, adding more salt and lemon juice as needed.

Make the salad
Trim any rogue leaves from the outside of 2 iceberg lettuces or

8 Little Gems, then leaving the root on, cut each iceberg or Little Gem into 4 wedges through the core. Break the wedges up into smaller chunks with your hands so you still have a few layers of lettuce but the dressing can get to them more easily. Spread a third of the dressing evenly over a serving platter, then put the wedges on top and season with salt and pepper, taking care to get in between the layers of lettuce leaves, then squeeze over an unwaxed lemon in the same way.

Put everything together
Spoon the rest of the tahini ranch very generously over the top of the lettuce leaves, then top with the breadcrumbs and remaining ½ a bunch each of chopped chives and dill. Serve immediately. You want this to be cold and refreshing.

Sesame ramen noodles

300g dried ramen noodles
    (I like Clearspring) or 800g
    fresh ramen noodles
250g spring or Asian greens or
    other green veg
150g tahini
1 tablespoon rice wine vinegar
1 tablespoon soy sauce
1 tablespoon chilli oil, plus
    extra to serve
1.5 litres good vegetable stock
4 spring onions, trimmed and
    finely sliced
2 tablespoons toasted white
    sesame seeds

Tantanmen is a Japanese noodle soup which uses Japanese sesame paste, coating the noodles in the savoury creamy broth it makes. If you can get or have Japanese sesame paste, then use that, but I have found tahini, which I always have in the cupboard, works well. I have deliberately left the recipe simple here, with just some greens, and given you a few seasonal ideas for what veg to add so you can cook this all year. A jammy egg, cooked in boiling water for 6 minutes, is a good addition too.

SERVES 4

Cook the noodles and veg
Bring a large pan of salted water to the boil, add 300g dried ramen noodles or 800g fresh and cook just less than the packet instructions – you want them to be al dente. About 30 seconds before they are ready, add 250g spring or Asian greens to the same pan, then drain the lot and rinse under cold running water to cool.

Make the broth
Whisk together 150g tahini, 1 tablespoon rice wine vinegar, 1 tablespoon soy sauce and 1 tablespoon chilli oil until you have a thick paste. Heat 1.5 litres good vegetable stock in a large pan over a medium heat until hot but not boiling. Turn off the heat and whisk in the tahini paste. Add more soy or salt if needed.

Prepare the toppings
Choose your toppings from the suggestions that follow this recipe and get them ready to go.

Finish the ramen
Divide the noodles and greens between 4 bowls, pour over the tahini broth, then top with 4 trimmed and finely sliced spring

onions, 2 tablespoons toasted white sesame seeds, some chilli oil and one of the seasonal vegetables below.

Spring
pan-fried asparagus/thinly sliced radishes/chopped spring onions

Summer
pan-charred sweetcorn/pan-roasted cherry tomatoes/chopped spring onions

Autumn
pan-crisped mushrooms/cavolo nero/crispy onions

Winter
thinly sliced sweet potato cooked with the noodles/pan-crisped tofu/chopped toasted nuts

Tahini

Smoky aubergines with tahini and spiced tomatoes

4 medium aubergines
100g tahini
1 clove of garlic, peeled
30g white sesame seeds
½ teaspoon chipotle flakes or
    chilli flakes
½ teaspoon sweet smoked
    paprika
¼ teaspoon ground cinnamon
1 jalapeño chilli, finely chopped
    (deseeded if you like)
2 large ripe tomatoes, roughly
    chopped
1 teaspoon maple syrup
½ a bunch of parsley (15g),
    chopped
½ a bunch of coriander (15g),
    chopped
juice of 1 unwaxed lime

Tahini and aubergines. They work. Here the aubergines are grilled until they almost collapse and become buttery, soft and everything an aubergine should be. Once they are peeled they are pale and sit on top of the punchy sauce that makes them sing. Richness comes from tahini over the top. Do not skip over this recipe; it's a favourite.

SERVES 4

Cook the aubergines
This can be done on a barbecue, griddle pan or in the oven (preheated to 200°C/180°C fan). Prick 4 medium aubergines 10 times with the tip of a knife to stop them exploding. To barbecue or griddle, heat your barbecue or griddle to super-hot, then add the aubergines and cook, turning every few minutes, until the skin is charred and the flesh is so soft it feels as if it might collapse. If you are using the oven, place the aubergines on a baking tray and cook for 30–40 minutes, turning halfway, until soft and collapsing.

Make the whipped tahini
Mix 100g tahini with 50–100ml ice-cold water in a bowl until you have a thick whipped-cream consistency. Grate in a peeled clove of garlic.

Toast the seeds and spices
Toast 30g white sesame seeds in a hot pan, or in the oven if you are using it, stirring them every few minutes until they are evenly golden. Stir in ½ teaspoon chipotle flakes or chilli flakes, ½ teaspoon sweet smoked paprika and ½ teaspoon ground cinnamon for the last 30 seconds.

Make the spiced tomatoes
Finely chop 1 jalapeño chilli (removing the seeds if you like) and put into a bowl. Roughly chop 2 large ripe tomatoes and add these to the jalapeño with the spiced sesame seeds, 1 teaspoon maple syrup, ½ a bunch of chopped parsley and the same of chopped coriander and the juice of 1 unwaxed lime. Taste and add salt and more syrup to balance out any flavours which feel too dominant.

Peel the aubergines
Once the aubergines are cooked, leave them to cool. Once they are cool enough to handle, hold them by the stem and peel the skin off.

Put it together
Take a platter or 4 plates, spoon the tahini on top, then use the back of a spoon to spread it around the platter or plates. Place the aubergines on top then pile on the spiced sesame tomatoes.

Tomato, peach and tahini sandwich

1 ripe peach
1 tablespoon apple cider vinegar
1 green chilli, sliced
1 teaspoon runny honey
2 ripe summer tomatoes,
    thickly sliced
zest of 1 unwaxed lemon
2 pieces of fresh bouncy
    focaccia (see page 156 for
    a recipe)
2 tablespoons tahini
1 bunch of wild rocket
extra virgin olive oil
½ a bunch of basil (15g), leaves
    picked

This was inspired by a recipe that landed in my inbox one summer morning. It was from the Natoora newsletter, by a chef called Daisy Bennett. I jumped up and made a simpler version of it almost immediately, and it became a summer staple. Putting peach in a sandwich might seem like a strange thing to do, but remember tomato is also a fruit. The tahini tempers the sweetness here. Please note that your sandwich will only be as good as your peaches and tomatoes.

SERVES 2

Dress the peach
Cut 1 ripe peach into 8 slices and put into a bowl with 1 tablespoon cider vinegar, 1 sliced green chilli and 1 teaspoon runny honey.

Season the tomatoes
Cut 2 ripe summer tomatoes into thick slices and put into a colander over a bowl with a good scattering of sea salt and a teaspoon of the liquid from the peach. Stir in the zest of 1 unwaxed lemon.

Make the sandwich
If your bread is not super fresh, warm it in the oven or toaster or in a hot, dry pan. Cut 2 pieces of fresh bouncy focaccia in half horizontally to form two 'sandwiches'. Spread one side of each focaccia sandwich with 1 tablespoon tahini and lay on half a bunch of wild rocket. Use a spoon to drizzle the other side with the juice from the tomato bowl, then some olive oil. Top the rocket with the peach, tomatoes and the leaves from half a bunch of basil and sandwich together. Eat with a napkin.

Add ons:
Mozzarella, burrata or feta would all work well as additions.

Tahini

Tahini, pear and honey flapjacks

100g white sesame seeds
100g sunflower seeds
350g jumbo porridge oats
100g dried fruit (I use a mixture
of golden raisins and dried
pears), roughly chopped
50g crystallised ginger, finely
chopped
250g unsalted butter, vegan
butter or flavourless coconut
oil, plus extra for greasing
200g soft light brown sugar
100g tahini
4 tablespoons runny honey or
maple syrup
zest of 1 unwaxed lemon

These flapjacks are a line-up of lots of my favourite things – tahini, toasted sesame, dried pears, crystallised ginger and brown sugar. Punch from the ginger (which I love so much I could write a book about it), chew from dried pears and raisins, sweetness from honey or maple, then the tahini rounds it all off with its buttery depth, just the right side of bitter, and stops it feeling too sweet.

If using coconut oil here, I would recommend using the one for cooking often marked 'odourless' or 'cuisine', as it doesn't have a strong coconut flavour.

MAKES 16

Preheat the oven and line your tin
Preheat the oven to 180°C/160°C fan. Grease a 20cm square tin with butter or oil, then line with baking paper.

Toast the seeds
Toast 100g white sesame seeds and 100g sunflower seeds until golden brown in the oven as it is preheating. Give them a stir every few minutes, keeping a close eye on them so they don't burn. They should take about 10–12 minutes in total.

Pulse the oats
Pulse 350g jumbo porridge oats in a food processor until broken down a little. Add 100g roughly chopped dried fruit and 50g finely chopped crystallised ginger and pulse until incorporated.

Melt the butter and sugar
Melt 250g butter, dairy-free butter or coconut oil, 200g soft light brown sugar, and 100g tahini in a large pan on a low heat. Once it's melted take it off the heat and stir in 4 tablespoons runny honey or maple syrup.

Mix the oats and butter
Mix the oats with the toasted seeds and the zest of 1 unwaxed lemon. Add a good pinch of flaky sea salt, pour in the butter and sugar mixture and stir again, until you have a sandy oaty mixture. Make sure all the oats are evenly coated.

Bake
Spoon the oat mixture into the lined tin. Use the back of a spoon to press down a little and level it out but don't pack it down too much. Bake in the preheated oven for 40–45 minutes or until golden brown (it will be slightly darker at the edges).

Cool and cut
Leave in the tin until cooled completely then cut into 16 squares. Will keep in a sealed container for up to a week.

Tahini

Apple galette with tahini frangipane

150g cold unsalted butter or non-dairy butter (I use Violife Vioblock), cut into small cubes
200g tahini
75g light soft brown sugar
1 large free-range egg, beaten, or 60ml sparkling water
1 tablespoon plain flour
500g sweet shortcrust pastry (vegan if needed)
6 medium firm, sweet apples (I like Red Delicious, Braeburn or Jonagold)
100g golden caster sugar
2 tablespoons Demerara sugar
crème fraîche, cream or ice cream to serve

I have made a lot of frangipane tarts. Their chewy, crisp bite is a perfect texture. As a young kid, I was unnaturally obsessed with cooking and made kirsch-soaked cherry frangipane tarts that my dad loved. In kitchens I made them stuffed with figs and peaches. This is a riff on the classic almond frangipane and instead uses tahini. It's all the better for it; the tahini offsets the sweetness of the pastry. This recipe works best with a homemade or thicker, more rustic tahini. If you struggle to get your tahini to whip, add another tablespoon of flour to the mix.

SERVES 8–10

Brown the butter (optional)
Add 150g cold cubed butter to a small pan and cook over a medium heat, stirring regularly, until the butter browns and smells nutty. Pour into a heatproof bowl and put into the fridge to chill for around 1 hour, or until the consistency of soft butter.

Make the tahini frangipane
In a stand mixer or with a hand-held electric whisk, whip 200g tahini on the highest setting for 4–5 minutes until it thickens. Then add 75g light soft brown sugar and whisk again, scraping down the sides of the bowl as you go, until you have a thick mixture and none of the sugar is visible. Add 4 tablespoons (60g) of the chilled butter bit by bit with the mixer running on medium speed.

Add 1 large egg, beaten, and a good pinch of sea salt, followed by 1 tablespoon plain flour and mix to combine.

Roll out the pastry
Roll out 500g sweet shortcrust pastry to about 35cm × 35cm, then transfer to a large baking-paper-lined square baking tray. Use a spoon or spatula to spread the tahini frangipane over the pastry, leaving a 3cm border around the edge, and put it into the fridge to chill.

Cut the apples
Top and tail 6 medium firm, sweet apples, reserving the trimmings, and cut the apples into rounds across the middle so you get thin circles with little star shapes. Stack them on top of each other in their apple shape – this will make it easier to lay your slices out on your tart. Add the apple tops and bottoms to a small saucepan with 100g golden caster sugar and 100ml water. Bring to the boil, turn down to a simmer and cook for 8–10 minutes, or until slightly thickened and glossy.

Make the tart
Take the rolled-out pastry out of the fridge and lay the apples on top, I like to lay them overlapping each other but any way you like will work. Fold the edges of the pastry back over the edge of the apples to create a roughly rectangular galette. Put it back into the fridge while you heat the oven.

Bake the tart
Preheat the oven to 220°C/200°C fan. Use the remaining butter to brush the pastry edge and sprinkle with 2 tablespoons Demerara sugar. Bake for 35–45 minutes in the middle of the oven, turning halfway, until golden brown and bubbling at the edges. Remove from the oven, brush all over with the apple glaze and serve with crème fraîche, cream or ice cream.

Georgie's tahinopita

1 × 7g sachet of active dried
    yeast
130g soft light brown sugar
1½ teaspoons Maldon sea salt
    (or other flaky sea salt – if
    using regular fine sea salt,
    use less)
600g strong white bread flour,
    plus extra for dusting
olive oil
100g tahini
6 tablespoons runny honey (or
    maple syrup if vegan)
1 tablespoon ground cinnamon
½ teaspoon sesame seeds

This bread is a recipe from my friend Georgina Hayden. We cooked, tested recipes and hung out together for years, and I was always in awe of Georgie's breads and baking. Tahinopita are the stars of the bakeries Georgie visits when she's back in Cyprus. The soft, fluffy, doughy-in-a-good-way bread twisted with a tahini, sugar and cinnamon mixture which catches and caramelises in some places where it gets hit by the heat of the oven, and in other places where it's hidden between the folds of the dough, gives it a frangipane crossed with cinnamon bun feeling. Tahinopita shows off tahini at its best, deep and moreish with a grown-up sweetness.

SERVES 10–12

Make the dough
Measure 400ml warm water into a measuring jug and whisk in 7g active dried yeast and 30g soft light brown sugar. Leave to one side for 5 minutes. Stir 1¼ teaspoons sea salt into 600g strong white bread flour in a bowl, then make a well in the middle. Pour the yeast mixture into the well, along with 2 tablespoons olive oil, and stir the flour into the liquid with a fork until all mixed together – you're looking for a slightly damp dough. If it feels dry add a splash more water. Turn the dough out on to a lightly floured surface and knead for 5–8 minutes until smooth and elastic.

Grease a mixing bowl with a drizzle of olive oil and pop in the dough, turning it over in the oil so it gets lightly coated all over. Cover with a clean tea towel and leave in a warm spot for around an hour to an hour and a half, or until doubled in size.

Make the tahini filling
When the dough is ready, make the filling by mixing together 100g tahini, 100g soft light brown sugar, 4 tablespoons honey (or maple syrup), 1 tablespoon ground cinnamon and ¼ teaspoon sea salt.

Shape the dough
Turn the dough out on to a lightly floured surface, knead it for a couple of minutes, then gently roll it out into a large rectangle, around 55cm × 30cm. Evenly dot and spread the tahini mixture all over the dough (it will be too thick to spread, so you'll need to use your hands for this bit – poking it and prodding it into place), and don't worry if it isn't completely covered; it'll spread as it bakes. Roll the dough into a large Swiss roll, starting with one of the long edges, as tightly as you can, then slice the whole thing in half lengthways. Press together two of the ends and then plait the two pieces so that the cut side is always facing up. Once you've finished plaiting the dough, join the two ends together to form a ring and place it on a lightly oiled baking sheet. Leave it to one side for 30 minutes to prove again. Meanwhile, preheat the oven to 180°C/160°C fan.

Bake the tahinopita
When the dough has finished its second prove, drizzle the dough with 1 tablespoon honey or maple syrup, and sprinkle with ½ teaspoon sesame seeds. Pop the tray in the middle of the oven and bake for 35–40 minutes, until golden all over and cooked through. When it is ready, remove from the oven and leave to cool for 10 minutes on the tray before transferring to a wire rack and drizzling with another tablespoon of honey or maple syrup.

Perfect any time of the day, with a small cup of strong Greek coffee or a mug of tea.

All about flavour

Flavour is just the vanilla in your ice cream or the turmeric in your dal. Flavour is both what we literally taste – the sweet, salty, sour, bitter and umami – and what we feel, see and remember when we eat. A bite of a ripe run-down-your-chin peach will be about its taste and sweetness but also about how we perceive a peach: where we are eating it, our memories of perfect holiday peaches and even how peaches play into our lives, families, childhoods and celebrations. Even the temperature or ripeness of the peach might trigger a specific memory, and all these things form part of the flavour of that peach.

Flavour goes deeper and it means different things to different people. It might jog a memory and transport us back to our homeland. It's about connection. It's about food shared. It's about being human. Flavour symbolises different things to different people. The same dish eaten by one person might remind them of how their mother cooked it, while for another it might remind them of a time when that food was a comfort. This all plays into how we perceive the flavour of food.

Packet ramen noodles make me think of late-home-from-school childhood dinners. Greengages remind me of the sun on my skin and browsing markets in the south of France. Cheese soufflés and puffy omelettes make me think fondly of my mum; banana sandwiches my dad. There is so much in each of these memories.

Nik Sharma in his excellent book *The Flavor Equation* makes sense of this bundle of tastes, senses and feelings.

Emotion + Sight + Sound + Texture + Aroma + Taste = Flavour

Nik spells out that what we deem delicious is actually a combination of all of these things coming together into one holistic experience.

Emotion

Your emotional state when you try a dish affects how you perceive the flavour. It has been shown that flavour can affect our emotions too: Nik Sharma says that the same news told to someone drinking a sweet drink and others drinking a bitter drink in a study evoked different reactions. For instance, I'll always remember the paella (or a version of it) on page 182 as the first dish my son taught me how to cook after making it at school.

Sight

We eat with our eyes: the colours and shapes and look of food are crucial in building our appetites and our perception of what we eat. We have learned to associate certain colours with certain flavours. Years of writing about and styling food has made me realise how much we rely on a photo to know what we are cooking. If food looks appetising, it begins to sate us even before we take a bite.

Sound

Sound is a forgotten element when it comes to both cooking and eating. A sound can be a marker that food is cooked: the crackle of a loaf of bread which tells you it is cooked, or the hollow tap on its bottom. But sound is more than a marker. It is an amplifying sensation that brings on appetite and tells us when something is going to be good: think of the snap of a chocolate bar or a biscuit.

Texture and temperature

From crunchy to soft and yielding, cool to hot, the delicate sensors in our mouth allow us to feel our food. An ice-cold slice of watermelon on a hot day will taste and feel wholly different to a warm one. It will feel crunchier, juicer and more delicious all round.

Aroma/smell

A huge part of how we taste food is actually how we smell it. Often, we refer to someone losing their taste, but almost always it's actually their ability to smell food which is affected.

Taste

Taste is an instinct. On a basic level, it guides us to foods that are safe and to reject those that aren't. It is connected to memory, and as we eat over time, memories build up that become part of how we taste. It's this that I am going to focus on.

The taste and flavour map on page 230–231 shows the commonly accepted matrix of flavours. I like to think of this as an interdependent system. Like a solar system where the main tastes are the planets that depend on each other to stay in balance, everything is dependent on the others to shine. On top of this, there is an added layer of senses and emotions, which I see as the sun, giving them life.

Sweet, salty, sour, bitter and umami are the commonly accepted tastes, the planets, but I have added a few outliers which I find useful to consider when I am thinking about flavour.

Greenness
herbs, greens, grassy, verdant flavours. Even grassy olive oil.

Heat and spice
warmth that comes from chilli, cinnamon, cumin and the endless list of spices.

Creamy richness
which comes from fat, oil or dairy, or plant-based yoghurt, cream or milk.

I can't put my recipes together without these elements, so I consider them the stars to the planets in my flavour solar system.

The flavours in this book

	Sweet	Salty	Sour	Umami	Bitter	Hot	Verdant	Creamy
Lemon	●		●		●			
Olive oil							●	●
Vinegar			●					
Mustard				●				
Tomato	●							
Capers		●	●					
Chilli						●		
Tahini					●			●
Garlic				●				
Onion	●							
Miso		●		●				
Peanut	●	●						●

All about flavour

How flavour works

Sight   Sweet

Sound   Sour

Smells   Salty

Feeling   Bitter

Memory   Umami

Culture   (Five tastes)

↓

Flavour

How taste works

Sweet

Verdant   Salty

Taste

Hot   Sour

Bitter   Umami

Layering flavour

What we define as a delicious flavour is a combination of lots of elements coming together. Knowing how and why our ingredients work together will make you a better cook. This book pulls out twelve ingredients which all sit within one of these flavour profiles. Cooking through each chapter and seeing how that ingredient can be used in different ways is a great way to build on your understanding of taste and how different ingredients are balanced.

Sour/acidity

Sourness or acidity is, to me, one of the most important parts of cooking, and it's often a key element to add or balance to make food taste good.

The acid in a food will affect how it cooks, not just how it tastes. An example is cooking red onions. If you add lemon or vinegar to onions, they change colour from deep purple to bright pink, and they cook more quickly.

Acid can

- Temper sweetness and saltiness: if a dish feels too sweet, acid will help. The same if a dish is too salty.

- Help counter bitterness: think of a chicory salad with a punchy dressing.

- Cut through fat: think gherkins in a burger or vinegar on chips.

Bright/acidic foods

Most foods have some level of acidity. Lemons and rhubarb are obviously acidic, but yoghurt, milk, honey and coffee are less obvious acidic foods. Here are a few I use most in my kitchen.

Citrus
In particular, lemons and limes. Limes are more acidic, with a stronger bright sourness than lemons, and lemons are sweeter. The juice and zest bring different types of acidity: the juice is sharp and fresh, and the zest is bright and sherbety, thanks to the oils in the skin. See page 16 for more.

Vinegar
Vinegar is a cheap and always available source of acidity. Its flavour and acidity can vary greatly. See page 78 for more on vinegar.

Tomatoes

Tomatoes have lots of citric acid, but they sweeten as they ripen. If you want to add tomato flavour but also some acidity, the best tomato will be tomato purée or tinned toms. See page 124 for more on tomatoes.

Yoghurt, kefir and buttermilk

Their sourness comes from the fermentation of bacteria in milk or non-dairy milk. They add a freshness and creaminess as well as acidity.

Tamarind

Comes from the tangy pulp inside tamarind pods. I use it most often in a glossy brown paste from a jar, which brings a more subtle sweet/sour acidity with caramelly notes. It's at home in curries and stews, and dressings for bright, crunchy salads.

How to use acid

- Add yoghurt to your food: yoghurt on the side of a curry, or to top a soup or on a flatbread.

- Add fruit to a salad: apples, apricots or sour cherries for a pop of acidity.

- Add citrus juice or vinegar at the very end of cooking for an acidic kick. A good way to balance a dish.

- Add citrus or vinegar to root vegetables as they roast for a mellow acidic note that sweetens as it cooks.

- Acid can be used to preserve: pickles and the natural acid foods create as they ferment naturally in foods like sauerkraut or kimchi.

- Dry ingredients like sumac, amchur (dried mango), dried lime and citrus zest all add sourness without liquid.

Salty

In this book, two chapters focus on capers and miso, but in my kitchen there are always cornichons, olives, stock and soy. These all have a natural saltiness to them, so if you're cooking with one of those ingredients it's important to remember that some salt is going to come from that, and you will need to adjust the seasoning accordingly. For more on salt, see page 10.

Salt can

- Reduce the intensity of bitterness: salting aubergines is an example of this.

- Acidity can enhance the perception of salt in food, so adding lemon juice or vinegar to your cooking means you might need to add less salt. For anyone who is trying to reduce salt, this is a really good technique.

- Umami-rich foods like soy or miso boost the perception of saltiness as well.

- Salt and sweet: I add a little bit of salt to things like my morning porridge but also to anything I bake with chocolate. It's just a small amount; you don't want a strong salty flavour, but you do want to have that sort of enhancement that salt brings.

How to use salt

- Seasoning
One thing I can't stress enough about salt and seasoning is to taste your food as you cook. It is the key difference as far as I've seen between professional cooks and home cooks. Chefs taste every part of the food throughout the cooking process. This will give you an idea of how the flavours are developing, how each individual element is tasting, and how they might come together. So if one element of your meal is tasting a bit salty, you can step in and make sure that you don't over-salt other elements of the meal, and, hopefully, it will balance out.

'Knowing how and why our ingredients work together will make you a better cook.'

- Texture
Salt can add texture if you're using a flaky salt – sprinkle it on top of a salad or even on the top of a chocolate tart or brownie to add crunch and texture as well as saltiness.

- Speed of cooking
Adding salt to a pot of boiling water not only seasons the vegetables as they're cooking but it also allows them to cook quicker. The loss of nutrients is also significantly reduced when vegetables are cooked in salty water rather than in just plain water.

Sweet

The natural sugars in foods are responsible for their sweet taste. Vegetables naturally have their own inherent sweetness and natural sugars. Think about a sweet potato or squash, for instance. So when it comes to sweetness in savoury cooking, you might add sweetness to a salad dressing that tastes a little bitter to bring balance. Or add sour cream to level out a very sweet roasted sweet potato.

Sweetness can

- Reduce the intensity of hot chilli heat – think super-hot Thai chillies with palm sugar (and lime).

- Sweetness can make acids less powerful – think lemonade: the sweeter it is, the less lemony it tastes.

- Temperature affects sweetness – the warmer something is, the sweeter it will taste. When making ice cream or anything served very cold, you may need to increase the sweetness of the room-temperature custard for it to taste as sweet when it's cold.

- Sugar can mask bitterness – think about stirring some sugar into a cup of coffee. It also helps with the bitterness of cabbage or bitter leaves.

- Sugar can enhance all flavours. I use it sparingly and always add it bit by bit, but it's a good balancing element to turn to if there is something missing in your food.

Sweet foods

Onions
Onions cooked slowly to bring out their natural sugars bring sweetness and depth. Raw onions have a hint of sweetness but also acidity. More on onions on page 264.

Lemons
Lemons have lots of natural sugar that sits against their acidity. When cooked, their sugar intensifies and their acidity mellows.

Maple
I use maple to sweeten savoury food, dressings, tofu, dipping sauces and sometimes add a splash to a soup or stew that needs balancing. I find maple (a liquid sweetener) much more versatile than sugar.

Honey
Honey brings a brighter, fresher sweetness with more nuance, and I use honey a lot in my cooking. Just a drop will often join up the dots and round out the flavour.

Sugar
The most obvious type of sweetness is sugar. My favourite is muscovado sugar, which has a deep, dark, almost black treacle caramel consistency.

Fruit
Adds freshness and sweetness and can be a good way to add sweetness subtly.

Sweet vegetables
From sweetcorn to sweet potato and squash. It's worth considering the sweetness of these vegetables as you cook.

'Bitterness splits opinion more than any other taste.'

Layering flavour

Bitterness

Bitterness splits opinion more than any other taste. As humans, we are very sensitive to bitter tastes at extremely low levels. Almost every culture in the world cooks with bitter foods, from tahini to bitter greens and radicchio. Our natural response is to steer clear of bitter foods to protect us from harm or damage. Our brains are hardwired to see foods that taste bitter as unpleasant, so we avoid them.

Bitter can
Salt, acid or sweetness will mellow bitter flavours, so if you're still getting used to bitterness in your food using one or more of them might be a good idea.

Bitter foods

Citrus fruit
Some fruit, like grapefruit, has more bitterness than other citrus fruits. Most of the bitterness comes from the white part under the skin, so when you zest a lemon or lime be careful to only use the brightly coloured top layer, unless you want to add bitterness.

Tahini
Tahini has a mildly bitter taste which is a great first introduction to bitter. It's also rich and rounded as well as slightly sweet, which balances the gentle bitterness.

Alcohol
Beer is bitter thanks to the hops it's made from and the fermentation process. Wine, especially red, can also be bitter.

Coffee
Coffee is a classic bitter taste. It is great in cooking: I add it to chillies, and it also enhances chocolate-flavoured desserts, brownies and cakes.

Cocoa and cacao
If you've ever eaten a raw cocoa bean, you will know how much natural bitterness is in cocoa or cacao. Cocoa has a bitter and acidic taste, but the addition of sugar and milk helps mask the bitterness. It can also be used in stews and chillies, echoing Mexican and ancient Incan and Mayan cooking.

Bitter lettuces
I love using bitter lettuces. For me, they have to be coated with a dressing that has some sweetness to offset the bitterness. These bitter leaves can actually help our digestive process, so they're a great thing to have on the side of a meal as well as being something interesting and delicious to eat.

Umami/Savouriness

Savouriness or umami, to use the Japanese word, is a recently discovered dimension of flavour. This is a newly recognised taste but is really nothing new. Think grating Parmesan over a plate of pasta or adding ginger, garlic and onions to soups, broths and curries.

A lot of umami flavours are created by ageing or fermentation, such as miso, soy sauce, mustard and kimchi. To me, umami is the hard-to-put-your-finger-on element that rounds off your dinner. Marmite on toast, gyozas dipped in a soy-heavy dipping sauce, the miso next to your plain rice.

Savoury/umami foods

Miso
A fermented soybean paste made using a koji, which is a bit like a miso sourdough starter. The type of miso you buy can be denoted by the colour, red or white, or the type of koji that is used, usually soy, barley or rice.

Mushrooms
Mushrooms are a great way of adding a savoury note. Dried mushrooms can be a particularly good umami hit, as their flavour is more concentrated than that of fresh mushrooms. Soak them in hot water

first to get maximum flavour and use the chopped, dried mushrooms and the water in your cooking.

Soy sauce/tamari
Soy is made by fermenting soybeans and salt and has a natural savouriness.

Parmesan cheese
True Parmesan is not vegetarian, so vegetarians should search out a vegetarian Parmesan that is made without using animal rennet. A deep umami flavour comes from the ageing process of the cheese.

Marmite
Marmite, or yeast extract, is a flavour that splits opinion. It's a great way of adding depth to vegetarian and vegan food. Marmite is a by-product of the beer brewing process, and Vegemite, which is similar (but not as good in my opinion), is a by-product of making brewers' yeast, so as well as eating something delicious you are using up something that would otherwise have been thrown away.

Seaweed
It was the study of seaweed by Japanese scientists that actually led to the discovery of this umami taste. There is a substance called glutamate which is found in seaweed and lots of other umami-rich foods. It varies depending on which seaweed you're talking about. I like using seaweed to flavour broths and stocks.

Fermented foods
These are a great way of adding umami – kimchi, sauerkraut and sambal will add flavour to soups and stews but also to dressings, sauces and sandwiches.

Heat/spice

Heat or spiciness isn't one of our five official tastes. It's the sensation of heat from eating something like chilli. What's actually happening when you bite a chilli, peppercorn or warming spice is that chemicals in the food attach to our sensory receptors, and those receptors get irritated and trick the brain into producing a sensation of heat or pain.

Foods with heat

Chillies
When we think about heat, we immediately think of chillies. The heat in a chilli is in the white pith or ribs which hold the seeds. To reduce the heat of a chilli, cut out this white rib and remove the seeds. There is more on chilli on page 174.

Pepper
There are lots of different types of pepper – from black peppercorns to long pepper and pink, white and green peppercorns. Black tend to be the spiciest. We can use black pepper to create heat in the same way as we might use chilli. Pink peppercorns are best used raw because heat destroys their spiciness. Green peppercorns are often sold pickled, and upgrade curries. Long pepper is a more fragrant pepper and comes in long, tiny pinecone shapes.

Ginger
Ginger is a favourite way to add heat both to savoury dishes and sweets and cakes – think gingerbread and ginger cake. I love cooking with stem ginger and its sugary syrup.

Horseradish and wasabi
These are two different plants, but I class the flavour as similar. They give a kind of different heat that goes straight into your nose, which some people love and others find overwhelming. Horseradish is particularly good with yoghurt and dairy in sandwiches. Wasabi I use with rice and noodles but also in dressings where I might use mustard.

Heat in the kitchen

- Peppercorns are great used in sweet cooking as well as savoury: grinding some pepper over a fruit salad will really enhance the flavour of the fruits.

- Raw onions and alliums like chives are also a great way of adding a slightly more subtle heat to anything you cook. I love adding them to rice and salads to give a subtle, gentle heat.

- Mustard powder and mustard seeds are another great way of adding a more subtle heat.

- The hotter the temperature of the food, generally the fierier the chillies or pepper are going to taste.

- Fried ginger
  A trick I learnt as a young chef was to fry very thin slices of ginger and scatter them over a dish, which gives a hit of texture and heat. The same can be done with garlic.

Fat

Some form of fat is used in almost everything we cook. It's not part of the accepted five tastes, but considering taste without it feels incomplete. Our food is only as good as the fat it is cooked in. I know that the deliciousness of the tomato sauce I make is entirely dependent on the amount and quality of olive oil I put into it.

Fat carries flavour. While some fats have flavours of their own, all fats coat our tongue and actually allow us to taste food.

Types of fat

Olive oil
Olive oil has a distinctive flavour that can range from fiery to buttery. There is as much variety in olive oil as there is in wine. It does not age well, so don't keep a bottle for more than a year. Olive oil has a lowish smoke point, but most of the food cooked in home kitchens, even when shallow frying, is below that smoke point, so it's safe to use.

Neutral oils
Oils like sunflower, vegetable, rapeseed or light olive oil (not extra virgin rapeseed or olive oil) are flavourless and good for cooking if you don't want to add the flavour of the oil. I use a light olive oil or rapeseed.

Ghee
A favourite of mine to cook with, it adds the depth that butter might, but because it's been clarified it doesn't burn or blacken in the same way. Ghee is great for browning, and I always use it for making pancakes and waffles.

Coconut oil
It comes in two types: one has a coconut flavour that's great in some dishes but overpowers others. Use unflavoured coconut oil if you don't want the coconut flavour. Coconut oil has a really high smoking point, so it's great to use if you are cooking at very high temperatures.

Yoghurt
I use organic full-fat Greek yoghurt a lot in my kitchen. I use yoghurt both for its gentle acidity and also as a fat to add creaminess. I often use it where you might use mayonnaise, such as in coleslaw, or in place of some or all of the oil in salad dressings to bring a fresher creaminess. Adding cold yoghurt to hot food is also a great way of adding richness as well as being a pleasing temperature contrast.

Using fats

Using oil to finish a dish is a complete game-changer. Every meal we eat has a drizzle of some sort of oil or yoghurt over it at the end. To me, it just rounds off the flavour and gives a final dimension of richness. I think this is particularly important when it comes to vegetarian cooking.

'There is as much variety in olive oil as there is in wine.'

Layering texture

When I think about what I'm going to cook, I think about the texture as much as the flavour. Balancing crispy, crunchy, creamy, chewy, soft, wet, crumbly, smooth or sticky is just as important as balancing flavour. Think toasted seeds tossed into a salad; charred, oil-drizzled bread next to a bowl of soup; the crunch of some peppery radishes inside a soft taco; the smooth, spoonable creaminess of Greek yoghurt; the chew of udon noodles.

Texture also hits our tastebuds and tells our brain that this is delicious food and helps us to feel satisfied. An array of different textures builds an interesting eating experience. Have you ever eaten an enormous bowl of porridge that feels texturally monotonous? A bowl with texture from seeds, the crunch of brown sugar and a drizzle of cold cream would send very different messages to your brain, and you would feel full, sated and satisfied in a completely different way.

When we talk about adding texture to food, it's often assumed that we are talking about adding crunch, such as breadcrumbs on top of a bowl of pasta or some crispy sage leaves. While crunch is perhaps the easiest way to think of texture, it is more nuanced than that.

Unlike flavour, though, which for the most part does need to be a balance of all or most of its elements, I don't feel like every dish needs to have a balance of every texture. Some foods, like a roast potato, for instance, will inherently have numerous different textures – the outside will be crisp and crunchy, the deep-golden edges might be a tiny bit chewy, and the inside will be fluffy and soft. So it's important that texture is not always about layering ingredient on top of ingredient. To achieve texture,

One of the most undervalued elements in cooking and eating is texture. Texture is just as key as flavour, particularly in vegetarian cooking. When children respond to food, so much of their response is about the texture rather than flavour; it's a primal part of how we eat. We are all tuned into texture. You might love the spoonable softness of a risotto, the crunch of a pickle or the chew of an udon noodle.

We can appreciate a texture thanks to specialised sensory receptors. The receptors can sense the pressure of something, such as the weight of a liquid like oil or the brittleness of a piece of crunchy food. Other receptors sense temperature and create a painful reaction if something is too hot. Scientists refer to four texture or mouthfeel categories – chewy, crunchy, suckable and creamy.

how you cook and what heat you cook at are key – thinking about what you have, and sometimes keeping things simpler, will amplify the textural sensations.

When we eat food, generally it's nice to have a mixture of at least two textures. Think patatas bravas dipped into alioli or udon noodles in a miso broth. It's having these different textures present on a plate that makes food exciting.

When putting together a plate of food, consider texture. Two opposing textures is a good place to start: crunchy and creamy or chewy and soft. But remember that sometimes one texture can be satisfying or comforting: a heap of mashed potato, a cheesy bowl of polenta, a scoop of ice cream. Here are the ways I think about texture, which I hope will help you consider the various elements of texture in your food too.

Crunch

Crunch is the easiest and quickest way to make a meal more exciting. When you put crunch next to soft, your tastebuds perk up.

Which crunch you add will depend on the texture you are pairing it with. Soft ricotta gnocchi works perfectly with crispy sage leaves. A bowl of soft, cold yoghurt pairs well with the dry crunch of granola. The juicy crunch of fresh sliced apple might work well next to some very creamy cheese.

- Dry crunch
  Granola, unbuttered toast, breadcrumbs, flaky sea salt, toasted flaked almonds, Demerara sugar, toasted spices.

- Shattering crunch
  Peanut brittle, crispy onions, flaky pastry, toasted coconut, fried sage leaves, fried garlic, crisps.

- Chewy crunch
  The edges of a cheese toastie, an olive oil crouton in a Caesar salad, crumble topping.

- Juicy crunch
  Crisp apples and pears, crunchy vegetables like carrots and celery, samphire.

Chewy

Chewy is the texture I crave the most, from the sugary pull of a chocolate chip cookie to the puffy chew of a bao bun. I love my food to have chew.

- Brownies, chewy chocolate chip cookies, udon noodles, tapioca pearls, dried fruit, good sourdough, marshmallows, bao buns, tofu, gummy bears.

Soft

Soft foods are gentle and smooth; a contrast to crunchy and chewy.

- Ripe mango or banana, soft-boiled or scrambled egg, ripe peaches, roast sweet potato, boiled carrots, pillowy whipped cream.

Creamy

When two liquids that don't usually mix come together to create something that feels and tastes like a perfect mixture of the two. If something is creamy and rich, then it's likely to be an emulsion of liquid and fat.

- Greek yoghurt, ice cream, panna cotta, vinaigrette, mozzarella, tahini, peanut butter, mayonnaise, buttery pasta sauce, fats and oils, coconut milk, hummus.

One ingredient
– many textures

One way to add texture without having to add cost or effort is to use the same ingredient two ways. Some corn for a chowder can be kept back and crisped in a pan with chilli to put on top. Raw cauliflower could be shaved on top of some roasted cauliflower soup. Leeks could be cooked slowly in butter and added to colcannon, and some could be kept to sizzle in butter and oil to scatter over the top. One ingredient can give you endless textures.

Heat and texture

Heat is the element of transformation; it takes food from raw to cooked and from soft to crisp, or vice versa. So far, we've just looked at the different ingredients that can add texture to our food, but how we cook our food also has a dramatic effect on its texture.

Heat and cooking in oil or fat create different types of texture in our food. For instance, if we steam a sweet potato we will get a soft, silky texture on the inside, whereas if we roast a sweet potato we will get a crispy outside and corners and a soft inside.

When you think about heat and texture, consider what you want to end up with and work back from there. It might be a bowl of buttery mashed potatoes, in which case boiling then mashing will give you the creamy effect you are after. But if you want a perfectly crunchy on the outside but melting on the inside cheese toastie, you might need to think more carefully. You may want to butter the outside of your sandwich and toast it in a hot pan until the edges are golden and crisp and the cheese inside is perfectly melted. You will want to eat it warm so that the cheese is still melty.

Garlic

I buy garlic five heads at a time. I bring it home and peel back the white, papery skin until I get to the stripy lilac cloves. Then it sits there, in the bowl with lemons and limes, pretty and purple. It will be happy there for weeks until I need it. Then a thwack with the side of the knife squashes the clove and loosens the skin. I run my knife through it quickly. I add it to hot butter or oil in the pan and immediately this purple garlic that asked so little of me unleashes its enormous hit of flavour. So much, it's almost not fair on the other ingredients in the kitchen.

On Garlic

Garlic's transformative power to make food tasty is unparalleled.

I use garlic sparingly, as an accent, not to overwhelm. Often, when I'm making tomato sauce, I will bash the clove with the side of the knife and let it sizzle whole and flavour the oil it's cooking in then lift it out. That hint of garlic is all I need (and is good if you are cooking for gentler palates). Adding a little garlic to your food can sharpen the taste of everything else; adding too much just makes everything taste like garlic.

The amount of garlic flavour you get from a clove will depend on how it is chopped. Kept whole but bashed it will be the gentlest hum of garlic. Finely sliced garlic will add a gentle garlic flavour and will give you pops of garlic flavour. Sliced garlic is also good cooked in oil until golden for a crisp garlic crunch. Minced garlic (or garlic crushed with a garlic press) will give you a more intense garlic flavour throughout what you are cooking. It's good raw too if you like a punchy salad dressing.

Burnt garlic has such a strong flavour it can easily ruin a dish. If you're prone to burning it, you can start your garlic and oil in a cold pan or add the garlic with other ingredients to soften the heat. Garlic really only needs a couple of minutes on a medium heat, less if finely chopped or minced, to cook. If you burn your garlic, start again – you will never get the taste of burnt garlic out of a dish.

I am not a fan of garlic bought peeled or pre-chopped: I think the flavour is acrid. If you find that chopping garlic is too much on a weeknight, chop a head and freeze it under oil in ice cube trays, or peel a head and keep the peeled cloves in a jar in the fridge for up to two weeks.

Hot, Nutty, Mustardy, Sweet

- Head of garlic
  The garlic we know is the picked, semi-dried bulbs of garlic.

- Young or wet garlic
  These are the white and purple bulbs picked and sold before they start to dry. It's milder, but you can use it in the same way as normal garlic.

- Elephant garlic
  Actually a member of the leek family – with enormous cloves and a milder taste.

- Wild garlic
  Is a different species of allium. It has a strong taste when it's raw that mellows when you cook it. It is highly seasonal and grows in woodlands from early spring.

- Black garlic
  Heads of raw garlic are fermented until they turn sticky, sweet and black. They go well with eggs and noodle dishes.

- Confit garlic
  Cloves of garlic cooked slowly in oil until they are soft, buttery and almost caramel-flavoured. Nothing like raw garlic.

Goes well with

almond	mushroom
aubergine	olive
basil	onion
broccoli	parsley
cauliflower	rosemary
cheese	shallot
chilli	thyme
coriander	tomato
ginger	walnut

Favourite uses

- Ajo blanco (see page 86)
- Smashed cucumber salad
- Fried into golden garlic crisps to top anything

- Confited and jarred for adding flavour to all my cooking
- In equal parts with ginger for a ying/yang feeling
- Fried with a chopped red chilli in oil for an aglio, olio e peperoncino pasta
- Rubbed on toast and topped with fresh tomatoes
- Grated into yoghurt with salt and lemon for serving with flatbreads

Storage

Store garlic at room temperature in a dry, dark place – this way it will stay fresh for up to six months. Remember, the longer you keep garlic, the stronger the flavour will become. Garlic is fresh and changes flavour as it ages. If it's old or left in a bright spot, a little green shoot will creep out of the top. I think the green sprouts add bitterness, so I always halve the clove, flick the green spouts out with the end of my knife and then use the rest of the clove normally.

Peeled garlic cloves can be stored for up to a week in a container in the fridge.

What to buy

If you're able, buy UK garlic (the Isle of Wight is a famous producer); cloves bought in the late spring and early summer will be fresher, milder new season garlic. Anything stored through the winter will be stronger. Spain, Italy and France grow good garlic – places like Natoora and good veg suppliers should be able to tell you about the variety and freshness of the garlic they sell.

In recent years, imported Chinese garlic is the main supermarket choice because of price and the fact there is little seasonal variation in flavour.

Confit garlic

4 whole heads of garlic
(about 240g)
350ml olive or rapeseed oil
a couple of sprigs of woody
herbs (5g), like bay, rosemary,
savory or thyme

Confit garlic is buttery, sweet and almost caramelly, an entirely different thing from raw or quickly cooked garlic. It can bring big and bold flavour to your cooking. While the word confit sounds like something you'd hear in a restaurant kitchen, it couldn't be simpler to make at home and keeps for months, meaning you have a hit of deep, sweet garlic on hand. Whether smudged over hot grilled toast or used at the start of making a comforting sauce, this is a great thing to have ready all year round, and the oil can be used too, so nothing is wasted.

MAKES 1 × 400G JAR

Peel the garlic
Peel 4 whole heads of garlic and add the cloves to a medium saucepan with 350ml olive or rapeseed oil. The garlic cloves should all be covered with oil. If they aren't, simply add a little more oil until they are.

Confit the garlic
Cook the garlic over a medium-low heat until the cloves just begin to sizzle gently around their edges, then lower the temperature slightly to maintain that gentle sizzle. Cook for 45 minutes, or until the garlic is completely soft and golden brown.

Store the confit garlic
Allow the oil to cool slightly, then add 5g woody herb sprigs to a sterilised jar large enough to hold the garlic confit and oil. Pour the cooked garlic and oil over the woody herbs (be careful, if the oil is too hot it may spit slightly as it hits the herbs) and seal the container. Store the confit garlic in the fridge, covered with the oil, for up to 6 months.

Garlic

Garlic and ginger pickle broth

80g fresh ginger, peeled (keep
    the peelings)
2 tablespoons red miso paste
a bunch of spring onions
    (about 8), trimmed but
    kept whole
6 cherry tomatoes
1 whole head of garlic (about
    10 cloves), cloves peeled
200g sushi rice, washed until
    the water runs clear
3 tablespoons groundnut or
    vegetable oil
1 fresh red chilli, finely sliced
1 teaspoon coriander seeds
2 tablespoons sesame seeds
1 tablespoon maple syrup
1 teaspoon soy sauce or tamari
150g jar pickled ginger, with
    the pickling liquid

This soup was made one day when Kitty (who helped me test the recipes for this book) and I were sitting around my kitchen table, talking through our day of testing. I was quite pregnant and full of cold, and everything seemed an effort. We settled on the idea of a broth with rice and lots of ginger. It revived me like no other soup I can remember. It was like an IV drip of goodness – plump sushi rice, a gingery garlic miso broth, and then a punchy pickle, half crispy garlic and half pickled and fresh ginger. I made it every day for the next three days. Thanks, Kitty.

SERVES 4

Make the garlic and ginger broth
Peel 80g fresh ginger and keep the peelings. Add 1.5 litres water to a saucepan, add 2 tablespoons red miso paste, a bunch of trimmed spring onions, 6 cherry tomatoes, 4 peeled cloves of garlic and the ginger peel. Bring to the boil, then turn down to a low simmer for 20–30 minutes.

Wash and cook the rice
Put 200g washed sushi rice and 300ml cold water into a saucepan with a lid. Bring to the boil, cover, then immediately turn the heat down to a very low simmer and cook for 10 minutes. Turn off the heat, wrap the lid of the pan in a tea towel and put it back on the pan, then leave the rice to sit for 10 minutes.

Slice the pickle ingredients
Thinly slice 6 cloves of garlic with a knife or very carefully on a mandoline. Chop the peeled ginger into matchsticks as thinly as you can.

Fry the aromatics
Put 3 tablespoons groundnut or vegetable oil into a small frying pan or saucepan, followed by the sliced garlic, ginger, 1 finely sliced fresh red chilli, 1 teaspoon coriander seeds and 2 tablespoons sesame seeds. Put the pan over a medium-low heat and allow everything to cook slowly for 5–7 minutes until the garlic and ginger are just golden and crisp. Once crisp, turn off the heat, add 1 tablespoon maple syrup and 1 teaspoon soy sauce and let it bubble. Set aside to cool slightly.

Finish the pickle
Empty 150g jarred pickled ginger into a bowl with its liquid (there should ideally be about 75ml of pickling liquid from the jar, but it will vary from jar to jar) then carefully pour in the ginger and garlic mix from the pan with all the liquid.

Finish the broth
Spoon the warm rice between four bowls and ladle over the broth. Put the bowl of garlic pickle in the middle of the table and let everyone spoon on as much as they like. Any leftover pickle will keep in a jar in the fridge for up to 2 weeks.

Add-ons
I like to eat this broth simply but if you wanted to add more veg, then some quartered pak choi, broccoli, shredded spring greens, or even very thin slices of sweet potato, would work well. Just add them to the broth for the last few minutes of cooking.

Confit garlic cauliflower cheese

75g butter or vegan butter

75g plain flour

900ml milk or oat milk

2 whole heads (about 20 cloves) of confit garlic (see page 244)

80g Cheddar or vegan Cheddar, grated

50g Gruyère or vegan Cheddar-style cheese, grated

1 large cauliflower, broken into chunky florets, smaller leaves reserved

150g fresh breadcrumbs

zest of 1 unwaxed lemon

a few sprigs of thyme (5g), leaves picked

a few sprigs of sage (5g), leaves picked and chopped

Confit garlic makes everything better, and I feel the same about cauliflower cheese, so together this is a blanket of a dish. Confit garlic, cheesy sauce and burnished cauliflower. Eat this with some lemon-dressed greens or a bitter leaf salad. This is always one of our Christmas Day sides.

SERVES 6

Make the béchamel
Preheat the oven to 180°C/160°C fan. Melt 75g butter or vegan butter in a medium saucepan over a medium-low heat, then stir in 75g plain flour until it forms a paste. Cook for a couple of minutes until the paste begins to smell toasty (this will cook the rawness out of the flour). Add 900ml milk or oat milk a little at a time, whisking continuously into a smooth, white sauce.

Add the confit garlic and cheese to the béchamel
Take about 20 cloves of confit garlic from their fragrant oil and stir half into the sauce. Add half the grated Cheddar (40g) and half the grated Gruyère (25g), or your vegan alternatives, season well with sea salt and freshly ground black pepper and stir to melt the cheese. It should be quite a loose sauce (it will thicken up as it bakes) so add a little more milk or oat milk if needed.

Arrange the cauliflower
Arrange the florets from 1 large cauliflower and some of the smaller cauliflower leaves in a baking dish that will fit everything in nicely, then add the remaining 10 cloves of confit garlic, dotting it into the spaces between the cauliflower.

Pour over the sauce
Pour the garlicky cheese sauce evenly over the cauliflower, then top with the other half of the grated Cheddar (40g) and grated Gruyère (25g).

Make the breadcrumb topping and bake
Mix 150g breadcrumbs with the zest of 1 unwaxed lemon, 5g thyme leaves and 5g chopped sage leaves, then sprinkle over the cheesy cauliflower. Finally, spoon over some of the oil from the confit garlic and bake for 1 hour, until the cauliflower is soft and golden.

Roast garlic and white bean soup

200g blanched almonds
1 litre good-quality vegetable
    stock (if using powder
    or cubes use half the
    recommended amount for
    800ml water)
1 large cauliflower (850g), cut
    into florets, leaves kept
a whole head of garlic
1 teaspoon fennel seeds
6 tablespoons olive oil
1 onion, peeled and finely
    chopped
1 stick of celery, finely chopped
200ml white wine or more stock
1 × 400g tin white beans,
    drained (either butter beans
    or cannellini beans)
4 sprigs of thyme, leaves picked

We made this soup one day on the shoot for my last book. It has the comfort of a silky spoonable soup but with a big bold flavour. Mostly on shoot days we eat what we have cooked to take pictures of and most days it's a feast. One of my favourite things about writing a book are these lunches eaten with the friends who help me put my books together.

This day, though, we must have started late or been making sweet things, so we whipped up this soup: buttery roast garlic, almonds, white beans and cauliflower. It was what we had that needed using, but it turned out to be a soup I have repeated a lot since. The tone-on-tone colours in this soup, white on white, had me thinking this is actually a good flavour lesson. Often I'll make something and then realise that every-thing I used was from one colour palette. I think there is some sense in this. Think squash, chilli and orange or peas, broad beans and mint. It's not a hard and fast rule but a way of cooking I sometimes enjoy.

SERVES 4

Toast the almonds
Preheat the oven to 200°C/180°C fan. Add 200g blanched almonds to a large shallow baking tray, then place in the oven and toast for 5–10 minutes until lightly golden. Remove from the oven then add three-quarters of them to 1 litre good vegetable stock to soak and leave the other quarter to cool separately.

Roast the cauliflower and garlic
Put the florets from 1 large cauliflower into the same tray with a whole head of garlic and add 1 teaspoon fennel seeds, 2 tablespoons olive oil, a generous pinch of flaky sea salt and some freshly ground black

pepper. Toss together so the florets are all evenly coated, then roast in the oven for 30 minutes until golden at the edges. Remove the cauliflower from the tray into a bowl and return the garlic to the oven for a further 15 minutes until it is soft inside.

Make the soup
Put 2 tablespoons olive oil, 1 peeled and finely chopped onion and 1 finely chopped stick of celery into a large saucepan. Sauté on a medium heat for 5–10 minutes until soft and sweet but not browned. Add 200ml white wine or more stock and cook until it reduces down to half the amount.

Add the cauliflower and stock
Add the roasted cauliflower, 400g tin of white beans, drained, the soaked almonds and vegetable stock to the saucepan with the onion and celery. Bring to the boil, then lower the heat and simmer for 10–15 minutes.

Squeeze in the garlic
Cut the top off the roasted head of garlic and squeeze out the soft flesh into the saucepan. Compost the papery skins, then blitz the soup with a hand-held blender until completely smooth, adding hot water if needed to loosen to the consistency of double cream.

For the topping and serve
Finely chop the cauliflower leaves and the remaining toasted almonds then add them to a frying pan with 2 tablespoons olive oil, a pinch of sea salt and 4 sprigs of picked thyme leaves. Fry on a high heat for 5–10 minutes until the leaves are crisp and tender and the almonds are more toasted and golden. Ladle the soup into bowls and finish with the crispy cauliflower and almond topping.

Creamy double garlic and broccoli rigatoni

1 large head of broccoli
(about 500g)
500g rigatoni
4 tablespoons extra virgin
olive oil
2 cloves of fresh garlic, very
finely chopped
10 cloves of confit garlic
(see page 244 for recipe)
60g Parmesan (I use a vegetarian
one) or vegan Parmesan-style
cheese, grated
zest of 2 unwaxed lemons and
the juice of 1
1 tablespoon black pepper, freshly
ground (about 10 grinds)

Think cacio e pepe here, but the creaminess comes from confit garlic, not a mountain of Parmesan (though we add some of that too). The confit garlic brings sweet, mellow, creamy garlic flavour which is backed up by a couple of cloves of fresh garlic for heat and spice. The broccoli is cooked almost to the point of collapse, which adds to the soft creaminess of the sauce. All that richness is backed up by a hit of black pepper and just enough umami from some Parmesan. An on-repeat pasta.

If you don't have confit garlic for this recipe (the recipe is on page 244) then you can add a couple of extra cloves of fresh garlic and more Parmesan. It won't be quite as rich or creamy but it will still be a bowl of pasta you will be very happy about.

SERVES 4

Chop and cook the broccoli
Cut 500g broccoli into small florets, then roughly chop the stalk into 1cm pieces. Bring a large pot of well-salted water to the boil, add the broccoli florets and stalks and cook for 8–10 minutes until soft. You want it well cooked so it breaks down into a sauce. Drain the broccoli with a slotted spoon and keep the water on.

Cook the pasta
Add 500g rigatoni to the same water and boil for a minute less than the packet instructions, which will be about 8–10 minutes.

Cook the fresh garlic and add the cooked broccoli
Meanwhile, put 4 tablespoons extra virgin olive oil into a frying pan on a medium-low heat and add 2 very finely chopped cloves of peeled garlic, frying for a minute before adding the cooked broccoli and a few

spoonfuls of the pasta water. Simmer slowly for 5–8 more minutes until it's really soft, mashing some of the broccoli as it cooks with the back of your spoon.

Make the confit garlic sauce
In a small bowl, roughly mash 10 cloves of confit garlic with 60g grated Parmesan or vegan Parmesan-style cheese, the zest of 1 unwaxed lemon and 1 tablespoon of black pepper, freshly ground, to make a thick paste. Squeeze in the juice of 1 lemon and add a few spoonfuls of the pasta water until you have a spoonable sauce-like consistency, about the thickness of double cream.

Finish the pasta
Drain the pasta, reserving a mugful of the pasta water, then add the pasta to the broccoli pan with the confit garlic sauce. Stir together over a low heat, adding more pasta water until you have a glossy sauce to coat everything, remembering that the sauce will thicken as the pasta sits. Serve immediately, with extra Parmesan, black pepper and lemon zest.

Confit garlic Caesar salad with herbs

2 slices sourdough bread, torn
into roughly 2cm pieces
8 cloves of confit garlic, plus
4 tablespoons of the confit
garlic oil (see page 244)
zest and juice of ½ an unwaxed
lemon
100g crème fraîche or oat
crème fraîche
50g Parmesan or vegan
Parmesan-style cheese,
grated, plus extra to serve
2 teaspoons Dijon mustard
1 teaspoon black pepper, freshly
ground, plus a little extra
2 tablespoons capers, plus
2 tablespoons caper brine
4 Little Gem lettuces or 2 heads
of Romaine lettuce
½ a bunch of parsley (15g), leaves
picked
½ a bunch of chives (10g), finely
chopped

Like a classic Caesar but fresher. I use
confit garlic here to add creaminess
to the dressing, with some crème
fraîche for bright acidity and lots of
herbs to lift it. The confit garlic oil is
used to roast the croutons, so there
is a mellow double garlic flavour.
I eat this as it is on the side, but if you
wanted to make it into a meal then
a tin of drained white beans, patted
dry and cooked until crisp in olive oil
in the oven while the croutons cook,
would round it out.

SERVES 4

Preheat the oven and make the croutons
Preheat the oven to 180°C/160°C fan.
Tear 2 slices of sourdough bread into
roughly 2cm pieces and place in a
large baking tray with 2 tablespoons
confit garlic oil, sea salt and freshly
ground black pepper. Toss so it's all
evenly coated in the oil, then bake
in the oven for 10–15 minutes until
golden and crisp but still a little soft
in the middle. Remove and set aside.

Make the dressing
In a bowl, mash 8 confit garlic cloves,
then mix with the zest and juice of
½ an unwaxed lemon, 100g crème
fraîche or oat crème fraîche, 50g
grated Parmesan or vegan Parmesan-
style cheese, 2 teaspoons Dijon
mustard, 1 teaspoon freshly ground
black pepper and 2 tablespoons caper
brine from the jar. Mix to a thick
dressing, about the same consistency
as yoghurt.

Put the salad together
Add the leaves from 4 Little Gem
lettuces or 2 heads of Romaine lettuce
to a serving bowl with the picked
leaves from ½ a bunch of parsley (15g),
½ a bunch of finely chopped chives
(10g), half the dressing (saving the rest
for another day), 2 tablespoons capers

and the croutons. Toss everything
together, then serve immediately
with some more Parmesan grated
over the top.

Crispy garlic egg-fried rice

500g cooked jasmine or
   basmati rice
1 cucumber
150g radishes, leaves trimmed
1 tablespoon crispy chilli oil or
   chilli crisp
3 tablespoons soy sauce or
   tamari
1 teaspoon maple syrup
zest and juice of 1 unwaxed lime
8 cloves of garlic, peeled and
   very thinly sliced (use a
   mandoline if you have one)
3 tablespoons neutral oil (such
   as groundnut)
2 tablespoons sesame seeds
4 free-range eggs
1 bunch of spring onions,
   very finely sliced

Egg-fried rice is made about once every two weeks here. It's a meal we know Dylan will eat and it's what I crave when I'm not feeling like thinking about food, which is surprisingly often. Here, some crispy garlic adds texture and sweet toasty flavour to the rice. Garlic crisped in oil like this will improve just about any meal, so once you have mastered it you can top all your meals with it (and trust me, you just might). The rice comes with an easy little smacked cucumber and radish salad which lifts and adds crunch. I've kept the rice simple, but if you wanted to you could add some shredded greens or blanched frozen peas as well. If you are vegan you could add some crumbled soft tofu instead of the eggs.

SERVES 2 GENEROUSLY, OR 4 AS PART OF A MEAL

Cook the rice if needed
If you don't have leftover rice, cook around 170g rice now, to give 500g cooked rice (see page 194 for a method).

Make the cucumber and radish salad
With a rolling pin gently smack 1 cucumber and 150g trimmed radishes so they split but don't break up completely. Chop the cucumber into 2cm pieces and put them into a serving bowl with the radishes. Add 1 tablespoon crispy chilli oil, 2 table-spoons soy sauce, 1 teaspoon maple syrup and the zest and juice of 1 unwaxed lime and mix until every-thing is coated in the dressing.

Make the crispy garlic
Thinly slice 8 peeled cloves of garlic with a knife or very carefully with a mandoline. Put 3 tablespoons of neutral oil into a small frying pan or saucepan and add the sliced garlic and 2 tablespoons sesame seeds. Put

the pan over a medium-low heat and allow everything to cook slowly for 3–5 minutes until the garlic is very lightly golden and crisp. Be careful here to cook until just golden. Taking the garlic too far or too brown will make it bitter, so don't be tempted to cook it on a high heat. Drain the garlic and seeds with a sieve (keeping the oil), then leave to cool on some kitchen paper.

Beat the eggs and fry the rice
Beat 4 eggs well with another table-spoon of soy sauce. Put the reserved oil in a large wok or frying pan over a high heat, then, once hot, add 500g cooked jasmine or basmati rice and spread it out in an even layer to heat through for a minute. Now stir until all the rice is coated in a little oil.

Add the eggs
Push most of the rice to one side of the pan. Add the beaten egg to the empty side, stir the egg quickly to fry and partly cook it, then stir it into the rice and cook for another minute or two. Take off the heat.

Serve the rice
Mix a quarter of the crispy garlic and sesame seeds into the cucumber and radish salad. Divide the rice between four bowls and put some of the salad on the side of each. Finish the rice with the remaining crispy garlic and sesame, and top with 1 bunch of very finely sliced spring onions.

Lemongrass dal with garlic and curry leaves

1 teaspoon coriander seeds,
   bashed
1 teaspoon cumin seeds
300g red split lentils, rinsed
6 garlic cloves, peeled, 3 left
   whole, 3 finely sliced
2 lemongrass stalks, bashed
1 teaspoon ground turmeric
½ teaspoon Kashmiri chilli
   powder
1 × 400ml tin coconut milk
200g greens, like spinach or
   shredded chard
2 tablespoons coconut oil
1 small red onion, peeled and
   finely sliced
1 teaspoon black mustard seeds
20 fresh curry leaves
1 unwaxed lemon
chapatis or rotis, to serve

The comfort of dal is unmatched, and this gently spiced one comforts as well as lifts, thanks to some lemongrass, greens and lemon. The real star here, though, is the garlic temper, the garlic, red onion, mustard seeds and curry leaves which are spooned over the dal to give tiny pockets of flavour on each spoon. This dal is inspired by one from Cynthia of Rambutan that I've been making a lot.

SERVES 4

Toast the spices
In a saucepan big enough to cook your dal, toast 1 teaspoon bashed coriander seeds and 1 teaspoon cumin seeds, then tip into a small bowl.

Rinse and cook the lentils
Rinse 300g red split lentils in cold water, then drain, put them in a pan and cover with 1 litre water (about 1cm over the top of the lentils). Add a good pinch of salt and bring to the boil. Once boiling, skim off any scum that has risen to the top, then reduce to a simmer. Add 3 whole cloves of garlic, 2 bashed lemongrass stalks, 1 teaspoon ground turmeric, ½ teaspoon Kashmiri chilli powder, the toasted coriander and cumin seeds and cook for 15 minutes, or until the lentils are velvety soft.

Add the coconut milk
Once the lentils are cooked, turn the heat back up to medium, add 400ml coconut milk and 200g spinach and cook for another 10 minutes, until creamy.

Make the temper
In a small pan heat 2 tablespoons coconut oil over a high heat, add 1 small red onion, peeled and finely sliced, and cook for 5–6 minutes

until golden brown. Add 3 finely sliced cloves of garlic, 1 teaspoon black mustard seeds and 20 curry leaves and cook for 1–2 minutes more until the curry leaves are crispy and shiny.

Finish the dal
Spoon the dal into bowls, top with the garlic and curry leaf temper, add a squeeze of lemon juice to lift everything and eat with roti or chapati.

Gurd's roasted tomatoes with crispy garlic

125ml olive oil

6 fat cloves of garlic, sliced into thin slivers

1 teaspoon dried chilli flakes

a bunch of parsley (30g), very finely chopped

zest and juice of ½ an unwaxed lemon

4 tablespoons panko breadcrumbs

3 tablespoons dukkah (see recipe below)

1 teaspoon fine sea salt

1kg large ripe tomatoes (I used 4 × 250g tomatoes, halved horizontally)

FOR THE DUKKAH
(MAKES A SMALL JAR)

45g blanched hazelnuts

2 tablespoons sesame seeds

1 tablespoon cumin seeds

1 tablespoon coriander seeds

1 tablespoon fennel seeds

1 teaspoon paprika

1 teaspoon dried oregano

1 teaspoon fine sea salt

2 teaspoons black pepper, coarsely ground

Spending time with Gurdeep feels like time spent in full colour, on fast forward in the most wonderful way. I trust Gurd's opinion on food completely. He is a genius with flavour, and these tomatoes are proof. To Gurdeep, garlic is a unique flavour amplifier whose multiple characters can take a dish into completely different directions depending which is pulled upon. 'Raw garlic imparts sharp spiciness and earthy pungency. Slowly roasted, it's transformed to a fragrant-fudgy butter; and when browned or blackened, it gives an intense tangy-bitterness that shatters with a crunch.' This recipe from Gurd celebrates garlic's diversity – first extracting its allium sweetness into olive oil for roasting with, then crisping it up for some textural peppery bite.

SERVES 4

Fry the crispy garlic
Preheat the oven to 195°C/175°C fan. Very gently heat 125ml olive oil in a frying pan, then add 6 fat cloves of garlic, sliced into thin slivers. Fry in the just bubbling oil, low and slow, for 3–4 minutes, watching it closely; you want the garlic to release its flavours into the oil without taking on any colour at all. When the garlic begins to clump together in the oil, add 1 teaspoon dried chilli flakes and sizzle gently for another 1 minute. Pour the oil through a sieve into a jug, keeping the garlic and chilli flakes to one side for now.

Make the topping
In a separate bowl, mix together a bunch of very finely chopped parsley and the zest and juice of ½ an unwaxed lemon. Next, stir through 70ml of the garlicky oil, keeping some behind to drizzle over later. Finally, mix through 4 tablespoons panko

breadcrumbs, 3 tablespoons dukkah and a teaspoon of fine sea salt to make a green-zesty crumb crust.

Prep and top the tomatoes
Slice 1kg large ripe tomatoes in half horizontally, spread out on a lined baking sheet and sprinkle each one with a pinch of sea salt. Spoon a thick layer of the dukkah-gremolata crust on to each and drizzle liberally with the last of the garlicky oil.

Bake the tomatoes
Bake in the oven for 45–50 minutes, until the tomatoes are soft and the tops start to brown. Remove from the oven, baste with the oils from the bottom of the tray, then sprinkle over the fried garlic and chilli flakes. Return to the oven for a further 5–6 minutes until the garlic just turns crispy and the crust is nicely baked. Serve with couscous or warm flatbreads. Enjoy hot or cold.

For the dukkah:
Preheat the oven and toast the spices
Preheat the oven to 180°C/160°C fan. Scatter 45g blanched hazelnuts, 2 tablespoons sesame seeds, 1 tablespoon each of cumin, coriander and fennel seeds on to a baking tray. Bake for 6–7 minutes until toasty and just browned. Remove from the oven and cool.

Grind and mix
Spoon the cooled nuts and spices into a spice grinder or food processor, along with 1 teaspoon each of paprika, dried oregano and fine sea salt and 2 teaspoons coarsely ground black pepper. Pulse for a couple of seconds to a coarse crumbly rubble. Keep in an airtight jar in a dark place, where it will store well for up to 4 weeks.

Olia's pampushky

15g fresh yeast or 7g active dry
    yeast
1 teaspoon caster sugar
225ml warm water
400g strong white flour, plus
    extra for dusting
8g fine sea salt
5 cloves (about 20g) wet or
    regular garlic, crushed or
    very finely chopped
3 tablespoons sunflower oil, plus
    extra for oiling
½ a bunch of parsley (15g), finely
    chopped
1 free-range egg, beaten, to glaze

Olia is a dear friend. She writes with great beauty on the food of Ukraine and the surrounding regions. Olia has also provided me and countless others with an unmatched heart-first perspective on the war in Ukraine – standing up and speaking out when it must have been immeasurably hard. Olia has been kind enough to share this recipe with me, and I put it here as a reminder to not forget the war still waged on Ukraine.

Olia tells me that the word 'pampushka' can be used to describe a gorgeous plump woman and is one of her favourite words. Pam-poo-shka! These pampushky are traditionally served with red borshch. In Ukraine, Olia says she would use regular garlic, so if you can't find wet (new) garlic, don't worry – it will still be delicious.

MAKES 8 BREADS

Make your starter
First make a 'sponge', which is a type of yeasty starter. Dissolve 15g fresh yeast or 7g active dry yeast and 1 teaspoon caster sugar in 225ml warm water (make sure it's body temperature – hot water would kill the yeast). Add 200g strong white flour and mix roughly. Cover the bowl and leave to prove in the refrigerator overnight or on the counter for 3 hours.

Make the dough
The next morning, or 3 hours later, add another 200g strong white flour and 8g fine sea salt to the starter and knead on a well-floured work surface until the dough is smooth and comes away from your hands easily.

Shape the dough
Divide the dough into 8 pieces and shape into round buns. Put them side by side in an oiled round ovenproof dish or a 24cm round cake tin, cover and let them prove again, this time in a warm place, until doubled in size. They will join together just like hot cross buns do.

Make the basting oil
Meanwhile, preheat the oven to 220°C/200°C fan. To make the basting oil, simply stir 20g crushed wet (new) or regular garlic through 3 tablespoons sunflower oil with a small pinch of sea salt and ½ a bunch of finely chopped parsley, then let it infuse.

Glaze and bake
When the pampushky look plump and ready, brush them generously with a beaten egg to glaze and bake for 20–25 minutes or until they form a glistening golden crust. Take them out and baste them with the garlic oil. Serve immediately.

Onions

Papery skin so thin you can see the light through it. Brown and purple, white and caramel. There is poetry in an onion. Tears when it's peeled, but after a slow cook transformed into a blanket of sweet comfort. Onions cross cultures. The start of so much. The smell of an onion cooking is the smell of promise, of good things to come. A steady assurance of flavour that we can rely on, and we all need something to rely on. Cooked under pastry with cheese and potato, sharp and tempered with acid to lift a tomato salad, charred and blackened but still sweet. All that from one papery allium that lives in the dark.

On Onions

Every cuisine uses onions. In my kitchen, they are used 100 ways. From slow-cooked and buttery to pickled and punchy. From crispy shards to buttery leeks. Onions and the other alliums (shallots, leeks, spring onions) make my cooking what it is.

To me, an onion needs some cooking: often a long, slow cook until soft and buttery, but I never cook a raw onion for anything less than 10 minutes, until it's softened, broken down and has lost its rawness.

I may be in the minority here, but I am not keen on completely raw onion. If I want the hit of onion freshness, I will quickly pickle it in lime juice and salt or a little vinegar and sugar, depending on what I am eating. The same with a shallot. As well as sweetness and acidity, using onions like this adds their own version of warmth and heat.

My love of nothing but a well-cooked onion has led me to use leeks and spring onions instead of onions when I want to cook quickly. It lends the same allium depth, but you can cook a spring onion in a couple of minutes and a finely sliced leek in five.

Types

- Mild
  Big onions with a soft, mild flavour.

- Yellow
  The most widely used onion in the UK – they have a rich flavour that makes them endlessly versatile.

- White
  More unusual in the UK, white onions are generally cleaner in flavour than yellow, but don't store quite as well as yellow onions do.

- Red
  Slightly sweeter but still punchy when raw. These pickle really nicely.

- Spring onions
  These are very young yellow, red or white onions that are pulled out of the ground before they can turn into onions.

- Leeks
  The milder, milky green cousin of the onion.

- Shallot
  Tapered with a coppery skin – milder and sweeter in flavour than red onions. A staple in French cooking.

Goes well with

beetroot	lemon
butter	lime
caper	mushroom
carrot	pea
cheese	potato
chilli	red pepper
ginger	sage

How to cook

- Baking
  Roasting onions turns them into something sweet, rich and earthy – a vegetable all of their own, not a supporting act.

- Soaking
  If you want to use raw onions, but are after a mellower flavour, soak them in a bowl of cold water for a few minutes before using.

- Sautéing
  To sauté an onion, cook over high heat with a little oil until golden brown. If they begin to catch on the bottom of the pan, adding a splash of water (not oil) will unstick them.

- Sweating
  This means cooking over a low heat until the onion becomes soft and transparent, without browning.

- Caramelising
  Caramelisation is a slow, delicate process that combines sweating and sautéing (see following page).

Storage and tips

Keep onions and shallots in a cool, dark place. Remove them from any plastic bag, as that makes them sweat and go off quicker.

Store a cut onion in the fridge, cut side down, on a plate covered with a bowl or in a jar or glass container so that other foods don't take on the taste of onion.

What to buy

Try to buy onions grown in the UK when you can.

Look for firm red or yellow onions with taut skin that feel heavy for their size, with no green sprouts.

I buy escallion shallots, also known as banana shallots. The flavour is sweeter, and they are less annoying to peel than the small shallots.

For leeks and spring onions, look for perky ones with no dry or browning bits.

Crispy shallots

6 banana shallots, peeled,
   halved and finely sliced
1 litre sunflower oil

Peel and halve 6 banana shallots, then remove their tops and finely slice. Add to a large bowl and, using your hands, move through the shallots separating as many individual slices as possible.

Put 1 litre sunflower oil into a large saucepan and heat to roughly 180°C, or until a large breadcrumb turns golden in 30 seconds in the oil. Add the shallots to the oil and cook, stirring continuously, for 10 minutes, or until the shallots are a light brown. The shallots will continue to cook and colour for a minute or so once they are out of the oil, so remove them just before they're looking done.

Drain on kitchen paper and allow to cool. Store in an airtight container in a cool dark place for up to 2 weeks. Perfect for topping salads, dressing fried vegetables or simply stirred through buttery pasta.

Here are a few easy ways to use your crispy onions
- They're great on top of a curry, a dal or a laksa.
- You can scatter them over a stir-fry or a noodle dish like a pad thai.
- Pile them into a cheese sandwich with some pickle.
- To finish scrambled eggs.
- They make any autumnal or winter soup much tastier.
- They'll improve a baked potato or sweet potato with crème fraîche and a pinch of chopped capers.
- Lastly, they are the perfect finish to a rich autumn tomato pasta.

Slow-cooked onions

1.2kg medium brown onions
   (about 6), peeled, halved and
   finely sliced
1 knob of butter
4 tablespoons olive oil
1 tablespoon apple cider vinegar
2 tablespoons light soft brown
   sugar (optional)

These slow-cooked onions bolster the base of pies, sauces and one-pot suppers. Make a large batch and keep them to hand, frozen in ice-cube trays. Simply knock out a couple of cubes straight into the pan as and when you need them.

Add 1 knob of butter and 4 table-spoons olive oil to a large casserole-style pot and set over a medium-high heat. As soon as the butter has melted and begins to sizzle, add the onions and a generous pinch of salt. Stir to evenly coat the onions in the buttery-oil mixture and turn the heat down to low. Cook, stirring every now and then, for 30–45 minutes, until the onions are translucent, sweet and soft. Add 1 tablespoon apple cider vinegar and stir to combine.

If you like, you can enhance the natural sweetness of the onions by adding 2 tablespoons light soft brown sugar at this stage. Add to the pan, stir to mix evenly and cook for a couple of minutes until the sugar has dissolved. Take the onions off the heat and transfer to a sterilised container where they will keep, covered in the fridge, for a week. To preserve them for longer, simply divide the cooked and cooled onion mixture between ice-cube trays and freeze until needed.

Sticky onion Eccles cakes with carrot chutney

1 tablespoon coriander seeds
1 teaspoon caraway seeds
400g carrots, peeled and grated
1 small thumb-sized piece of
  ginger, grated
50g caster sugar
zest and juice of 2 unwaxed
  lemons
1 tablespoon butter or olive oil
4 shallots, peeled and finely
  chopped
75ml white wine vinegar
2 cloves of garlic, peeled and
  finely chopped
6 pitted dates, roughly chopped
150g Lancashire cheese,
  crumbled, or a vegan hard
  mature-style cheese
50g almonds, toasted and
  roughly chopped
2 × 320g ready-rolled puff pastry
  sheets (use non-dairy if
  needed)
1 organic egg, beaten (or
  3 tablespoons of non-dairy
  milk)
4 tablespoons mixed seeds
  (I use a mix of poppy and
  sesame)
2 tablespoons Demerara sugar

Eccles cakes are my favourite. There is a bakery in Anglesey, where John is from. The Eccles cakes are off the chart, the bottom sweet and sticky from the filling running out where the pastry joins. I've wanted to try a savoury version for ages. The filling is based on John's mum's carrot chutney.

This Eccles cake brings together a sticky shallot and carrot filling, which is really like a chutney, and some Lancashire cheese topped with Demerara and seeds which form a crunchy seeded top. These travel well.

MAKES 12 ECCLES CAKES

Mix the spices and carrot
Bash 1 tablespoon coriander seeds in a mortar and tip into a saucepan. Add 1 teaspoon caraway seeds, 400g peeled and grated carrots, 1 small thumb of grated ginger, 50g caster sugar and the zest of 2 unwaxed lemons. Cover with a lid and set aside while you cook the onions.

Cook the shallots
Melt the butter in a frying pan and fry 4 finely chopped shallots with a pinch of salt over a medium-low heat until soft and beginning to turn golden – about 10 minutes.

Make the carrot chutney
Add the carrot and spices to the pan with the shallots and place over a medium heat and measure in the juice of 2 unwaxed lemons and 75ml white wine vinegar. Slowly bring to a boil, then reduce the heat and simmer for 10 minutes, until the carrots are tender.

Make the filling
Add 2 finely chopped cloves of garlic, 6 roughly chopped pitted dates and 200ml water to the pan and cook until

the dates are completely soft and broken down and almost all the liquid has evaporated. You want a thick chutney consistency. This should take 10–15 minutes, and you will need to keep stirring here so it doesn't stick. Leave aside to cool. Once cool, crumble in 150g Lancashire cheese, or a vegan hard mature-style cheese, add 50g toasted and roughly chopped almonds and stir to combine.

Roll out the pastry
Unroll 1 × 320g ready-rolled puff pastry sheet on to a well-floured surface and cut it into 6 equal squares. Pile 2 heaped tablespoons of the filling in the middle of one of the squares. Bring the four corners together over the filling to form a sealed round. Repeat with the other 5 squares. Turn the cakes over and, with the pinched side on the work surface, use a rolling pin to gently flatten, then place on a lined baking tray. Repeat with the other pastry sheet.

Finish and bake the Eccles cakes
Mix the 4 tablespoons seeds with 2 tablespoons Demerara sugar. Brush the top of each Eccles cake with beaten egg or non-dairy milk. Dip the eggwashed side into the seed and sugar mixture to completely cover the top of the pastry. Transfer the seeded pastries to a baking sheet as you work. Chill in the fridge for at least 20 minutes. When you are ready to bake, heat the oven to 200°C/180°C fan, remove the cakes from the fridge and use a sharp knife to make a couple of slashes in the top of the pastry. Bake them in the oven for 25–30 minutes until deep golden and flaky.

Onions

Spring onions with bread sauce

700ml whole milk or oat milk
1 onion, peeled and halved
5 cloves
5 black peppercorns
2 bay leaves
250g stale sourdough, blitzed
   to breadcrumbs
90ml double cream or oat cream
⅛ of a nutmeg, grated
a bunch of dill (or fennel tops),
   leaves picked and finely
   chopped
12 spring onions or calçots,
   trimmed and green tops
   finely sliced
4 tablespoons extra virgin
   olive oil
½ teaspoon Dijon mustard
2 teaspoons apple cider vinegar
a little runny honey or agave
   syrup (optional)
rapeseed or sunflower oil,
   for frying
3 shallots, peeled and finely
   sliced into rounds

This is based on a fine plate of food I ate at 40 Maltby Street last year. You know a dish is good when you crave it so much you have to recreate it yourself. This has a roast dinner feeling to it. I use dill a lot in this recipe. If you are not a dill fan, use fennel or parsley instead for a more mellow herb hit. I won't hold it against you.

The bread sauce can be made up to two days ahead and kept in the fridge. Reheat and loosen with a little milk if it's too thick.

SERVES 4

Infuse the milk
Pour 700ml whole milk or oat milk into a medium saucepan. Spike 1 peeled and halved onion with 5 whole cloves and lower into the milk. Add 5 black peppercorns and 2 bay leaves and bring the milk to the boil over a high heat. Remove from the heat, cover and allow the flavours to infuse for half an hour.

Finish the bread sauce
Sieve the aromatics from the milk and put the milk back into the saucepan. Add 250g stale sourdough breadcrumbs and bring to a gentle simmer. Stir in 90ml double cream or oat cream and grate in ⅛ of a nutmeg, then season well with sea salt and pepper. Continue to cook over a low heat until the sauce has thickened. Stir in half the finely chopped leaves from a bunch of dill (or fennel tops), then remove from the heat. Keep warm if you are planning to eat it soon. If not, allow to cool before transferring to a covered bowl until you're ready to serve.

Griddle the spring onions
Heat a dry pan over the highest heat until smoking hot. Dry-fry

12 trimmed and finely sliced spring onions or calçots, not overloading the pan, for 10 minutes, turning often, until charred all over but soft inside. Add 200ml water to allow the onions to soften, and cook until it's evaporated.

Make the onion dressing
Meanwhile mix 4 tablespoons extra virgin olive oil with ½ teaspoon Dijon mustard and 2 teaspoons apple cider vinegar. Taste and add a squeeze of honey or agave if needed. Once you're happy with the balance, drizzle the dressing over the charred onions and keep warm in a low oven.

Cook the shallots
Heat 2cm of oil in a shallow frying pan. Separate 3 shallots cut into rounds into rings. When the surface of the oil looks as though it's shimmering, fry the shallot rings in batches until crisp and deep golden. Use a slotted spoon to lift them out on to a plate lined with kitchen paper.

Loosen the bread sauce and serve
If you have let it cool, reheat the bread sauce in a saucepan, loosening with a little milk if it's too thick. Spoon a couple of generous tablespoons of the sauce on to warm plates or a platter, top with a heap of the spring onions or calçots, dill or fennel tops, and thinly sliced spring onion tops and some of the crispy shallots and serve with roast or boiled, buttered potatoes.

Potato, cheese and sticky onion pie

50g butter
4 tablespoons olive oil
2 large white onions (400g), peeled and thinly sliced
1 tablespoon apple cider vinegar
850ml whole milk
½ a bunch of thyme (10g) and/or oregano
zest of 1 unwaxed lemon
2 cloves of garlic, peeled and finely sliced
1kg potatoes (waxy), peeled and cut into 2mm-thick slices
300g good strong melting cheese (e.g. Ogleshield, Coolea, Cheddar, Gruyère), grated
1 × 320g ready-rolled puff pastry sheet

This recipe came from Hugo Harrison, a brilliant chef who helped me test the recipes for this book. I ate a version at a dinner he cooked and was blown away. It's a lesson in how simple can be the best. The onions bring sweetness to the double carb pastry and potato. It's a rich pie, think dauphinoise inside a crisp pastry crust, so I want it with lemon-dressed greens or a punchy lemony salad to offset the richness.

SERVES 4–6

Caramelise the onions
Add 50g of butter and 4 tablespoons olive oil to a large heavy-based pan and set over a medium-high heat. As soon as the butter has melted and begins to sizzle, add 2 large white onions (400g), peeled and thinly sliced, and a generous pinch of salt. Stir to evenly coat the onions in the buttery-oil mixture and turn the heat down to low. Cook, stirring every now and then, for 30–40 minutes, until the onions are translucent, sweet and soft. Add 1 tablespoon apple cider vinegar and stir to combine. Scoop the onions out of the pan and set aside to cool.

Cook the potatoes
While the onions are cooking, put 850ml milk into a medium saucepan with ½ a bunch of thyme (or oregano), the zest of 1 unwaxed lemon, 2 finely sliced cloves of garlic, and a pinch of salt and warm over a low heat. Add 1kg waxy potatoes, peeled and cut into 2mm-thick slices, turn the heat up to medium and cook for 8–10 minutes, or until the potatoes are just cooked and tender when tested with a knife. Drain in a colander set over a bowl to catch all the infused milk. Set aside to cool.

Assemble the pie
Preheat the oven to 210°C/190°C fan. Layer the bottom of a 25cm pie dish with an even layer of potatoes, followed by a couple of spoonfuls of the slightly cooled milk mixture. Cover with a third of the onions, followed by 100g strong melting cheese like Ogleshield, grated. Repeat this process, finishing with a layer of potatoes on top, until all the potatoes, onions and the cheese have been used up.

Cook the pie
Cover the pie with baking paper, pressing down so that it is directly covering the potatoes, then bake on the middle shelf of the oven for 35–40 minutes, or until a knife easily passes through the potato. Remove from the oven, take the paper off and quickly but carefully top the pie with a 320g ready-rolled puff pastry sheet, trimming the edges with the back of a knife. Poke a hole in the centre to allow steam to escape and liberally brush with any remaining infused-milk mixture. Place back in the oven and continue cooking for another 40 minutes, or until the pastry has risen and is a deep golden brown.

Allow to cook slightly before serving and eat with lots of greens or lemony salad.

Sticky shallot pappardelle

8 banana shallots (600g), peeled
and finely sliced
75ml olive oil
a knob of butter (optional)
2 cloves of garlic, peeled and
finely chopped
1 small carrot, peeled and grated
4 tablespoons tomato purée
1 tablespoon sherry vinegar
a small bunch of woody herbs
(1 sprig each of thyme,
rosemary and sage)
400g pappardelle (or tagliatelle)
100g Parmesan cheese, grated,
to serve
½ a bunch of parsley (15g),
finely chopped

This pasta came from a craving for a rich pappardelle ragù, but mine obviously has to be made with veg, and I wanted it to cook quickly, as I was making it for a weeknight dinner. Here, shallots cook down to form a super-sweet and rich ragù, backed up by tomato purée, woody herbs and garlic. It's inspired by a Rachel Roddy recipe that my kids love. The sauce tastes like it's taken much more work than it has. If you are cooking for fewer than 4, the ragù will keep in the fridge for up to a week.

SERVES 4

Prep and cook the shallots
Peel, trim and finely slice 8 banana shallots. If you have one, a mandoline or a food processor with a slicing attachment can be useful here. Add to a cold pan with 75ml olive oil, a pinch of salt and a knob of butter if you are using it. Cook the shallots slowly over a medium-low heat for 20–25 minutes until they have softened but not browned.

Finish the ragù
Add 2 cloves of garlic, peeled and finely chopped, 1 small carrot, peeled and grated, and 4 tablespoons tomato purée, and cook for 5–6 minutes, until the tomato purée is beginning to look sticky and thick. Then add 1 tablespoon sherry vinegar and 200ml water. Add a small bunch of woody herbs and cook for another 10 minutes until you have a soft, caramelly ragù.

Cook and finish the pasta
Cook 400g pasta in plenty of boiling, well-salted water for a minute or so less than the packet instructions. You want it just before al dente. Drain it, reserving a mug of pasta

water, or use tongs to lift the pasta from the pasta pot into the ragù pan. Remove the woody herbs from the pan and season the ragù with salt and freshly ground black pepper. Add enough pasta cooking water to bring it together into a creamy sauce which coats each noodle. If you drained your pasta in a colander rather than using tongs you will need to add a bit more pasta water. Finish in the pan with 100g grated Parmesan. Top with ½ a bunch of finely chopped parsley.

Onions

Esme salad with grapefruit

2 ripe vine tomatoes, finely chopped
1 red onion, peeled and finely chopped
1 clove of garlic, peeled and finely chopped
2 pink grapefruits, peeled and segmented
2 red peppers, deseeded and finely chopped
½ large cucumber, finely chopped
2 tablespoons capers
zest and juice of ½ an unwaxed lemon
2 tablespoons pomegranate molasses
2 tablespoons olive oil
1 tablespoon harissa paste
½ teaspoon sumac
a pinch of chilli flakes
½ a bunch of parsley (15g), leaves picked and chopped

Esme salad is a staple of Turkish cooking. You'll find a bowl of this bright salad in most Turkish mezzes in the restaurants that line the streets of Hackney. I first tried it in one of those places, alongside falafel, Turkish feta and stewed runner beans. I think the onion is key here. It brings sweetness, a bit of savoury and some acidity to balance out the other punchy flavours which make an esme salad. Here it's best to leave the finished salad to mingle for a couple of hours before eating if you can. Mine is not as finely chopped as the ones in the ocakbaşı near my house, and capers are wildly untraditional but I like them. The grapefruit is inspired by a trip to Bubala in London; they put grapefruit in their version.

SERVES 4 AS A SIDE

Prep the salad
Put 2 finely chopped ripe vine tomatoes, 1 peeled and finely chopped red onion, 1 peeled and finely chopped clove of garlic, 2 peeled and segmented pink grapefruits, 2 deseeded and finely chopped red peppers, ½ a finely chopped large cucumber and 2 tablespoons capers in a serving bowl.

Make the dressing
In a jar or small bowl, mix or shake the zest and juice of ½ an unwaxed lemon, 2 tablespoons pomegranate molasses, 2 tablespoons olive oil, a pinch of salt and pepper and 1 tablespoon harissa paste together. Pour this over the salad ingredients, toss together, then sprinkle over ½ teaspoon sumac and a pinch of chilli flakes.

Serve the salad
The salad is best if left to sit for a couple of hours before serving. If you leave it to sit, drain off most of the liquid before adding ½ a bunch of chopped parsley and a little more olive oil. I serve it with flatbread and dips like hummus, cacik (a Turkish cucumber and garlic dip) or labneh. Any leftovers can be stored in the fridge for up to 2 days and brought to room temperature before eating.

Jaya's Utsav paneer

1 large white onion, peeled
2 tablespoons thick strained
    yoghurt
½ teaspoon ground red chilli
    powder (ideally Kashmiri
    chilli powder)
½ teaspoon ground turmeric
½ teaspoon ground black
    pepper
½ teaspoon ground kasoori
    methi (dried fenugreek
    leaves)
2 tablespoons vegetable oil
    or ghee
400g paneer, cut into cubes
1 red or green pepper (or half of
    each), deseeded and cut into
    chunks
1 red onion, peeled and cut into
    eighths, or a handful of small
    red onions, peeled
coriander leaves, to serve
garam masala, to serve
rice or chapatis, to serve

FOR THE CURRY BASE
2 tablespoons vegetable oil
    or ghee
2 green cardamom pods, split
2 bay leaves
5cm piece of cassia bark or
    cinnamon stick
½ teaspoon cumin seeds
1 green chilli, pierced and
    left whole
2cm thumb of ginger, grated
2 cloves of garlic, peeled and
    grated
½ teaspoon ground coriander
½ teaspoon ground fennel seeds
½ teaspoon ground cumin
1 × 400g tin good-quality
    chopped tomatoes
½ teaspoon ground red chilli
    powder, to taste (ideally
    Kashmiri chilli powder)

This recipe was kindly passed on to me by Jaya Chandna and her mum. It is insanely moreish and so perfectly spiced, and for days after making it I couldn't think of much else. Jaya tells me this was a recipe developed by her mum and named after Utsav café in Jaipur, where Jaya would go for lunch with her grandad.

She says, 'This was towards the end. Gone were the days of motorcycle rides to eat pakoras on Delhi streets or painting with him in his studio or hearing my mum shout at him for climbing on the wheelie bins to fix the shed roof (!); replaced by quiet walks pushing his wheelchair round the garden, sitting in the late afternoon sun discussing the antics of the other members of the care home and trips to Utsav café for paneer curry and hot rotis. Where somehow there'd always be a reason to share a pista ice-cream afterwards.'

According to Jaya, it's the onions in this recipe that really bring it to life – the juice of the onion tenderises the paneer, and the grated white onion forms the base of the curry. The small red onions add a lovely sweetness and crunch.

SERVES 4, WITH RICE OR CHAPATIS

Marinate the paneer
Grate 1 large white onion, place in a muslin cloth or sieve, and squeeze out all the juice into a bowl. Set the onion aside and mix the juice with 2 tablespoons thick strained yoghurt and ½ teaspoon ground red chilli powder, ½ teaspoon ground turmeric, ½ teaspoon ground black pepper and ½ teaspoon ground kasoori methi. Marinate 400g cubed paneer in this mixture for at least 1 hour.

Make the curry base
Heat 2 tablespoons vegetable oil or ghee in a heavy saucepan and add 2 split green cardamom pods, 2 bay leaves, 5cm cassia bark or cinnamon and ½ teaspoon cumin seeds. Watch that they don't burn. Once fragrant, add the grated squeezed onion and 1 green chilli, pierced but left whole, and fry until light brown. Add a 2cm thumb of ginger, grated, and 2 grated cloves of garlic and fry. Add ½ teaspoon ground coriander, ½ teaspoon ground fennel seeds and ½ teaspoon ground cumin and a pinch of sea salt, allow to cook briefly, then add 1 × 400g tin of good-quality chopped tomatoes. Fry well until the oil separates. Add a little more sea salt and ground red chilli powder to taste.

Char the peppers and onions
Char 1 red or green pepper, cut into chunks, and 1 red onion, peeled and cut into eighths, in a frying pan and add the curry base sauce. Cook the sauce for a few minutes so the vegetables retain their crunch. Tip the curry with the onions and peppers into a bowl and wipe out your pan to cook the paneer.

Cook the paneer
Put the pan back on the heat, add 2 tablespoons ghee or oil, then fry the marinated paneer until speckled brown all over. Add the curry to the pan.

Finish the curry
Add half a cup of water to the pan and simmer until the paneer is plump and the sauce has thickened. Sprinkle with coriander leaves and garam masala (if you want to add a kick!) and serve with rice or chapatis.

Mushroom shawarma with sumac onions

½ teaspoon smoked paprika
½ teaspoon cumin seeds, ground
½ teaspoon coriander seeds, ground
½ teaspoon whole allspice, ground
9 tablespoons extra virgin olive oil
5 cloves of garlic, left whole and unpeeled
4 white onions, peeled and quartered, plus 1 more onion peeled, halved and very thinly sliced, to serve
450g oyster mushrooms
½ teaspoon ground turmeric
250g thick natural yoghurt
1 teaspoon sumac
½ teaspoon red chilli flakes
zest and juice of 1 unwaxed lemon
½ a bunch of parsley (15g), roughly chopped
4 flatbreads, to serve

I crave this shawarma – the crunchy edges of roasted mushrooms and onions next to the moreish onion and garlic yoghurt that has an serious amount of flavour. This recipe to me feels like a real celebration of onions. They come roasted with the mushrooms, blitzed into the unreasonably delicious yoghurt and in a lemony onion salad on top.

SERVES 4

Make the spice rub
In a small bowl, mix ½ teaspoon smoked paprika, ½ teaspoon cumin seeds, ground, ½ teaspoon coriander seeds, ground, ½ teaspoon whole allspice, ground, and 4 tablespoons extra virgin olive oil with a good pinch of flaky sea salt and freshly ground black pepper to form a loose paste.

Roast the onions
Preheat the oven to 200°C/180°C fan. Crush 5 unpeeled cloves of garlic slightly with the back of a knife. Put 4 peeled and quartered white onions, all the garlic and the spiced oil into a large, low-sided baking tray and toss together until the onions and garlic are all evenly coated. Roast in the oven for 30 minutes until a little charred and softened.

Add the mushrooms
Tear 450g oyster mushrooms into rough bite-sized pieces. Remove the onions from the oven and put half into a bowl with the garlic cloves, then set aside. Add the mushrooms to the baking tray with the remaining onions and toss together so the mushrooms are coated, adding a little more oil if needed. Return to the oven for another 25 minutes until the mushrooms are crisp and golden and the onions are slightly charred and really soft.

Prepare the onion yoghurt
Meanwhile, add the cooled onions to a food processor or blender. Squeeze in the garlic flesh from its papery skins and discard the skins. Add 4 tablespoons extra virgin olive oil, ½ teaspoon ground turmeric, 250g thick natural yoghurt and a pinch of flaky sea salt. Blitz until you have a semi-smooth mixture.

Make the onion salad topping
Peel, halve and very finely slice 1 onion and add to a bowl with 1 teaspoon sumac, ½ teaspoon red chilli flakes, the zest and juice of 1 unwaxed lemon, ½ a bunch of roughly chopped parsley, 1 table-spoon extra virgin olive oil and a pinch of sea salt and freshly ground black pepper.

To serve
Warm the flatbreads and top with the yoghurt, onions and then the mushrooms and more parsley.

Miso

Sweet, gentle, caramel-coloured white shiro miso sits next to a red miso and a dark barley miso on the top shelf of my fridge. It sits undisturbed for weeks and months until needed, asking nothing. I would wager it would last years. A teaspoon of miso fills a pot with flavour like nothing else. Miso comes from a culture that is not my own, and I have much to learn about how to cook with it. But it holds a place deep in my heart. I stir it into Cheddar for cheese on toast. Beat it into creamed corn with green chilli. Mash it with toasted walnuts for a soupy udon inspired by Shuko. Bake it into scones and whip it with cream and bananas. Learning as I go.

On Miso

Miso fills a pot with flavour with very little effort. It's great in soups, stews, broths, dressing and marinades and is even good in sweet things like caramel.

Miso is such a useful ingredient in vegetarian cooking, as it brings a hit of umami that can be hard to get with veg alone. It's sweet, nutty, earthy, umami, savoury and briny. Sometimes even with notes of barley, banana or chestnut. Adding miso to a dish gives a flavour that implies whatever it is in has been cooking for hours.

Whilst there is very little miso made in the UK, what is imported generally arrives by sea. If you buy carefully, you support the artisans who make it. It's also quite easy to make yourself, see page 288. As it's fermented, it's also good for your gut. If you want to keep its beneficial properties, you can add it right at the end of cooking.

Salty, Umami, Sweet, Earthy

Types

Buying miso can be confusing, as there are so many types out there. I am no expert, but here are the three I buy the most.

- White miso
  Lighter in colour and taste, good for light broths, dressings and in baking or caramel.

- Brown rice miso
  Generally darker in colour and a little saltier, good for more punchy dressings to stand up against chilli and for tossing roast veg in for the last 5 minutes of roasting.

- Red miso
  Often made from barley; it's salty and deep in flavour, good for stews, noodle soups and gravies.

Goes well with

aubergine	ginger
avocado	honey
banana	kale
caramel	kimchi
chilli	leek
chocolate	mushroom
egg	

Favourite uses

- In a simple miso soup with spring onions and tofu
- As the base for a ramen
- In dressings
- A tablespoon added to soup for depth
- To round out vegetable stock
- In brownies or cookies
- Stirred through roasted squash or new potatoes for the last 10 minutes
- Smothered over aubergines before roasting

Storage and tips

Miso keeps well as it's already fermented. Store tightly sealed in the fridge for a year or longer. It can discolour, so a layer of greaseproof paper directly on the surface will slow the oxidisation.

If you are using your miso in a soup or a stew, be sure to add miso towards the end of cooking, as it helps retain all its goodness. I mix all of the miso needed with some cold water until I have a thick but pourable paste and then stir it into a soup or a stew once I have turned the heat off.

What to buy

All of the misos from Clearspring are consistently good. I also like Hikari Organic Miso Paste and Umasa Red Miso.

Homemade miso

200g dried pulses – soybeans,
    chickpeas, cannellini beans, etc.
40g dried rice koji
40g fine sea salt
15g white miso paste

Making your own miso is really not as complicated as it sounds and it gave me such an insight into the different kinds and flavours. If you make a white miso then you will only need to ferment it for a couple of months rather than the year or so needed for a darker, richer miso. Either way, once you have jarred it up it's completely hands off. The only special thing you need is dried rice koji. I buy mine from souschef. co.uk, but you could buy it from any Japanese food store.

MAKES 2 LARGE JARFULS

Cook the pulses
Soak 200g dried pulses in plenty of cold water, cover and leave overnight (they'll double in size). The next day, drain and rinse them a couple of times in fresh cold water. Put in a large saucepan, cover with water, add a good pinch of salt and bring to the boil. As soon as the water is boiling, reduce the heat to a simmer, skim away any white foam from the top and cook for 1–2 hours, or until the pulses are cooked through and they break when squeezed between your fingers. Drain and allow to cool completely.

Mix the miso
Put the cooked pulses, 40g dried rice koji, 40g fine sea salt and 15g white miso paste into a large clean bowl and scrunch it all together with your hands. Keep scrunching until everything is well mixed. Measure out 200ml warm water then add a little water a bit at a time, scrunching as you go, until the mixture has the consistency of a thick hummus.

Ferment
Put the miso mixture into a clean sterilised 1-litre jar and push it down with your hand to remove any air pockets. Cover with a circle of baking paper and weigh it down (so the liquid which becomes the by-product, 'soy sauce', covers the miso) with something (I use baking beans), then set aside in a cool dark place for 8–12 weeks, checking and tasting each week or two until it's fermented to your liking. The 12-week mark should produce a slightly sweeter 'white' miso, and you can continue fermenting it for anything up to a year for a dark and rich miso. Once it's fermented to your liking, you can store it in the fridge to stop it fermenting any further. It will be happy there for up to a year, probably longer.

Miso rarebit with Asian herbs

4 thick slices sourdough bread
200g mature Cheddar, grated,
    or vegan-style Cheddar
    cheese
200g crème fraîche or oat crème
    fraîche
3 unwaxed limes
4 spring onions, trimmed and
    finely sliced
1 red chilli, finely chopped
2 tablespoons red miso paste
½ a cucumber
½ a bunch of mint (15g),
    leaves picked
½ a bunch of coriander (15g),
    leaves picked

This is the rarebit/toasted cheese of my dreams. Creamy and rich, umami from miso and a fresh hit of herbs and cucumber to lift it all. We eat it for lunch, but it's filling and interesting enough to eat for any meal. I use red miso here as I like its richness against the cheese. I've tried it with white or shiro miso too, which give a sweeter, more mellow umami note.

SERVES 4

Prepare the toast
Preheat the oven to 240°C/220°C fan. Place 4 thick slices of sourdough bread on to a large, flat tray then put in the oven to toast slightly on both sides, turning halfway. This will take about 5 minutes, depending on your oven. Remove from the oven and set aside.

Make the cheese mixture
In a bowl, mix together 200g grated mature Cheddar or vegan-style Cheddar cheese, 200g crème fraîche or oat crème fraîche, the zest of 2 unwaxed limes and juice from 1, 4 finely sliced spring onions, 1 finely chopped red chilli and 2 tablespoons red miso paste. Spread the mix over the 4 pieces of toast and place back in the oven for 8–10 minutes until golden and bubbling.

For the salad
Split ½ a cucumber lengthways, scoop out the watery centre using a teaspoon and finely chop. Put the cucumber and the picked leaves from ½ a bunch of mint and ½ a bunch of coriander into a bowl with a pinch of salt, the zest of 1 unwaxed lime and the juice from 2, then toss together. Serve the bubbling rarebit next to the herb and cucumber salad.

Creamed corn and white bean mash with miso butter

4 corn on the cob
2 onions, peeled and very
    finely sliced
1 tablespoon olive oil
2 × 400g tins butter beans,
    drained
75g unsalted butter or vegan
    butter
2 teaspoons white miso paste
2 green chillies, 1 deseeded
    and very finely chopped,
    1 thinly sliced
2 unwaxed limes
a few sprigs of coriander,
    to serve
Parmesan cheese, grated, to
    serve (I use a vegetarian one),
    optional

This is my comfort food. The butter beans and half the corn come together to make a slightly sweet, velvety mash that's served with the other half of the corn, which is crisped in a pan with some of the onions to create a double-textured spoonable bowl of happiness. White miso brings everything together and adds a roundness. Think the texture of polenta with the comfort of creamed corn and you are in the right place. I serve this with a tomato salad and some flatbreads.

SERVES 4

Cut the corn from the cobs
Carefully slice the kernels off 4 corn cobs. I do this by putting the base of each cob in a mixing bowl and carefully cutting down the length of each one to remove the kernels. This stops them flying everywhere.

Cook the onions
Put 2 peeled and very finely sliced onions into a medium saucepan with 1 tablespoon olive oil and a pinch of flaky sea salt. Cook over a medium-low heat for 15–20 minutes until really soft and beginning to brown, then scoop out 2 tablespoons and put on one side.

Add the corn and beans
Add 2 × 400g tins of butter beans to the pan of onions with half the corn kernels and 50ml water. Simmer over a medium heat for 10 minutes, then blitz in a food processor or with a hand-held blender until you have a creamy mash, seasoning with salt and freshly ground black pepper as you go. Put it back into the pan and keep warm.

Make the miso corn topping
Put a frying pan over a medium heat, add 75g unsalted butter or vegan butter, 2 teaspoons white miso paste and the remaining corn and cook for 4–5 minutes so the butter browns slightly and the corn becomes slightly soft and bright yellow. Now stir in the reserved onions.

Finish
Add 1 finely chopped green chilli to the brown butter and miso pan, along with the zest and juice of 1 unwaxed lime. Scoop the creamy beans on to a platter or plates and spoon over the buttery corn topping, followed by the thinly sliced green chilli, the zest and juice of 1 unwaxed lime, plus freshly ground black pepper, a few coriander leaves and a grating of Parmesan if you like.

Shuko's celeriac with clementine and miso

a 5g piece of dried kombu kelp (to make the dashi)
1 unwaxed clementine
1 large or 2 small celeriac
50g unsalted butter, at room temperature, plus a little extra for roasting
50g white miso paste, ideally saikyo
10g mustard – Japanese powdered mustard mixed with water, or English mustard
20ml rice vinegar

Shuko's food at her restaurant Koya is some of my favourite in London. I've sat at the bar at Koya many times. Her food has healed colds and broken hearts. To me, this recipe tells the tale of Shuko and Koya's food so perfectly – it sits exactly where comfort and brightness meet.

Shuko tells me that miso soup is what she first learned to cook when she was nine years old, and so it was a starting point in her cooking journey. Shuko tells me, 'Miso, like soy sauce, is made from soya beans by mixing them with koji bacteria and fermenting them, and it is a fundamental element of Japanese cooking and meals. There are countless variations of miso, depending on region, and a wide range of methods for how you can use them. This recipe uses a particularly sweet miso called saikyo miso, which has been matured longer than normal miso, and I think it is a great combination with roasted celeriac and citrus.'

SERVES 2 AS A MAIN, 4 AS A SIDE

Make the kombu dashi
You need to start this the night before you want to eat the celeriac. Add 5g dried kombu kelp to 40ml cold water and leave it to soak overnight, then take out the kombu before using the dashi.

Make the dehydrated clementine
Preheat the oven to 50°C. Peel the zest from 1 unwaxed clementine with a sharp vegetable peeler and spread it in a single layer on a baking paper-lined baking sheet. Bake until the zest is hard but not darkened, about 30–45 minutes. Once cool, blitz it in a clean coffee grinder or blender until you have a coarse powder. Set aside.

Roast the celeriac
Turn the oven up to 160°C/180°C fan. Wash and dry 1 large or 2 small whole celeriac, then use your hands to rub with a knob of unsalted butter. Wrap it in foil and place on a roasting tray. Roast for 2 hours or until it feels soft when you squidge it.

Make the miso mustard
In a bowl combine 50g saikyo or white miso with 10g mustard, 20ml rice vinegar, 40ml of the kombu dashi and 50g unsalted butter at room temperature and whisk together well.

Dress and serve
Once the celeriac is cooked, peel away the skin with a knife, then cut the flesh into bite-size wedges and mix the pieces with the miso mustard butter, enough to dress them generously. Dust with a generous amount of ground clementine peel.

Miso maple beetroot with goat's curd

2 tablespoons maple syrup
  or runny honey
3 tablespoons white miso paste
3 teaspoons wholegrain mustard
2 unwaxed limes
4 raw beetroot, peeled and
  quartered
3 tablespoons extra virgin
  olive oil
1 sharp, crunchy apple, halved,
  cored and thinly sliced
3 sticks of celery, finely sliced,
  and some leaves if possible
200–300g goat's cheese or curd
sourdough bread, to serve
  (optional)

We so often think of miso for Japanese dishes, but miso is such a versatile flavour that I have found it works incredibly well in lots of other countries' cuisines, from satay sauces to salad dressings. Here, miso pairs with some classically British ingredients. Roasting beetroot in this maple, miso, lime and mustard dressing creates a crispy, crunchy, caramelised umami-sweet coating to the beetroot which counters the earthy character inside. Paired with a crunchy celery and apple salad and served with crumbled goat's curd or cheese, this plate has got all the textures and flavours in one place.

SERVES 4

Make the miso maple dressing
In a small bowl, mix together 2 tablespoons maple syrup or honey, 3 tablespoons white miso paste, 3 teaspoons wholegrain mustard and the zest and juice of 1 unwaxed lime.

Roast the beetroot
Preheat the oven to 220°C/200°C fan. Quarter 4 peeled raw beetroot and put them into a shallow baking tray. Pour over 2 tablespoons extra virgin olive oil and roast in the oven for 20 minutes. Remove from the oven and toss in the miso maple dressing, making sure all the beetroot pieces are evenly coated. Return to the oven for a further 20 minutes.

Make the celery and apple salad
Halve, core and thinly slice 1 sharp, crunchy apple. Put in a bowl with 3 finely sliced sticks of celery, the zest and juice of 1 unwaxed lime, 1 tablespoon of extra virgin olive oil, a pinch of flaky sea salt and some freshly ground black pepper. Add the celery leaves too, if you have some.

To serve
Serve the beetroot with 200–300g soft goat's curd, a pile of the celery and apple salad and, if you like, some toasted sourdough for scooping things up.

Walnut miso udon

100g walnuts
2 spring onions, trimmed and
    left whole
a thumb-size piece of ginger,
    peeled and grated
4 tablespoons mirin
1 teaspoon runny honey or agave
    syrup, plus 1 tablespoon
2 tablespoons soy sauce
300g dried udon noodles
2 teaspoons red miso paste
2 teaspoons white miso paste
4 handfuls of mushrooms –
    I use a mix of shimeji and
    enoki mushrooms
1 head spring greens or
    sweetheart cabbage,
    destemmed and finely
    shredded

This is my homemade version of the walnut miso udon from Koya in Soho. Their udon noodles are from the gods, just the right side of chewy. But it's the walnut miso paste that comes next to them in a little bowl that really makes it. This is a version that I made at home to quell cravings when I first had my son and it was hard to get to the restaurant. This recipe appeared in another form in my first book but it's my favourite way to eat miso, so I felt it needed a spot in this chapter. Be generous when stirring in the walnut miso; the broth is quite simple so it needs a good hit of the miso.

I sometimes add a poached egg. Most vegetables will work well in this broth – chard, asparagus, sugar snaps, spinach. Don't be tied to what I have suggested here.

SERVES 4

Toast the walnuts
Put 100g walnuts into an ovenproof frying pan and toast in the oven at 180°C/200°C fan, or in a pan over a medium heat, for 3–5 minutes, until just toasted and smelling great. If any look too dark, you can rub off their skins and discard those bits. Leave to one side to cool.

Make the broth
Now get the broth going. Put 2 whole trimmed spring onions and a thumb of peeled and grated ginger in a pan with 2 litres water and bring to the boil. Reduce the heat and simmer for 10 minutes. Turn off the heat then add 4 tablespoons mirin, 1 teaspoon honey or agave syrup and 2 table-spoons soy sauce. Taste the broth and add some sea salt if needed. Put a lid on and turn down the heat to the lowest setting to keep warm.

Cook the udon noodles
Meanwhile, bring another pan of water to the boil. Add 300g dried udon noodles and cook for 6–8 minutes (or follow the instructions on the packet). Drain and rinse under cold water.

Make the walnut miso
While the udon are cooking, bash the toasted walnuts in a pestle and mortar until they resemble very coarse breadcrumbs. Add 2 tea-spoons red and 2 teaspoons white miso paste and 1 tablespoon of honey or agave syrup and mix to a paste.

Add the vegetables to the broth
Remove the spring onions from the broth, add 4 handfuls of mushrooms and leave to cook for a couple of minutes, then add 1 head of destemmed and finely shredded spring greens or sweetheart cabbage and take off the heat.

Put everything together
Divide the noodles between 4 bowls, ladle over the broth and the vegetables and serve with little bowls of the walnut miso to generously stir in.

Miso, lime and sweet potato bake

1 × 400ml tin coconut milk
100g cherry tomatoes
1 green chilli, roughly chopped
a large thumb-sized piece of
    ginger, peeled and roughly
    chopped (about 60g)
3 cloves of garlic, peeled
2 stalks of lemongrass, roughly
    chopped
2 tablespoons white miso paste
750g sweet potatoes, sliced
    about ½cm thick
2 unwaxed limes
a small bunch of Thai or
    normal basil

This has become a favourite dinner. Everyone in our house loves sweet potatoes, and the mellow miso, ginger and coconut flavours of the gratin are universally loved too. This is a gratin with a bit of attitude. White miso brings sweetness but also umami depth here. We eat this with plain rice and some greens (usually cavolo nero) shredded and cooked in a hot pan until the edges are crisp and finished with a squeeze of lime.

SERVES 4

Make the miso, ginger and coconut sauce
Put a 400ml tin of coconut milk into a blender with 100g of cherry tomatoes, 1 roughly chopped green chilli, ⅔ (40g) of a large thumb-sized piece of peeled and roughly chopped ginger, 3 peeled cloves of garlic, 2 roughly chopped stalks of lemongrass and 2 tablespoons white miso paste. Blend on high until you have a smooth, fragrant sauce.

Prepare the sweet potatoes
Preheat the oven to 180°C/160°C fan. Slice 750g of sweet potatoes about ½cm thick; you can do this by hand or using a mandoline. Season with sea salt then layer them into a round, shallow cast-iron pan or oiled baking dish about 28cm across if round and about A4-sized if rectangular. I like to layer the sliced sweet potatoes overlapping each other in rows or circles to echo the shape of the dish I am using.

Add the sauce
Pour over the coconut miso sauce and add the remaining ⅓ (20g) of chopped ginger. Use a couple of spoons to toss the potatoes in the coconut milk to make sure everything is coated.

Bake the bake
Cover the dish with foil and bake for 40 minutes until the top is browned and the potatoes are cooked through. Take off the foil and put back into the oven for 15 minutes.

Finish the bake
Grate over the zest of 1 unwaxed lime. Toss a small bunch of Thai basil leaves in a little oil and scatter them over the top, then put the bake back into the oven for another 5 minutes. Serve with 2 limes (including the one that has been zested) cut into wedges for squeezing over.

Mushroom dumplings with crispy kale seaweed

1 stalk of lemongrass, bashed and roughly chopped

1 clove of garlic, peeled

4 spring onions, trimmed and roughly chopped

a small thumb-sized piece of ginger, peeled and roughly chopped

a bunch of coriander (30g), leaves picked and chopped, stalks separated

4 Szechuan peppercorns, toasted

1 teaspoon Chinese five-spice powder

300g shiitake mushrooms

5 tablespoons neutral oil (I used coconut oil)

3 tablespoons dark miso paste

1 teaspoon runny honey or maple syrup

1 teaspoon Chinese rice wine

50g unsalted peanuts, toasted and roughly chopped

24 × 10cm round Chinese dumpling wrappers, defrosted if frozen

juice of 1 unwaxed lime

½ a shallot, peeled and finely chopped

1 tablespoon red miso paste

1 teaspoon toasted sesame oil

¼ teaspoon dried chilli powder

FOR THE CRISPY KALE

400g curly kale, roughly shredded and tough cores removed

1 tablespoon light soft brown sugar

1 tablespoon sesame seeds

½ teaspoon ground turmeric

The food I crave most often is a dumpling. The almost gummy wrapper, steamed or fried to a crisp, a just-the-right-side-of-salty filling and a dipping sauce both sharp and sweet. When I was pregnant they were all I wanted to eat. Since they are not the kind of thing you can whip up in 20 minutes (they take a little more planning), I make them for friends. These dumplings make the most of mushrooms, with the aromatics of lemongrass, ginger and coriander. I serve them with a great dipping sauce and some kale, cooked like the crispy seaweed served in the Chinese takeaways of my childhood.

The dumplings can also be prepared in advance and kept in the fridge or freezer uncooked. Once steamed, serve immediately. If you steam them from frozen, steam for a total of 15 minutes rather than 12. If you want crispy dumplings you could fry them in a little oil in a non-stick pan on a medium heat for 2–3 minutes on each side until golden brown.

The paste makes more than you need. Freeze it to make this again, or use as a base for a fresh coconut curry.

SERVES 6 (MAKES 24 DUMPLINGS)

Make the paste
Put 1 bashed and roughly chopped stalk of lemongrass, 1 peeled clove of garlic, 4 trimmed and roughly chopped spring onions, a small thumb of peeled and roughly chopped ginger, the stalks from a 30g bunch of coriander, 4 toasted Szechuan peppercorns and 1 teaspoon Chinese five-spice powder into a food processor. Add a pinch of salt and pulse five or six times to break everything down, then blitz on a high speed for a couple of minutes, stopping the machine and scraping

down the sides every so often, until you have a deeply fragrant paste. Add 300g shiitake mushrooms and pulse until roughly chopped, being careful not to chop too much – you don't want them to make a paste.

Make the dumpling filling
Melt 2 tablespoons neutral oil in a large frying pan over a medium heat. When the oil is hot, add the mushroom paste to the pan with a pinch of salt. Fry, stirring regularly, for 7 minutes until the paste is beginning to brown and everything smells fragrant. Remove from the heat and immediately stir in 1 tablespoon dark miso paste, 1 teaspoon honey or maple syrup and 1 teaspoon Chinese rice wine. Tip into a mixing bowl and mix in 50g toasted and roughly chopped peanuts and the picked and chopped leaves from the 30g bunch of coriander.

Preheat the oven and prepare the steamer
Preheat the oven to 200°C/180°C fan. Get a large lidded frying pan ready to cook your dumplings.

Make the dumplings
Place a dumpling wrapper on a clean work surface and place a heaped teaspoon of the mushroom filling in the centre. Use your finger to wet the edge of the wrapper and bring one side over the other to make a half-moon shape. Pinch the pastry at the top of the half moon to seal, then pinch and pleat from one edge to the other to seal the top completely. Do this with the rest of the wrappers until you have 24 dumplings.

Continued over...

Cook the dumplings
Heat your large frying pan over a medium heat, add a tablespoon of coconut oil and once hot, add the dumplings flat side down and cook for 2–3 minutes. Then add 150ml water, put the lid on and cook for 5–7 minutes until all the water has evaporated. Take the lid off and cook for another 3–4 minutes until the bottoms are golden and crispy. You may need to do this in batches.

Make the crispy kale seaweed
Meanwhile, spread 400g roughly shredded curly kale, with the tough cores removed, over 2 large roasting trays. Mix 2 tablespoons neutral oil with 1 tablespoon light soft brown sugar, 1 tablespoon sesame seeds, ½ teaspoon ground turmeric and 1 tablespoon dark miso paste and pour over the kale. Scrunch everything together, then spread out again so the kale is in a single layer. Place in the oven for 5–10 minutes, opening the oven door once during this time to release the steam. Remove from the oven and toss well before returning to the oven for another 5 minutes, opening the oven door a couple of times to release the steam and help the kale to crisp up. Remove from the oven and scrape into a large serving bowl.

Make the dipping sauce and serve
Mix the juice of 1 unwaxed lime, ½ a finely chopped shallot, 1 tablespoon red miso paste, 1 teaspoon toasted sesame oil and ¼ teaspoon dried chilli powder together to make a dipping sauce. Taste and adjust the seasoning if necessary.
    Serve the dumplings immediately alongside the crispy kale seaweed and dipping sauce.

Miso banana caramel whip

2 medium ripe bananas, peeled and mashed
75g soft light brown sugar
1 tablespoon white miso paste
200ml organic double cream or whippable vegan cream
200g thick Greek yoghurt or oat yoghurt
4 ginger nuts or digestive biscuits
2 tablespoons white sesame seeds, toasted
a little dark chocolate, grated, to serve (optional)

Imagine banoffee pie but ready in 15 minutes and spooned into a glass like a sundae. I'm on the fence about bananas but I love them in this caramel. If you are into bananas, some sliced banana with a little lemon squeezed over could be a nice addition. Here, the miso adds a salty back note that offsets the richness of the banana and brown sugar caramel. I think miso and banana are one of the best sweet combinations.

SERVES 4

Make the banana caramel
Put 2 peeled and mashed ripe bananas and 75g soft light brown sugar into a small saucepan over a medium heat and cook for 5–7 minutes until the sugar has dissolved and caramelised, stirring all the time until thick and glossy. Stir in 1 tablespoon white miso paste and take off the heat. Remove from the heat and leave to cool.

Whip the cream
Use a hand-held whisk or stand mixer to whip 200ml organic double cream or whippable vegan cream a little shy of soft peaks, so you are beginning to see the trail of the whisk but before it feels 'whipped'. It's best to under-whip it slightly, as the yoghurt will make it thicker. Now gently fold in 200g thick Greek yoghurt or oat yoghurt, taking care not to mix it too much. Put to one side.

Make the sesame crunch topping
Crumble 4 ginger nuts or digestive biscuits with your hands into a bowl and add 2 tablespoons toasted white sesame seeds.

To serve
Spoon a tablespoon of the banana caramel into the bottom of four glasses, then add a layer of the pillowy cream. Repeat the layers, ending with the sesame ginger crunch topping, and finish with a little grated chocolate if you like.

Miso, date and honey scones

180ml whole or oat milk, plus extra for brushing on top
zest and juice of 1 unwaxed lemon
450g plain flour, plus extra for dusting
1 teaspoon baking powder
½ teaspoon bicarbonate of soda
1 teaspoon ground ginger
150g cold unsalted butter or vegan butter, cubed
2 tablespoons miso paste
75g soft light brown sugar
5 Medjool dates, roughly chopped
2 tablespoons Demerara sugar
salted butter, runny honey, crème fraîche and some seasonal fruit, to serve

These scones are light and soft, buttery and sweet and sort of treacly all at once. The flavour comes from the combination of miso, ginger and dates. Adding the miso here gives them an underlying sweet and salty depth, which I am sure is why they are so moreish. Once the dough is made, I use a stacking method to build up layers in the scones, which makes them super-short and buttery.

MAKES 8 SCONES

Make the buttermilk
In a jug, mix together 180ml whole or oat milk and the zest and juice of 1 unwaxed lemon and set aside to thicken up.

Mix the dry ingredients
In a large mixing bowl, combine 450g plain flour, 1 teaspoon baking powder, ½ teaspoon bicarbonate of soda and 1 teaspoon ground ginger.

Mix the butter into the flour
Add 150g cold unsalted butter or vegan butter in cubes to the dry ingredients, along with 2 tablespoons miso, then, with your fingertips, gently rub them into the flour until you have a sandy breadcrumb-y texture, leaving some larger petals of butter as this will make the scones more flaky. Stir in 75g soft light brown sugar.

Add the dates and the buttermilk
Add 5 roughly chopped Medjool dates to the scone mix, working quickly so the butter stays cold. Make a well in the centre and pour in the thickened buttermilk, roughly mixing it together with a fork so as not to overwork it.

Bring the dough together
Tip the rough mixture on to a lightly floured surface, then, without kneading too much, bring it together to form a dough and shape it into a rectangle, neatening the sides with your hands.

Stack the dough to create layers
Cut the dough into three equal pieces, then stack these on top of each other. Press down on the top with a rolling pin or your hands, then roll or press out into a 3cm-thick rectangle about 16cm × 16cm.

Cut the scones
Cut the dough into 4cm squares using a knife and put on to a baking tray lined with baking paper. Brush the top of each one with a little extra milk or oat milk and sprinkle with 2 tablespoons Demerara sugar. Chill in the fridge for 30 minutes or the freezer for 15 minutes to firm up. At this point you can keep them in the freezer to bake in smaller batches from frozen.

Preheat the oven and bake the scones
Preheat the oven to 200°C/180°C fan. Bake the scones for 20–25 minutes until crispy and golden. Bake for another 5–7 minutes if frozen.

To serve
I've served the scones with butter, honey, crème fraîche and some fresh cherries, but you could serve them just with honey and butter, or clotted cream and jam if you wanted to keep it more traditional.

Peanuts

It started when I was four with peanut butter and jam sandwiches, eaten from a Strawberry Shortcake lunchbox. Always requested then and still eaten now. Rich, buttery, creamy and crunchy. I buy it in huge tubs, but when I make it myself it's the best. I roast the peanuts to the point just before they go too dark, a risk worth taking for the deeply golden butter. Swirled with soy, ginger, chilli sauce and rice vinegar, it makes a sauce we eat with rice and greens so often. It's folded into cookies. Spooned into smoothies. It adds a backbone of deep, creamy flavour to so many meals we eat. And the PB&Js remain.

On Peanuts

Peanut butter is something I crave. It was part of my childhood, eaten on toast or rice cakes for a snack. The hollows of crisp lengths of celery filled with smooth peanut butter and topped with a few raisins – ants on a log. I make the same things now for my own children. The sweet but not sugary flavour of peanut butter is so pleasing to a small person's palate.

Now, though, I use it most in cooking. From a quick cheat's satay sauce to cookies and cakes. Good in soups and stews, it adds a very good creaminess to tomato soup, for example, as well as a richness to a variety of soups and stews. It's especially good whenever I've used a can of coconut milk.

While peanuts are always imported to the UK, most peanut butter comes by sea. There has been a lot of discussion regarding the sustainability of nuts due to the water needed for them to grow, but peanut butter has a relatively low carbon count thanks to how peanuts help to rebuild soil. The shells and peanut plants can be used for energy generation and to feed animals, so if you buy from the right place there is little waste.

To me, making your own peanut butter (see page 314) is worth it. You can control the roast (I like mine deeply roasted), the level of salt and how crunchy or smooth it is.

Nutty, Fatty, Sweet, Salty

Flavour notes

Peanuts have a nutty, vegetal flavour, to state the obvious. They get a warmer sweetness when they're roasted.

Peanut butter has a nutty, salty and earthy flavour, with a fatty richness.

Goes well with

apple	coriander
banana	crunchy veg
berries (jam)	cucumber
broccoli	lemon
carrot	lime
celery	potato
chilli	soy
chocolate	tomato
coconut	vanilla

Favourite uses

- Stuffed into dates and dipped in chocolate
- Spooned from the jar
- Ants on a log
- Quick cheat's satay – with soy, rice vinegar, chilli sauce, ginger
- Smoothies – date, banana, coffee, vanilla
- In tomato soup
- Added to a coconut-based curry
- Dressing for salad
- In a quick salsa macha
- With banana pancakes
- Spooned next to fruit and yoghurt
- Swirled through brownies
- On top of roast sweet potato with lime and coriander

Storage

- Peanut butter
  Store out of sunlight and stir before each use to make sure the oil is mixed with the butter. Keeps for months.

- Whole peanuts
  Store in a cool, dark and dry cupboard in a sealed container; buy in small packets as the oil in the nuts can go off. Like all nuts, only keep for a few months.

Favourite brands and where to buy

Buy the best peanut butter your budget allows; try to steer clear of those containing palm oil, additives and sugars. I buy mine in huge tubs or from refill stores. I buy organic peanut butter from Whole Earth and Clearspring. I am also a fan of ManiLife Deep Roast and Pip & Nut. Koeze from Virginia, USA, is also very good. Asian supermarkets or wholefood stores are a good place to look for whole unsalted peanuts for cooking and to make your own peanut butter with.

Easy homemade peanut butter

500g blanched unsalted peanuts
groundnut oil, to loosen

Coating noodles, bolstering a salad or keeping an apple company for an afternoon snack, peanut butter has to be one of my most reached-for ingredients when cooking. It's a perfect example of a couple of things becoming more than the sum of their parts, and this homemade version couldn't be easier. Whether you like it chunky or smooth, you can whip up a batch that's exactly how you like it. This recipe also works with almonds, hazelnuts, macadamia nuts and brazil nuts. You might need to add a little more groundnut oil to loosen, as the amount of oil in the nuts will vary.

MAKES 2 MEDIUM JARS

Roast the peanuts
Preheat the oven to 200°C/180°C fan and put 500g blanched unsalted peanuts on to two baking trays so they are in one layer. Roast in the oven for 10 minutes, or until the nuts are golden brown and smelling fragrant. Set aside to cool.

Blitz and add the oil
Add the roasted and cooled peanuts to a food processor with a generous pinch of sea salt. Blitz for 3–4 minutes or until all the oil has been released from the nuts and the mixture has turned into a butter. If you're after a chunkier nut butter, then stop blending sooner. In this case, not all the oil from the nuts may have been released, so to get a spreadable consistency add a little groundnut oil and pulse until mixed well.

Store the peanut butter
Transfer the peanut butter to 2 sterilised jars and store in a cupboard for up to a month.

Aubergine, peanut and tamarind curry

2 medium aubergines, cut into
   3cm pieces
2 tablespoons coconut oil
   or ghee
1 tablespoon black mustard seeds
1 tablespoon cumin seeds
1 tablespoon fennel seeds
1 tablespoon garam masala
1 teaspoon ground turmeric
½ a bunch of coriander (15g),
   including stalks
a bunch of spring onions
   (about 6)
4 cloves of garlic, peeled
a thumb-sized piece of ginger,
   peeled and roughly chopped
1 × 400ml tin coconut milk
4 tablespoons crunchy peanut
   butter
2 tablespoons tamarind paste
4 vine tomatoes, roughly
   chopped, or 1 × 400g tin
   chopped tomatoes
200g paneer or firm tofu,
   cut into 2cm pieces
basmati rice, to serve
parathas, roti or chapati,
   to serve
pickled onions and raita,
   to serve (see introduction)

This curry is unreasonably good. The peanut butter mixed with coconut milk and tamarind makes an easy sauce in the tray which is so so moreish. As it's all cooked in the oven it's hands off and pretty quick. I love how the butteriness of aubergine stands up well to lots of spice. You could use squash or sweet potato in place of the aubergines in winter (you will just need to cook them for 10–15 minutes longer initially). Vegans can use firm tofu instead of the paneer; you can cook it in exactly the same way.

I make some quick pickled red onions to go on top. Finely slice a red onion, then scrunch the slices with a pinch of salt and the juice of ½ an unwaxed lime (or lemon). They will keep in a sterilised jar in the fridge for 10 days or so. I also make a quick raita by mixing roughly chopped cucumber with yoghurt, lime juice, chopped coriander and a good pinch of salt.

SERVES 4–6

Roast the aubergines
Preheat the oven to 220°C/200°C fan. Cut 2 medium aubergines into 3cm pieces and put into a large baking tray with a couple of tablespoons of coconut oil or ghee, 1 tablespoon black mustard seeds and a good pinch of sea salt. Put into the oven for a few minutes to melt the coconut oil, then remove, toss the aubergines until all the pieces are coated, and roast for another 20 minutes until golden.

Toast the spices
Meanwhile, toast 1 tablespoon cumin seeds and 1 tablespoon fennel seeds in a dry pan over a medium heat until they smell fragrant.

Make the paste
Put the toasted spices into a food processor with 1 tablespoon garam

masala, 1 teaspoon ground turmeric and the stalks from ½ a bunch of coriander. Trim the very bottoms of a bunch of spring onions and discard, then add them whole to the processor. Finally, add 4 peeled cloves of garlic and a peeled and roughly chopped thumb of ginger and pulse to a paste. Add 400ml coconut milk and blitz again before stirring in 4 tablespoons crunchy peanut butter and 2 tablespoons tamarind paste. Taste and season with salt if needed.

Add the tomatoes and paste to the baking tray
Once the aubergines have had their 20 minutes' cooking, add 4 roughly chopped vine tomatoes or a 400g tin of chopped tomatoes, and 200g paneer or firm tofu, cut into 2cm pieces, to the tray and pour over the peanut and coconut mixture. Toss to make sure everything is coated in the sauce, then carefully (it will still be hot) cover the tray with foil and put back into the oven for 15 minutes.

Remove the foil
After 15 minutes, remove the foil and put the tray back in the oven for 15 minutes.

Prepare the rice, flatbreads and toppings
Now is the time to cook your rice and warm your bread. If you are making the pickled onions and raita, get on with those too (see introduction).

Finish the curry
Once the curry has had its time, serve it next to the rice and breads with the onions and raita and any chutneys or pickles you like.

Spring onion pancake with peanut sauce

250g gram flour

2 tablespoons olive oil, plus
    extra for frying

1 shallot or small red onion,
    peeled and thinly sliced

zest and juice of 1 unwaxed lime

½ a small red cabbage (300g),
    finely shredded

1 large carrot, peeled and
    coarsely grated

a bunch of coriander (30g),
    chopped

2 tablespoons toasted sesame
    seeds, plus extra to finish

4 tablespoons soy sauce or
    tamari

4 tablespoons rice wine vinegar

2 tablespoons maple syrup

2 × 20g pieces of ginger, peeled

125g peanut butter

3 tablespoons sriracha

a bunch of spring onions,
    trimmed and finely sliced

350g tofu

This has got a California vibe to it, the kind of thing which feels bright and fresh but filling and satisfying all at once. I crave this kind of food and I miss the California cafés it transports me back to. The crossover of cultures here also reminds me of Californian cooking – a little bit Italian farinata and a little bit spring onion pancake with some Indonesian influence from the peanut sauce. It is similar to something I used to order at a now closed but much-loved café in Hackney called Palm Greens. It was always a good place to eat and people watch.

SERVES 4

Make the pancake batter
Put 250g gram flour into a bowl with up to 450ml cold water, and mix until you have a thick crêpe batter; gram flour will differ in how much water it will absorb. Whisk in 2 tablespoons olive oil and a generous pinch of sea salt. Leave to sit for at least 30 minutes but ideally for an hour.

Make the slaw
Finely slice 1 peeled shallot or small red onion, mix it with the zest and juice of 1 unwaxed lime in a small bowl and leave to sit. Put 300g finely shredded red cabbage into a large mixing bowl with 1 large peeled and coarsely grated carrot, ½ a bunch of chopped coriander and 2 tablespoons toasted sesame seeds.

Dress the slaw
Mix 2 tablespoons soy sauce or tamari with 2 tablespoons rice wine vinegar and 2 tablespoons maple syrup, then grate in 20g peeled ginger. Pour over the slaw and leave to sit.

Make the peanut sauce
Mix 125g peanut butter with 2 table-spoons soy sauce, 2 tablespoons rice

wine vinegar and 3 tablespoons sriracha, then grate a 20g piece of peeled ginger. Loosen with a little water until the mixture has a drizzling consistency.

Cook the pancakes
Once the batter has rested, add a bunch of finely sliced spring onions, reserving a few for serving. There should be enough batter to make 4 large pancakes. Heat a little oil in a frying pan over a medium heat, add a ladleful of the batter and angle the pan so the batter covers the base. Cook for 2–3 minutes until golden brown, then carefully flip on to the other side and cook for another 2–3 minutes until golden. Remove to a plate and keep warm in a low oven while you cook the other 3 pancakes in the same way. You might need to add a little more oil between each one.

Cook the tofu
Once all the pancakes are cooked, add a little oil to the same pan, put on a medium-high heat and roughly crumble 350g tofu into the pan in chunks. Cook until golden brown all over, then turn the heat down to low, add 2 tablespoons of the peanut sauce, toss for a minute to coat, then take off the heat.

Finish the slaw
Add the limey shallots/onions to the slaw and mix.

Put everything together
Serve the pancakes with the slaw and tofu piled on top, with ½ a bunch of coriander, the last of the spring onions and sesame seeds and some of the peanut sauce.

Peanut and charred tomato broth

400g cherry or small vine
    tomatoes
1 green chilli
2 cloves of garlic, unpeeled
    and bashed
1 tablespoon white miso paste
a thumb-sized piece of ginger,
    peeled and grated
250g soba or egg noodles
1 tablespoon toasted sesame oil
4 tablespoons crunchy peanut
    butter
2 unwaxed limes
½ a bunch of coriander, mint or
    basil (15g), leaves picked, or 5g
    of each
50g roasted peanuts, roughly
    chopped (optional)

We made this one day when I was feeling less than 100 per cent, and it brought me back to life. I love it when food can do that. It can be everything you need in a bowl. This hit all the flavours I needed that day: lots of ginger, garlic, chilli and lime to liven me up, charred smoky flavour from the tomatoes which adds instant depth, and peanut butter to round it all out with some creaminess. All those flavours sit on top of a simple base of soba noodles.

SERVES 4

Char the tomatoes
Start by putting 400g cherry tomatoes and 1 whole green chilli into a large heavy-based saucepan (that you will later cook the broth in) on a high heat. Char the tomatoes and chilli all over, turning often with tongs for about 5 minutes. Add 2 cloves of unpeeled and bashed garlic for the last minute or so, taking care that the garlic doesn't burn.

Make the broth
Add 1 litre of freshly boiled water to the tomatoes and chilli along with 1 tablespoon white miso paste and a thumb-sized piece of ginger, peeled and grated. Use the back of a spoon to break up the tomatoes a little, then bring to a boil and simmer for 30 minutes.

Cook the noodles
Meanwhile, boil 250g soba or egg noodles according to the packet instructions, then run under cold water for a minute to remove any starchiness. Toss in 1 tablespoon toasted sesame oil and divide between 4 bowls.

Finish the broth
Season the tomato broth with salt and pepper, then, once you're happy with the flavour, remove from the heat and fish out the garlic cloves and the chilli. Stir in 4 tablespoons crunchy peanut butter and the zest and juice of 1 unwaxed lime.

Serve the broth
Ladle the tomato peanut broth over the noodles and serve with more lime zest and juice and the leaves from ½ a bunch of herbs. Top with 50g roasted peanuts, roughly chopped, if you like.

Sweet lime and peanut slaw

1 large or 2 small red cabbages (850g)
5 tablespoons olive oil
3 unwaxed limes
2 tablespoons runny honey
2 tablespoons soy sauce
a small thumb-sized piece of ginger, grated
1 red chilli, roughly chopped
2 tablespoons smooth peanut butter
1 kohlrabi, leaves trimmed off then peeled and cut into chunky matchsticks
1 pear, cut into chunky matchsticks
100g unsalted roasted peanuts
½ a bunch of coriander (15g), leaves picked and roughly chopped

Cabbage pairs so well with peanuts. The creamy fattiness of peanut butter is a contrast to the fresh, watery crunch of the cabbage. I've added lime, coriander and ginger too, some of peanut's soulmates. In the winter I make this a deeper-flavoured warm salad by charring the cabbage. In the summer I skip the charring part and keep it more crunchy.

SERVES 4–6

Char the cabbage (optional)
Remove any wilted outer leaves and chop 1 large or 2 small red cabbages into quarters if small and eighths if large. Season them with some salt and 2 tablespoons of olive oil. Heat a pan or a griddle pan over a high heat, and once it's smoking hot add the cabbage and cook for about 8 minutes on each side until charred and crisp.

Make the dressing
Mix the zest of 1 unwaxed lime and the juice of 3 with 2 tablespoons honey or sugar and 2 tablespoons soy sauce. Grate in a small thumb of ginger, roughly chop 1 red chilli and add it too. Pour a quarter of the dressing into a small bowl and set aside, then mix 2 tablespoons smooth peanut butter into the remaining three-quarters of dressing until creamy.

Chop the fresh vegetables
Trim the leaves off 1 kohlrabi, if it has them, and peel away the tough outer green or purple skin. Cut this and 1 pear into chunky matchsticks. Roughly chop 100g roasted peanuts and the leaves from ½ a bunch of fresh coriander.

Dress the cabbage
Chop the cabbage wedges into smaller pieces. While still warm (if you charred it), pour over the peanut dressing. Pour the remaining soy and honey dressing over the kohlrabi and pear.

Put everything together
Put the cabbage on to a big platter and top with the pear and kohlrabi, then the chopped peanuts and coriander.

Hetty's ginger-peanut warm kale salad

4 heaped tablespoons smooth
  peanut butter
2 tablespoons tahini
2 teaspoons toasted sesame oil
2.5cm piece of ginger, peeled
  and grated
2 cloves of garlic, peeled
  and grated
3 teaspoons tamari or soy sauce
2 tablespoons rice wine vinegar
1 tablespoon runny honey or
  maple syrup
2 bunches of kale (320g), stalks
  removed and leaves roughly
  torn
200g (1 cup) quinoa, rinsed
500ml (2 cups) vegetable stock
  or water
300g extra-firm tofu
extra virgin olive oil
1 red onion, peeled and thinly
  sliced
1 cup unsalted peanuts, roasted
  and roughly chopped
a handful of coriander leaves

Since I discovered this recipe from my friend and cook Hetty McKinnon, it's been one of the meals I have craved most. With this recipe, Hetty manages to tread that elusive line between something tasting so delicious that you can't stop eating it and making you feel so good after eating that you crave it all the time. Hetty says herself, 'This salad comes with a warning: eat at your own risk, as it is very addictive. The combination of kale, tofu and ginger-accented peanut sauce is unexpectedly irresistible.' Hetty wrote this recipe for all the peanut butter obsessives who, like her, are often caught surreptitiously sneaking spoonfuls straight from the jar.

SERVES 4–6

Make the ginger-peanut sauce
Place a medium saucepan on a low heat and add 4 heaped tablespoons smooth peanut butter, 2 tablespoons tahini, 2 teaspoons toasted sesame oil, a 2.5cm piece of ginger, peeled and grated, 2 peeled and grated cloves of garlic, 3 teaspoons tamari or soy sauce, 2 tablespoons rice wine vinegar and 1 tablespoon honey or maple syrup, along with 1 cup water. Cook until the peanut butter and tahini have melted, stirring until the sauce is smooth and creamy. If the sauce 'freezes' or is too thick, add more water, a tablespoon at a time, until it's smooth and the consistency of thickened cream. Taste and season with sea salt and black pepper.

Fold the kale into the sauce
Fold 320g de-stalked and roughly torn kale leaves into the hot peanut sauce. The heat from the sauce will wilt and cook the kale. Set this aside.

Cook the quinoa
Put 200g rinsed quinoa and 500ml vegetable stock or water (if using water, season it with 1 teaspoon of sea salt) into a large pot. Bring to a boil, then reduce the heat, cover and cook for 15–18 minutes, until all the liquid has been absorbed and the quinoa is translucent and you can see the twirly grain. Turn off the heat and set aside, uncovered, while you prepare the rest of the salad.

Fry the tofu
Put 300g extra-firm tofu on a chopping board and season well with sea salt and black pepper. Heat a large non-stick frying pan on medium–high, and when it's hot, drizzle with 1–2 tablespoons olive oil. Working in batches, place the tofu in the pan and fry for 2–3 minutes on each side until lightly golden. When all the tofu is cooked, allow it to cool, then slice it into 5mm-thick strips.

Cook the onion
Rinse and dry the tofu pan and place it back on a medium heat. Drizzle more olive oil into the frying pan, add 1 peeled and thinly sliced red onion and cook for 12–15 minutes, stirring occasionally, until it is softened and sweet.

Finish the salad
Combine the peanut-kale mixture with the quinoa, tofu and onion. Transfer to a large serving plate and top with 1 cup roasted and chopped peanuts and a handful of coriander leaves.

Peanut butter Rice Krispie bars

110g runny honey
175g smooth or crunchy peanut
butter
100g Rice Krispies (I use the
brown rice ones)
50g unsalted roasted peanuts,
chopped
200g dark chocolate
a pinch of flaky sea salt

These started as a craving for a peanut Tracker bar, if you are in the age range to get that reference. They ended up some way from their original inspiration, as I wanted to keep them full of things which are somewhat good for you. These are a grown-up version of Rice Krispie treats mixed with the flavours of a Snickers.

MAKES 12 BARS

Prepare your tin
Depending on how thick you want your bars, line a rectangular or square tin with baking paper (20 × 20cm square, making thick bars, or 20 × 30cm rectangular brownie tin, making medium-thick bars).

Combine the ingredients
In a small pan, warm 110g runny honey and 175g peanut butter on a medium heat for a minute until runny, then pour into a large bowl with 100g Rice Krispies and 50g unsalted roasted chopped peanuts. Mix well until everything is evenly coated.

Pour into the tin
Pour into your chosen lined tin and press down heavily with the back of a spoon, or even the bottom of a glass, so the mix is evenly compressed into the tin. This will ensure a neat slice once set.

Melt the chocolate
Put 200g dark chocolate in a heat-proof bowl set over a pan of barely simmering water, making sure the base of the bowl does not touch the water. Stir occasionally and take off the heat just before it melts – the chocolate will finish melting in the residual heat.

Add the chocolate
Pour the chocolate over the Rice Krispies in the tin and spread into an even layer. Place in the fridge to set for 30–60 minutes.

Peanut butter chocolate-chip cookies

200g plain flour
1 teaspoon bicarbonate of soda
100g rolled oats
250g unsalted butter or vegan
    butter, softened
200g soft light brown sugar
100g caster sugar
125g crunchy peanut butter, well
    mixed
1 teaspoon pure vanilla extract
3 organic or free-range egg yolks
250g dark milk chocolate
    chips or your favourite bar,
    broken up

To me these are the perfect cookies. They have a chewiness from the brown sugar, texture from the oats, melting pools of chocolate, and crunch and saltiness from the peanut butter. Crisp-edged with the perfect chewy bite, these are a mixture of two of my all-time cookies – the Nora Ephron sandwich cookies from *The Dahlia Bakery Cookbook* and Violet Bakery egg-yolk cookies.

MAKES LARGE 18 COOKIES

Get yourself a baking tray
Line a baking tray with baking paper. It should be one that will fit into your fridge or freezer.

Mix the dry ingredients
In a bowl whisk together 200g plain flour and 1 teaspoon bicarbonate of soda. Stir in 100g rolled oats and ½ teaspoon sea salt and put to one side.

Mix the butter and sugar
In the bowl of a stand mixer fitted with the paddle attachment, or with a hand-held mixer, beat 250g softened unsalted butter or vegan butter with 200g soft light brown sugar, 100g caster sugar and 125g crunchy peanut butter until combined but not fluffy and creamy. Too much air will make the cookies cakey, not chewy. Add 1 teaspoon pure vanilla extract and 3 egg yolks and mix in until just combined.

Finish the cookie dough
Add the dry mixture to the butter and sugar mixture and mix until it just comes together to form a dough (don't overmix), then stir in 250g dark milk chocolate chips or 250g of your favourite chocolate, broken up.

Scoop out the cookies
Use a tablespoon or an ice-cream scoop to scoop out 18 even portions of dough, rolling each one into a rough ball and putting them on the lined tray. Put into your freezer for 2 hours if you have time. If not, it's not a disaster; they will just be a bit flatter.

Preheat the oven and bake the cookies
When you are ready to bake, preheat the oven to 180°C/160°C fan. Line a large baking tray or tin with baking paper and put however many cookies you'd like to bake on the tray, leaving enough space between them for them to double in size.

Bake for 7 minutes, then take the tray out and bang it gently on the work surface to remove any pockets of air (this helps make them chewy). Cook for a further 7 minutes until the centre of each cookie is still slightly soft but the edges are crispy and nicely golden. Remove from the oven and allow to cool on the tray for 10 minutes before serving.

Storing and freezing
The baked cookies will keep in an airtight container for up to 5 days. The cookie dough balls can stay happily in the freezer for up to 3 months and you can bake them as you need them. To store in the freezer, once the dough balls are frozen remove from the tray and put into a sandwich bag. If you are baking from frozen, allow the cookies 5–10 minutes out of the freezer before placing in the oven.

Cherry and chocolate peanut butter sundae

400g fresh or frozen cherries
3 tablespoons maple syrup
2 tablespoons smooth peanut
    butter
1 tablespoon cocoa powder
a big pinch of flaky sea salt
8 scoops vanilla ice cream or
    frozen yoghurt, about
      1 × 400ml tub (vegan if
      needed)

There is something about a sundae. They take me back to diners as a kid, waitresses with name badges, fried things on checked paper in red plastic baskets. They feel fun. This is the quickest pudding – the peanut and chocolate sauce is so easy and requires no skill. Peanut butter, chocolate and cherry together is a favourite. Serve the sundaes in tall frosted (pop them in the freezer for 10 minutes) glasses with long sundae spoons for digging right to the bottom of the glass. Any unused chocolate sauce keeps well in the fridge and can be reheated at a moment's notice (or eaten cold by the spoonful).

SERVES 4

Prepare and cook the cherries
If you have 400g fresh cherries, congratulate yourself, then stone and halve them and set aside. If you are using frozen cherries, put them into a small saucepan with 1 tablespoon maple syrup and cook on a medium-low heat until they are warm and soft, still with a little liquid. Remember the liquid will thicken as they cool.

Make the peanut and chocolate sauce
In a bowl, whisk together 2 table-spoons smooth peanut butter with 2 tablespoons maple syrup (or 3 tablespoons if using fresh cherries), 1 tablespoon cocoa powder and a big pinch of flaky sea salt. You might need to add a little water here if your peanut butter is thick.

Make the sundaes
Get yourself 4 glasses or bowls, scoop some cherries into the bottom of each glass, then add a scoop of ice cream, the peanut chocolate sauce, more cherries, another scoop of ice cream and the rest of the cherries and chocolate sauce.

Dylan's chocolate oat bars

2 tablespoons coconut oil
¼ cup (70ml) maple syrup
1 cup (250g) well-stirred peanut
    butter (I like crunchy)
2 cups (180g) porridge oats
    (gluten-free if needed)
½ cup shelled/hulled hemp
    seeds or sunflower seeds
⅓ cup (60ml) oat or other plant-
    based milk
150g dark chocolate, broken into
    pieces

This is a super-simple recipe that gets made once a week in our house. It stops us buying so many after-school snacks but also means we have something sweet on hand during the day. I make batches for people who are feeling ill or need some quick nourishment, like new parents. The peanut butter is the linchpin that these bars are built around; it brings richness to what is a drastically simple recipe. I do feel it's worth saying that while the peanut version is the best, most schools are nut-free, so it's useful to know these also work well with sunflower seed butter. I have kept the measurements in cups as well as grams here, as I find cups an easy way to measure these forgiving bars.

MAKES 24 MEDIUM BARS

Melt the oil and mix the dry ingredients
Put 2 tablespoons coconut oil into a small saucepan over a low heat and allow it to melt. Once melted stir in ¼ cup (70ml) maple syrup and 1 cup (250g) peanut butter. Put 2 cups (180g) porridge oats and ½ cup shelled hemp seeds into a mixing bowl.

Mix and make the oat base
Pour the peanut butter mixture over the oats and seeds and mix well until everything is coated. You will have a rough sandy texture which will set in the fridge as the coconut oil cools. Line a 23cm square loose-bottomed baking tin with baking paper, press the mixture into the tin and use the back of a spoon to flatten it out.

Make the chocolate topping
Put ⅓ cup (60ml) oat milk and 150g dark chocolate into a small saucepan and warm over a very low heat to melt the chocolate. Once the chocolate looks melted, gently stir the milk and chocolate together until you have a thick melted topping. Pour on top of the oats and spread out with the back of a spoon.

Chill and store
Put the tin into the fridge to firm up for at least 30 minutes, then cut into pieces. I go for medium bars, but you could do small bite-sized squares if you like. The bars store well in the fridge in a covered container for up to 10 days.

	Dill *soft*	Coriander *soft*	Parsley *soft*
Flavour profile	Almost sweet, licorice-like flavour and feathery texture	Gingery Peppery Lemony Floral	Green Fresh Vibrant
Info	In German folklore, brides put dill and salt in their shoes for luck.	The classic love it or hate it herb. A staple in Latin American and Asian cuisines.	One of the most versatile fresh herbs. I prefer the flat leaf to the curly one.
Goes with	Anything creamy/sour Broad bean Butter Carrot Cucumber Egg Mushroom Pickles Potato	Avocado Chilli Coconut Cumin Garlic Lemon Lime Mint Peanut Peppers Potato Tomato	Caper Carrot Cheese Egg Garlic Lemon Mushroom Potato
Favourite uses	I prefer dill raw to cooked. I like to use it bravely in salads, pickles and stews.	There is a huge amount of flavour in the stems, so use them in the base of a curry or soup.	Salsa verde is one my all-time favourites; tabbouleh and gremolata are also classics.
Swap with	Feathery fennel fronds.	Not the same but often can be swapped with basil, parsley or mint, depending on the recipe.	Chervil for the same mildness, celery leaves for savouriness or lovage for texture and a close(ish) flavour.

Mint	Basil	Tarragon	Oregano
soft	*soft*	*soft*	*medium*
The cleanest flavour of all the herbs	Gently spiced Peppery	Warming licorice	Slightly bitter Aromatic Medicinal
There are so many beautiful varieties, but mainly they fall into peppermint and spearmint (garden mint). Peppermint has a much higher menthol content, making it brilliant for teas and desserts.	Known as the king of herbs, there are over 150 varieties of basil – from Thai to lemon, and each has a slightly different flavour and leaf shape.	Used widely, from France to Syria, Iran to Armenia.	All marjorams are oreganos, but not all oreganos are marjorams.
Chocolate Coriander Cucumber Feta Garlic Lime Parsley Pea Pineapple Potato Strawberry Tomato Yoghurt	Coconut Egg Garlic Goat's cheese Lemon Lime Mint Mozzarella Nuts Olive Oil Peach Strawberry Tomato	Artichoke Beetroot Capers Cornichons Cream Egg Goat's cheese Mustard Pear Potato Raspberry	Aubergine Courgette Garlic Honey Lemon Mushroom Orange Peppers Potato Tomato
Make a peppermint tea with any wilting leaves.	I tear rather than chop basil to stop the edges blackening.	An unusual pairing is with sweet fruits: try raspberries, strawberries, peaches.	Too strong to eat raw, use it in the base of a cooked dish or sauce, or fry in olive oil until crisp to top.
Basil is often a good swap in dishes that use fresh mint; thyme can be a good swap for dishes that use it cooked.	Marjoram Mint (good with tomatoes) Oregano	Chervil Tarragon Dill	Thyme Marjoram Basil

	Marjoram *medium*	**Rosemary** *hardy*	**Thyme** *hardy*
Flavour profile	Flowery Sweet Medicinal	Slightly bitter Strong Taste of nutmeg	Earthy Slightly woodsy Flowery Trace of lavender
Info	All marjorams are oreganos, but not all oreganos are marjorams.	Traditionally thrown into graves for remembrance.	A bouquet garni is a bundle of herbs that is added to casseroles and soups. Traditionally parsley, a few sprigs of thyme and a bay leaf.
Goes with	Chickpea Chilli Egg Garlic Lemon Mozzarella Orange Pasta Tomato (especially sauces)	Chocolate Olive Onion Orange Parsnip Potato Plum Squash Tomato	Carrot Cheese Cinnamon Cream Garlic Leek Mushroom Squash Strawberry Sweet potato Tomato
Favourite uses	Always add at the end, as it loses flavour in heat.	Remove whole stems before serving/eating.	Za'atar is the Middle Eastern name for thyme, and also the name given to a seasoning blend containing wild thyme, salt, sumac and sesame.
Swap with	Thyme Oregano Basil	Thyme Sage	Rosemary

Sage	Bay	Lime leaves	Curry leaves
hardy	*hardy*	*hardy*	*hardy*
Earthy	Balsamic aroma	Bright, sherbety	Hard to place, grounding,
Eucalyptus	Mellow eucalyptus flavour	lemon/lime citrus tang	earthy, rounded flavour
Lemon		with aromatic almost	but with an enlivening
		floral freshness	backnote
Good with sweet-savoury foods like squash.	Before vanilla was ubiquitous, bay was used to flavour custards and puddings.	Lime leaves, also known as Makrut lime leaves, are the leaves from a bobbly green citus plant called *Citrus hystrix*.	Curry leaves bear no relation to curry powder. They are the leaves of the curry leaf tree. They are used in ayurveda.
Apple	Allspice	Chilli	Cauliflower
Blue cheese	Black bean	Cinnamon	Garlic
Egg	Cashew	Coconut	Mustard seeds
Onion	Chestnut	Coriander	Onion
Polenta	Chilli	Cumin	Potato
Potato	Cinnamon	Ginger	Rice
Squash	Fennel	Mango	Spice
Tomato	Fig	Noodles	
	Lemon	Peanut	
	Lentils	Squash	
	Potato		
	Rice		
	Tomato		
Crispy fried sage leaves make most things better, from fried eggs to pasta.	It's best to use fresh leaves. A small bay plant will last forever.	I use whole leaves in curries or broths; very finely shredded fresh leaves can also be used in small amounts as you would a fresh herb like coriander.	They can be added at the beginning of cooking as you would a lime leaf or bay leaf, or cooked in a temper: in hot oil with other spices to be spooned over at the end of cooking.
Bay	Sage	Lemon	Nothing is comparable, just
Thyme		Lemongrass	leave them out.
		Lime	

	Cardamom *pods and ground*	Cinnamon *sticks and ground*	Coriander *seeds and ground*
Flavour profile	Warm Sweet Citrussy	Warm Earthy	Citrussy Lemony Floral Earthy
Info	Seed pods from various plants in the ginger family. They can be used whole or ground, or just the seeds. There is black, green and white cardamom (bleached green). Green is the most commonly used.	The dried inner bark of the young shoots of the cinnamon tree, an evergreen tree in the laurel family. Dried and rolled into cigar-shaped scrolls. It was so precious to ancient communities that its source was kept a secret.	The fruit from the same plant as the bright, fresh coriander leaves. It's a member of the parsley family, native to the Mediterranean and south-west Europe.
Goes with	Apricot Banana Cauliflower Chocolate Coconut Coffee Lentils Pear Root vegetables Rose Vanilla	Apple Banana Chocolate Coconut Coffee Cream and dairy Onion Root veg Stone fruit Tomato Squash	Aubergine Blueberry Broccoli Cabbage Cauliflower Celery Citrus Garam masala Goat's cheese Potato Pulses
How to use	Whole or ground or scrape out the seeds. Toast pods in oil first. Grind the seeds in a pestle and mortar for the best results.	Use as a stick or ground. Ground is less strong/punchy and loses flavour quickly.	Seeds should be toasted and ground, as they are tough/chewy whole, though they are often used whole in pickling and brining.
Swap with	Hard to match. Leave it out or use more lemon.	Half the amount of nutmeg or allspice.	Caraway seeds, cumin seeds, fennel seeds, or a combination of the three.

Cumin	Fennel	Mustard	Nigella
seeds and ground	*seeds*	*seeds: yellow and black*	*seeds*
Warm	Citrussy	Hot	Earthy
Earthy	Warm	Warm	Heat
Tangy		Lemony	Smoky
Musky		Earthy	Grassy
			Verdant
Dried seeds of the cumin plant, part of the parsley family, used in Latin American, Middle Eastern, North African and Indian cooking.	Native to the Mediterranean, with a stronger flavour than fennel fronds or root. Often chewed instead of chewing gum, it tastes fresh and aniseedy.	Mustard seeds are the tiny seeds from mustard plants, and are grown worldwide. There are three common types: yellow, brown and black.	From the seed casings of the *Nigella sativa* plant, native to the Mediterranean and the Middle East.
Apricot	Beans	Cinnamon	Breads and savoury bakes
Beetroot	Cakes and seeded bread	Coconut	Carrot
Citrus	Cheese	Cream	Coconut
Chickpeas	Courgette	Cumin	Curry
Coriander	Cream	Curry leaves	Date
Curry and stew	Cucumber	Pickles	Fennel
Squash	Potato	Potato	Lentils
Stone fruit	Rye	Preserves	Pickles
Yoghurt	Spice blends	Tomato	Pulses
	Sweet bakes		Root veg
	Walnut		Sesame
			Squash
			Tomato
Whole or ground. Whole in a roasting tray with veg, or toasted in oil. A little heat/dry roast is required before grinding the seeds. Add early in the recipe if using seeds.	Toast lightly in a dry pan or fry whole in oil. Always benefits from being ground a little to release its own oils.	Make sure to fry until they pop or they can be bitter.	Use in a spice blend; use to garnish a salad. They don't keep well ground. Grind in a blender, rather than in a pestle and mortar.
Caraway seeds	Anise	Mustard	Celery seed
Coriander seeds	Aniseed	Mustard powder	Cumin seed
Garam masala			

	Nutmeg *whole*	Peppercorns *whole: white and black*	Pul biber *flakes*
Flavour profile	Nutty Earthy Warm	Hot Earthy	Hot Fruity Smoky
Info	Nutmeg is the inner seed of the nutmeg plant, *Myristica fragrans*, native to Indonesia. It's dried out in the sun.	These are the dried fruits of the pepper plant. Black, white and green peppercorns are all the same seeds of the same plant, just in various stages of development and processed differently. Black pepper is made from picked and dried unripe pepper berries.	Pul Biber is an umbrella term for Turkey's chilli (hot pepper) flakes, which include Aleppo pepper (from the Halaby pepper) and Urfa (cultivated in the Şanlıurfa region, near the Syrian border).
Goes with	Cheese Cream Kale Lemon Pastry and cake Ricotta Spinach Squash White sauce	Cheese Dairy Egg Parmesan Pasta Potato Tomato Turnip	Avocado Cheese Chickpeas Couscous Dairy Egg Melon Muhummara Stew Walnut
How to use	It's best when grated fresh, and gives a fresher, cleaner taste. I like to use a micro-plane. It can be bought ground and is particularly good for baking. It lasts longer as a seed than as a ground spice.	Buy whole peppercorns for the best flavour and scent. Overcooking can make it bitter.	Doesn't need to be heated to remove any rawness, so it's great as a final flourish on soups, salads, eggs. It is traditionally 'bloomed' in hot oil then poured over dishes.
Swap with	Allspice	White and black pepper can be substituted for each other in small quantities.	A small amount of chilli flakes.

Star anise	Smoked paprika	Turmeric	Vanilla
whole	*ground*	*ground and fresh*	*pods, paste and extract*
Sweet	Smoky	Peppery	Sweet
Warm	Sweet	Heat	Warm
	Oaky	Earthy	Floral
		Floral	

Star anise	Smoked paprika	Turmeric	Vanilla
The dried fruit of the Chinese magnolia tree. Star-shaped with eight points, each containing a seed. Both the seeds and the pods are used in cooking and contain the anise flavour.	Chillies smoked in large kilns over fire in the Extremadura region of Spain, then ground to a powder. You can buy picante (hot), dulce (sweet) and agridulce (bittersweet) varieties.	Bright yellow, used in most Indian cooking. You can use it in its fresh form (wear gloves), but most commonly we buy it in powdered form. It's boiled and dried in the sun for a couple of weeks, before being ground.	The second most expensive spice in the world, after saffron. We've been through a vanilla shortage over the last few years, thought to be down to deforestation and the working conditions in Madagascar, where most of the world's vanilla is grown. Vanilla pods are the fruit of certain kinds of orchid.

Star anise	Smoked paprika	Turmeric	Vanilla
Cabbage and greens	Beans	Aubergine	Apple
Citrus	Grains	Cauliflower	Banana
Chocolate	Lemon	Coconut milk	Blackberries
Cream	Mayonnaise	Dairy	Citrus
Leek	Parsley	Egg	Melon
Noodles	Pasta	Lentils	Pear
Pear	Rice	Onion	Rhubarb
Pho	Root vegetables	Root vegetables	Stone fruit
Rice	Tomato	Squash	Tomato
Root veg		Tomato	
Soy		White chocolate	
Squash			

Star anise	Smoked paprika	Turmeric	Vanilla
Like a bay leaf, it needs to be infused rather than eaten.	A great way to build up smoky flavour. I use a teaspoon in the base of soups and stews and toss root vegetables in a couple of pinches before roasting. It is a good swap for chorizo.	Fresh turmeric keeps for a few weeks in the fridge; dried ground turmeric has a shelf life of at least a year without losing character.	Avoid essence if you can. A good-quality extract is great for baking; look for the plumpest little black vanilla pods you can find. If cooking with the pods, slice lengthways and scrape out the small seeds with a knife. Store in a sealed container, in a dry, dark place.

Star anise	Smoked paprika	Turmeric	Vanilla
Anise – 5 spice powder.	Other smoked chillies or smoked chilli pastes like chipotle.	Nothing matches it.	Extract for pods in a pinch. 1 tablespoon = 1 pod.

Index

Acknowledgements

A book is written by many people, not just the one named on the cover. This book was written during a bright spring and boiling hot summer heavily pregnant, and when Esca was tiny and was only possible thanks to this tapestry of people.

I feel it is so important to acknowledge the support that allows me to do the work I do. Pretending it all happens with no help feeds the narrative that women must be everything all at once.

First thanks must go to Louise Haines, our fifth book together. For always championing me, being a trusted ear and for never compromising. And for your patience; I feel very lucky to be on your list.

Adriana Caneva, you have approached this book with the care, style and attention to detail I could only have dreamed of. Its beauty is in large part down to you.

Thanks to Mia Colleran for holding the book so completely. Alex Gingell for expertly editing me and Imogen Benson and Victoria Pullen.

Michelle Kane, my heart is full for you, and my thanks are endless. Patrick Hargadon, I feel very lucky to have you on this one. Thanks too to Sarah Bennie for what's to come. Matt Clacher and your team.

To David Roth-Ey and all at 4th Estate, very happy to be part of the 4th collective for five books.

Proofreaders Annie Lee and Laura Nickoll, copy editor Louise Tucker (the safest of hands), and indexer Hilary Bird.

Typesetter Gary Simpson.

To Felicity Blunt, dear friend and excellent person. Thank you for it all. Gracefully supported by Rosie Pierce and Flo Sanderson.

Jess Lea Wilson and Rachael Pilston, I bow down to you both. Jess, ten years and counting and grateful for every one. I am in awe of your endless talents. Rach, your holding and patience this last year have meant so much to me. I strive to be as kind, calm and creative as you. And for your hands – they look excellent.

Hugo Harrison, this book is in large part down to you. Weeks spent testing and retesting recipes, and talking about flavours and food. Your patience, brilliance and grace are endless. Thanks to El Kemp and Chloe Glazier for help testing.

Emily Ezekiel, Aunty Lemony. Five books and everything in between, our friendship has been through it all. No one brings creativity, vision, honesty and Loewe like you.

Rosie Ramsden. Thank you for bringing your painterly ways with food and your steady, uplifting friendship to my life. Golden.

Kitty Coles. 10/10. Always. Thanks for loving egg mayo as much as me and for countless other things.

Christina Mackenzie. Close to twenty years now. Lucky to know and love you. Jodene Jordan, oh babe, the care and love you put into everything, next level. Joe Carey, vibes. Thank you.

Matt Russell, it's been a while since the heady days of the vodka luge. Feel lucky to have called you a friend for so long. You have brought your talent, kind soul and jokes. Thanks to Claudia Gschwend, Aloha Shaw and Gareth Williams. Very lovely to have you.

To the wonderful people who came along on work experience; Hannah Roberts-Owen, Karina Borowiec, Ida Carlins, Freya Pinkerton, Lou Cottle.

Ali Dunwell, a saviour, for my face and my soul.

To the kind people who have allowed me to feature their recipes in the pages of this book, some friends, some just people I greatly admire. All writers and cooks you should know. Jaya Chandna, Maunika Gowardhan, Georgina Hayden, Olia Hercules, Jeremy Lee, Gurdeep Loyal, Hetty McKinnon, Nadya Mousawi, Shuko Oda, Mersedeh Prewer, Sarit and Itamar, Cynthia Shanmugalingam, Kitty Travers, Stanley Tucci and Karla Zazueta.

Thank you to fellow cooks and writers Samin Nosrat (*Salt, Fat, Acid, Heat*), Nik Sharma (*The Flavour Equation*) and Niki Segnit (*The Flavour Thesaurus*) and Mark Diacono (*Herb and Spice*) whose books have informed my writing.

Nadya Mousawi, an actual angel. You came into our lives with Esca, and I know you are here to stay. I am certain without you this book would not exist. Thank you too to Ewa Borowiec who cares for us like family.

Dear friends, many already above, I can feel you cheering me on, always. Special mention to Naomi Annand, Lisa Pfleger and Kate Sessions.

To Mum and Dad, Rog and Gez, you continue to be the life and soul, the friendliest pair and the parents and grandparents who set the bar. I am thankful for you both every day and can't believe my luck.

Laura, having you nearby now is like having half my heart back. I love you. And Jasmin and Jean. Owen, a kind and knowing force in my life. There is so much good to come for you, Hannah and Eli.

Special mention to Liz and Sian Dale for the early days.

John Dale. I am not sure what I did to deserve you. The kindest, steadiest, strongest and funniest. It's been a wild few years. Thanks for holding on to the hope when I couldn't and for making me laugh when I needed it most. For living by example. No words come close.

Dylan, my boy. I am your home, and you are mine. I couldn't be prouder or happier you are my son. I am so excited for a life of great adventures with you.

Esca. I longed for you, and here you are against the odds. With your earnest knowing and ear-to-ear smiles. You fill my heart and our family. Also please sleep a bit more.

To you for buying this book. It will always feel like the greatest thing in the world that you might pick this book up and cook a meal for the people you love. I'll never get over how good that feels.

Conversion chart

UK cups

¼ cup	62.5ml
½ cup	125ml
1 cup	250ml
1½ cups	375ml
2 cups	500ml

US cups

¼ cup	60ml
½ cup	120ml
1 cup	240ml
1½ cups	360ml
2 cups	480ml

Gas	F°	C°	Fan C°
1	275	140	120
2	300	150	130
3	325	170	150
4	350	180	160
5	375	190	170
6	400	200	180
7	425	220	200
8	450	230	210

4th Estate
An imprint of
HarperCollinsPublishers
1 London Bridge Street
London SE1 9GF
www.4thEstate.co.uk

Macken House,
39/40 Mayor Street Upper,
Dublin 1, D01 C9W8, Ireland

HarperCollinsPublishers

First published in Great Britain
in 2024 by 4th Estate

A catalogue record for this book
is available from the British Library
ISBN   978-0-00-852665-8

Always follow the manufacturer's
instructions when using kitchen
appliances.

Design and art direction
Caneva Nishimoto

Typesetting
GS Typesetting

Printed in Italy

This book is produced from
independently certified FSC™
paper to ensure responsible forest
management.

For more information visit:
www.harpercollins.co.uk/green

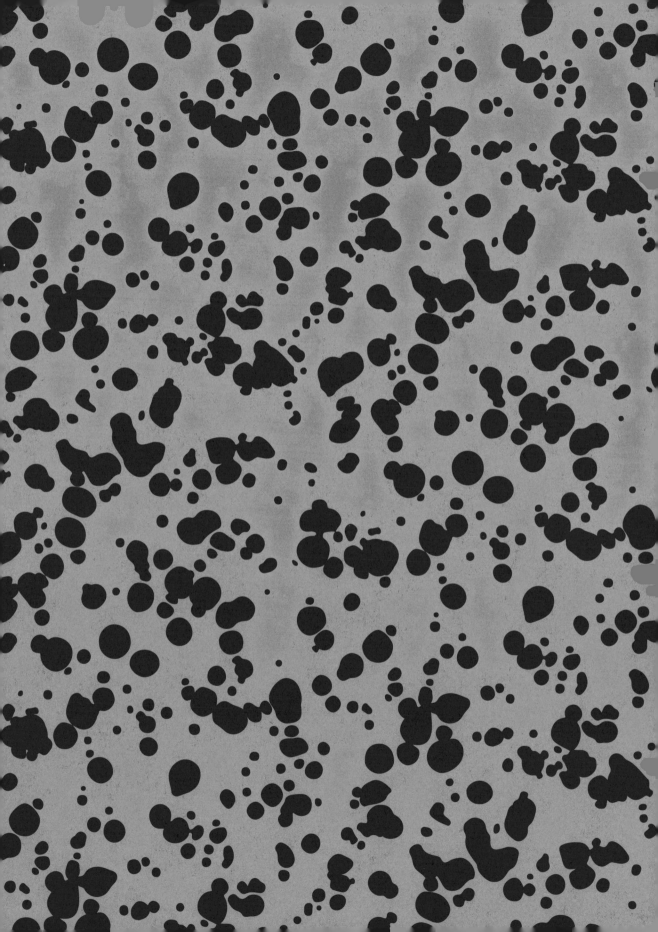

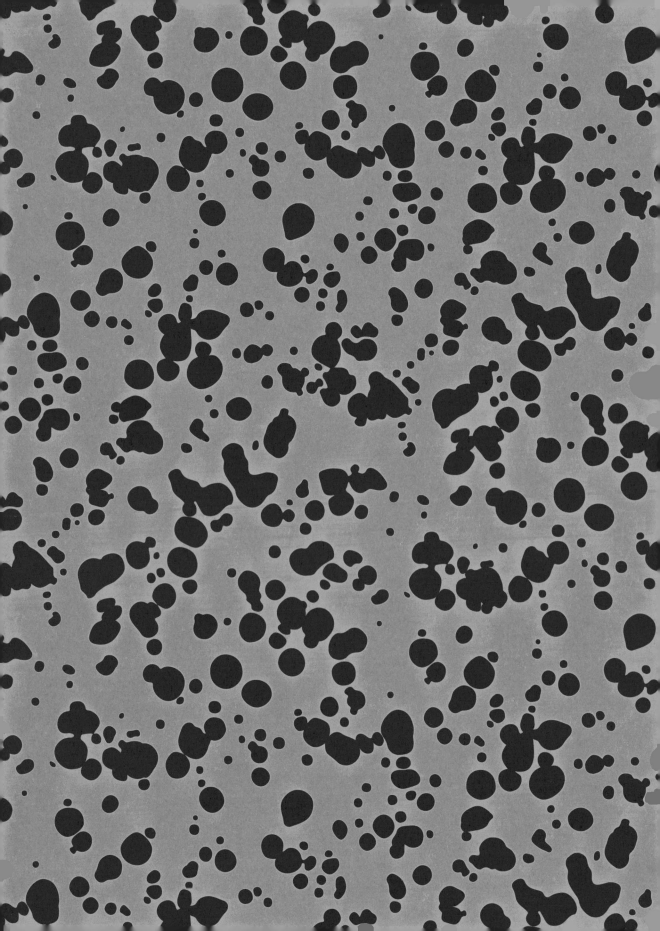